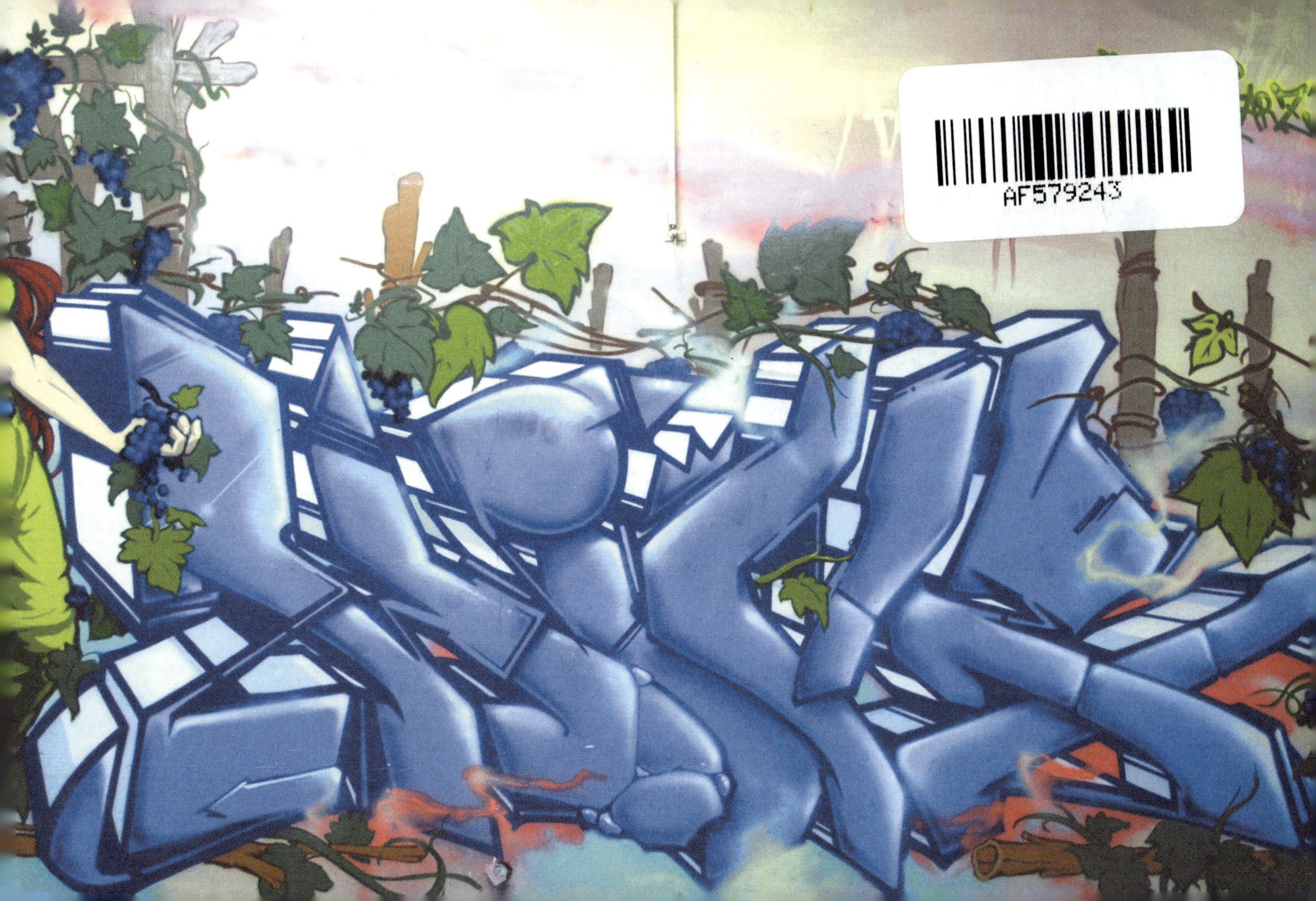

more of the best graffiti from around the world

Graffiti Planet 2

compiled and introduced by KET

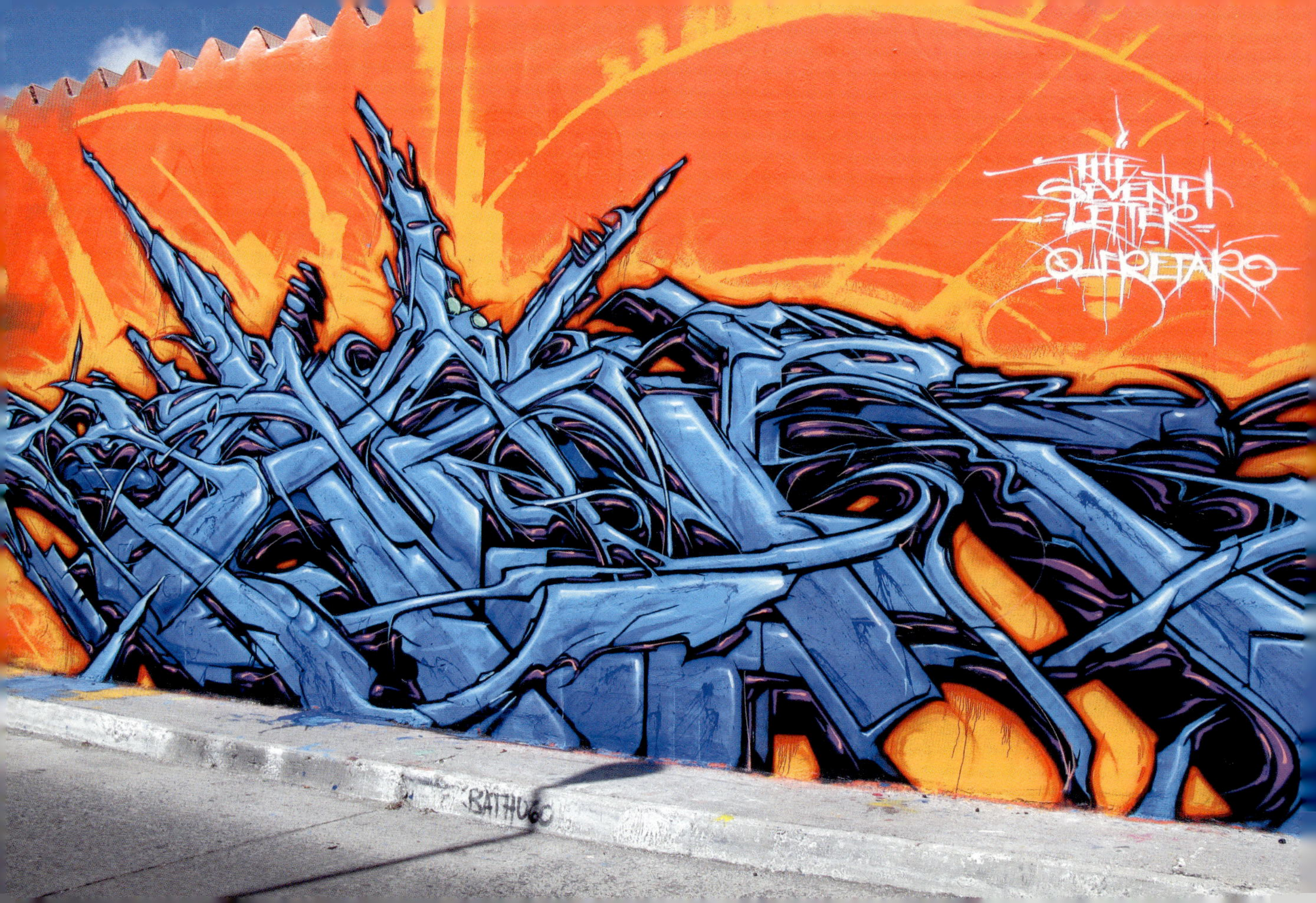
THE SEVENTH LETTER
QUERETARO

more of the best graffiti from around the world

Graffiti Planet 2

compiled and introduced by KET

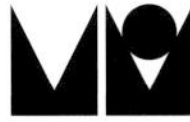

Michael O'Mara Books Limited

First published in Great Britain in 2009 by
Michael O'Mara Books Limited
9 Lion Yard
Tremadoc Road
London SW4 7NQ

A CIP catalogue record for this book is available from the British Library.

Papers used by Michael O'Mara Books Limited are natural, recyclable products made from wood grown in sustainable forests. The manufacturing processes conform to the environmental regulations of the country of origin.

ISBN: 978-1-84317-346-5

1 3 5 7 9 10 8 6 4 2

www.mombooks.com

Page 2 image: Saber, Queretaro, Mexico
Endpapers: Wine (Zeus 40), Pencil, and Wine (Opium), Naples, Italy (front);
Knows COD and Ewok One 5MH, Brooklyn, New York, USA (back)

Designed by Joanne Omigie (joanneomigie.com) after an original design by Envy Design

Printed and bound in Italy by L.E.G.O.

Special thanks

Special thanks to the following people who were instrumental in reaching out to other writers and helping me connect the dots: Wane COD, Dmise, Rew, Frame DTK, Alice Han, Sen 2, Ergo from www.Bucharestbusiness.ro, Host 18, Kasino, Egs, Thor, Ghost, Artiskfunk, Lunar, Mickey TFP, Zeb SB, Part One TDS, Cern, Kelp, Gökhan93, Kripoe, Curve, Jee BTC, Kane HSA, Scheme, Myre, and Freddy Mack.

Introduction

Walking the streets of Berlin, São Paulo, Paris, and the Bronx, it is easy to see that the aerosol art and writing movement is alive, well, and consistently growing. In such places there are distinct schools of thought amongst graffiti artists. Some favour 'bombing'– in other words the sport of tagging, which is all about getting your name around town quickly and prolifically. Another school, specifically in Berlin, has gone for an 'anti-style' approach, where the names are created in simple designs reminiscent of New York, circa 1973. Another development has been the growth of the 'street art' phenomenon, either where writers have turned to art that avoids the traditional use of letters, or art school students have decided that they too want to be part of the excitement of being public outlaws with their work. Yet, everywhere around the world, the style writing tradition continues to be the most respected and lasting in the existence of the graffiti movement.

Writing your name with elaborate style and beauty is the pinnacle of this art form. The collection gathered here has been selected with that in mind, with occasional departures to include some of the greatest street artists and bombers. And, in some rare cases, the artists featured here are masters of all three styles.

Long live the style writers, throw up kings, and bombers . . .

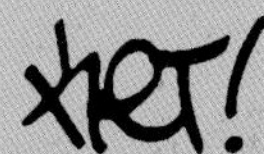

KET ONE/RIS/TFP/AOK/COD/MTK
On tour in Berlin, Germany

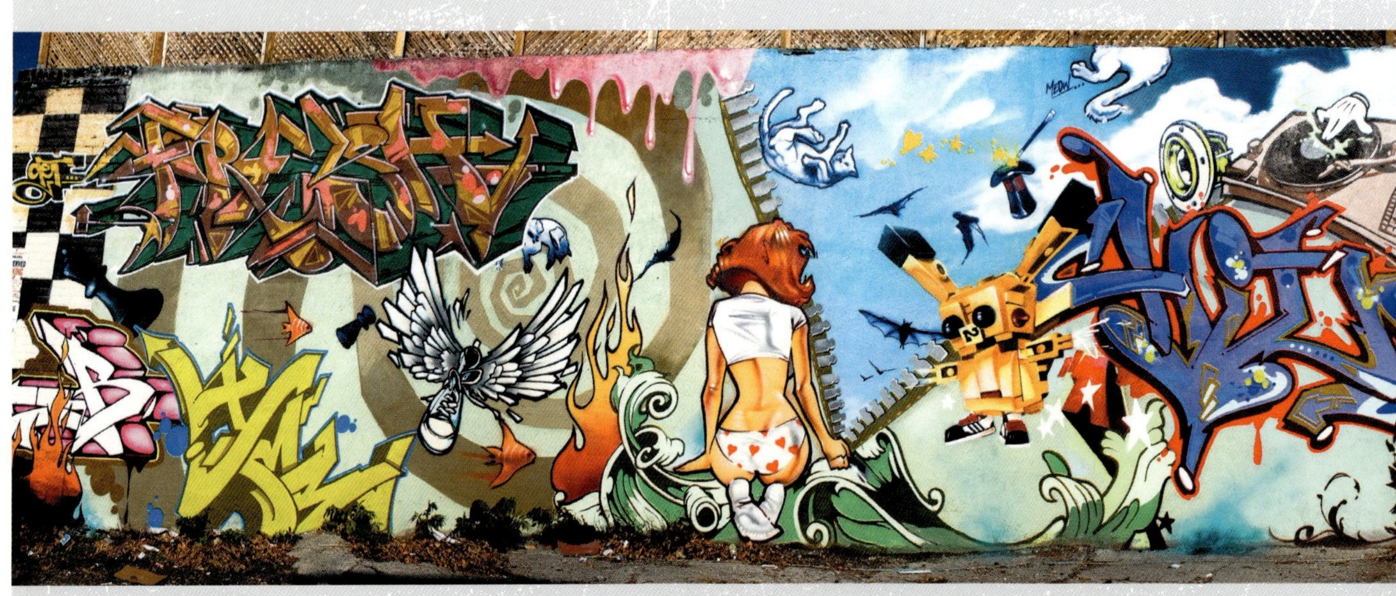

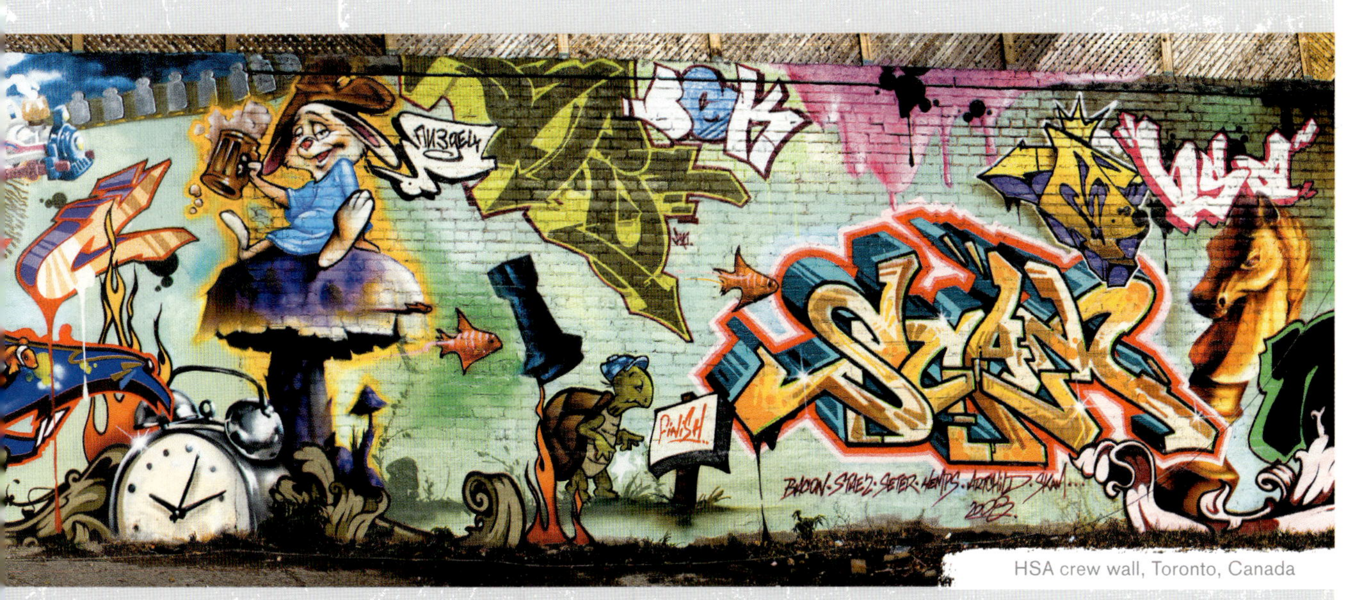

HSA crew wall, Toronto, Canada

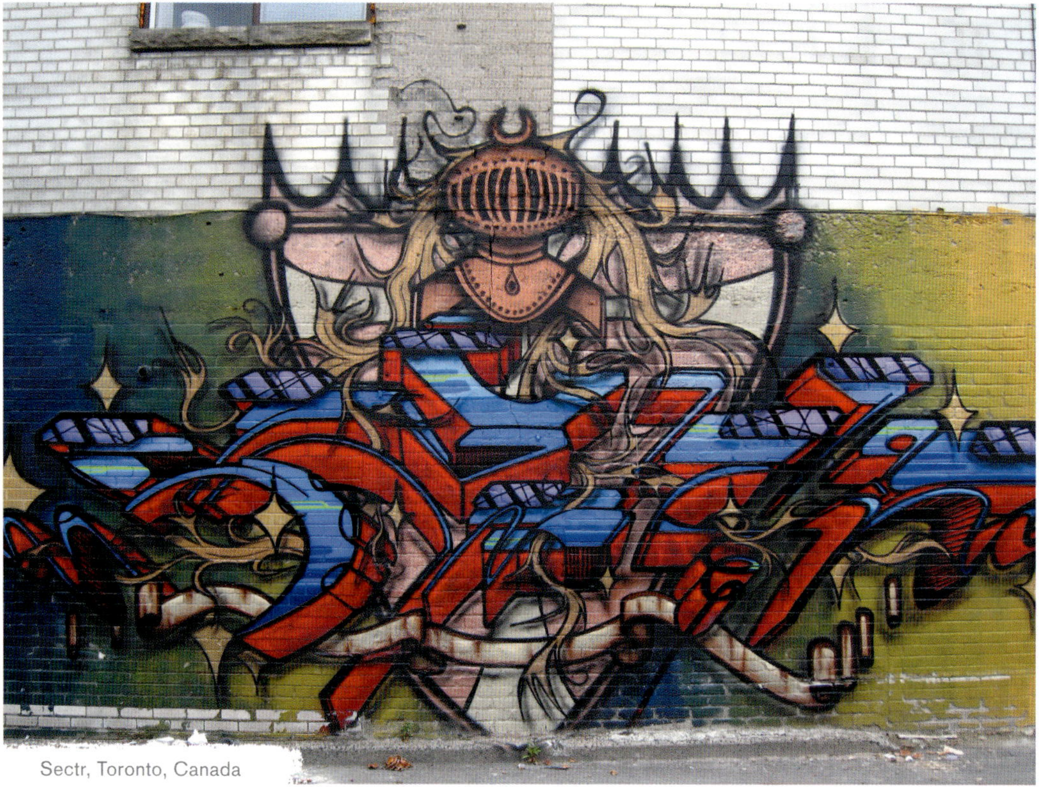

Sectr, Toronto, Canada

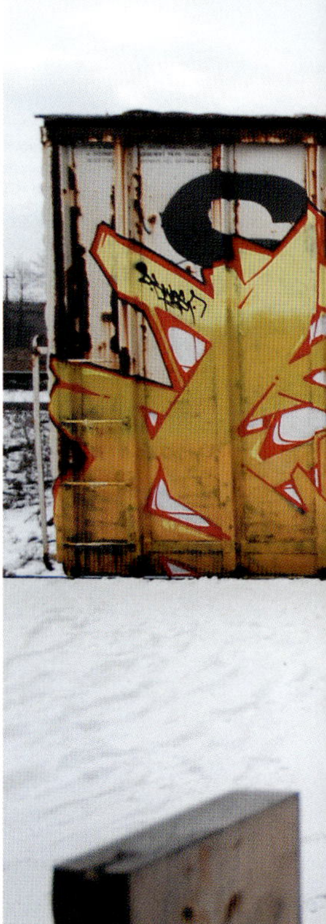

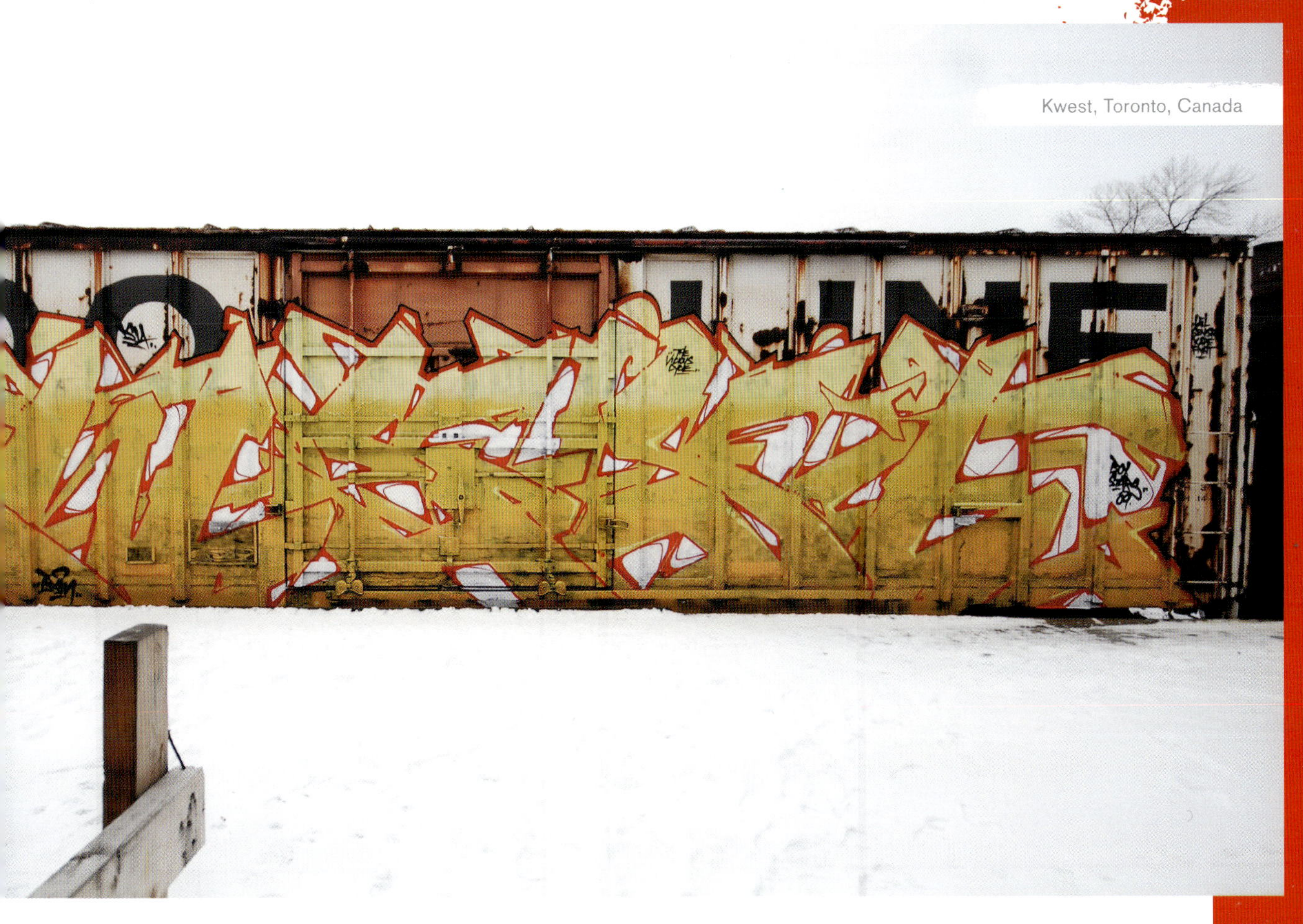

Kwest, Toronto, Canada

Virus TC5 and Knows, Montreal, Canada

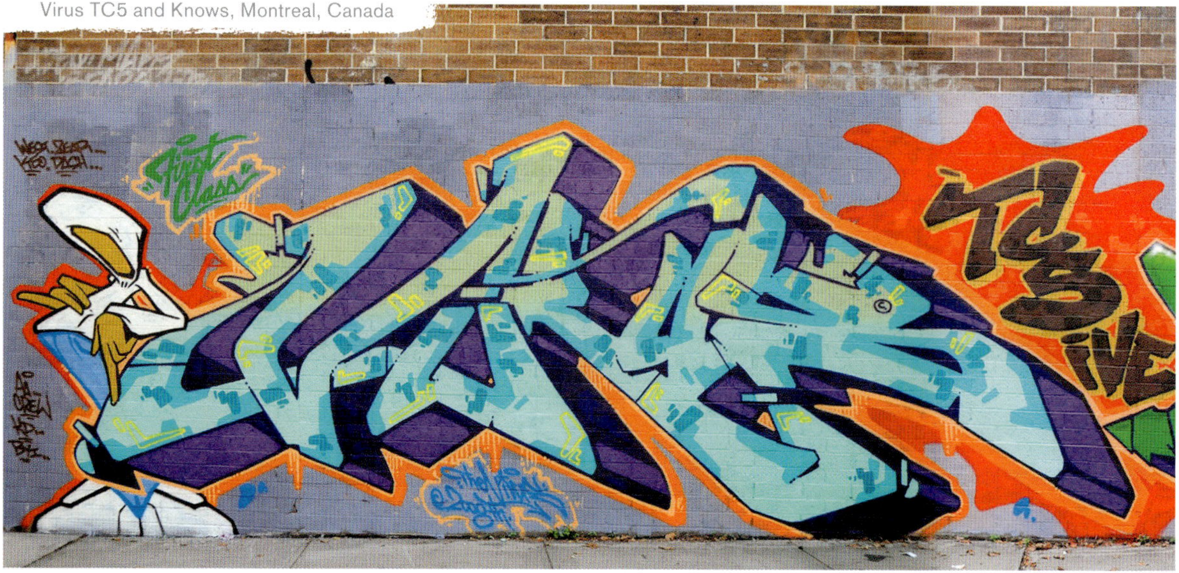

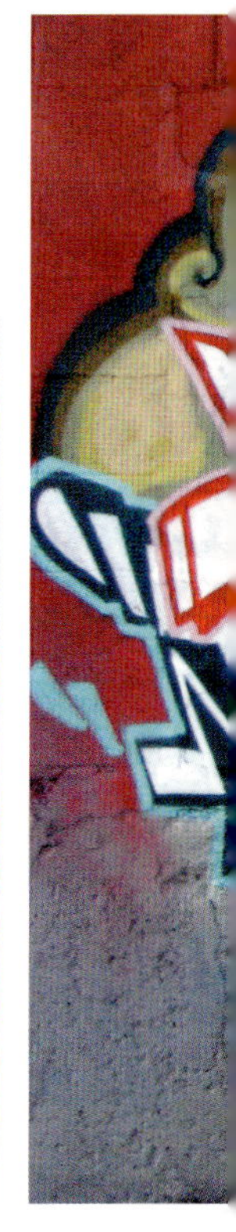

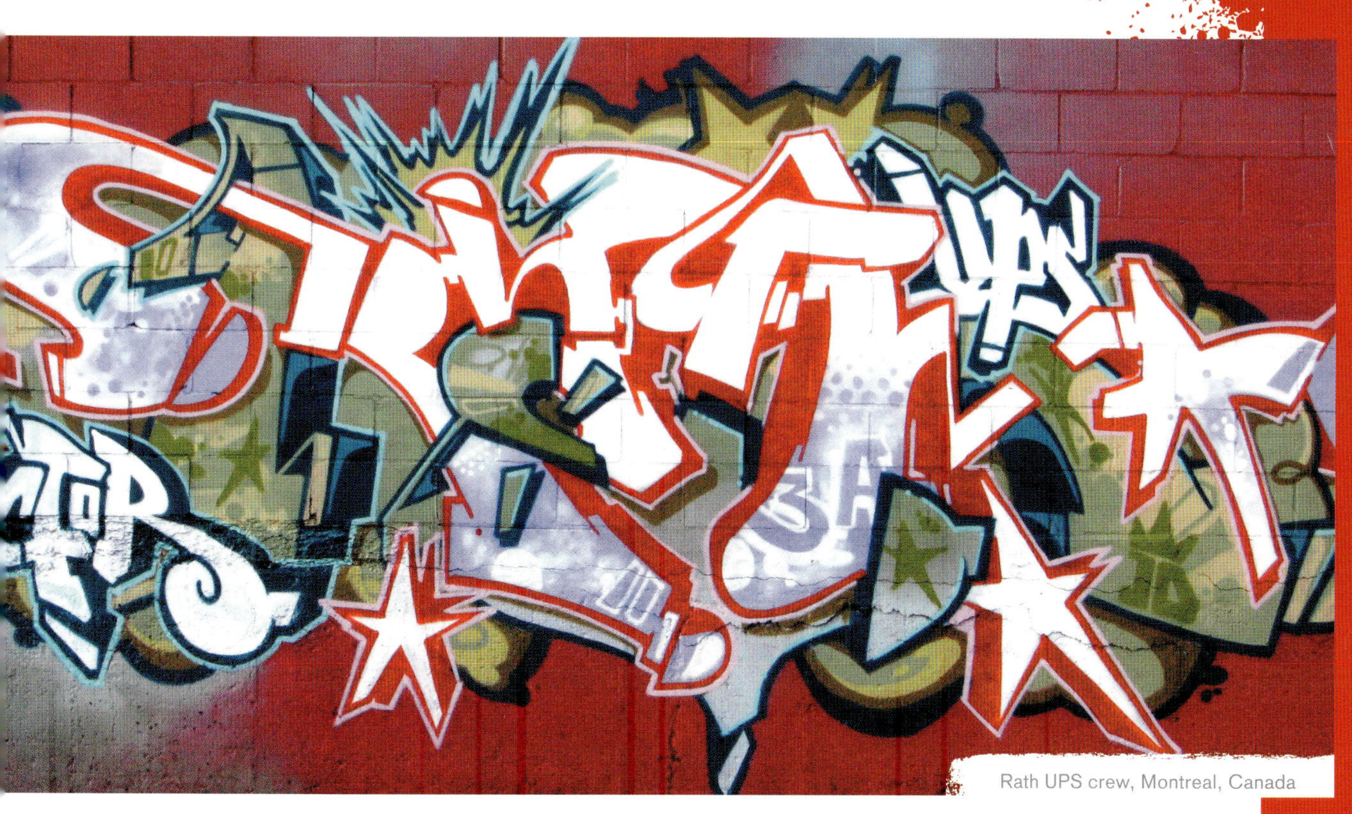

Rath UPS crew, Montreal, Canada

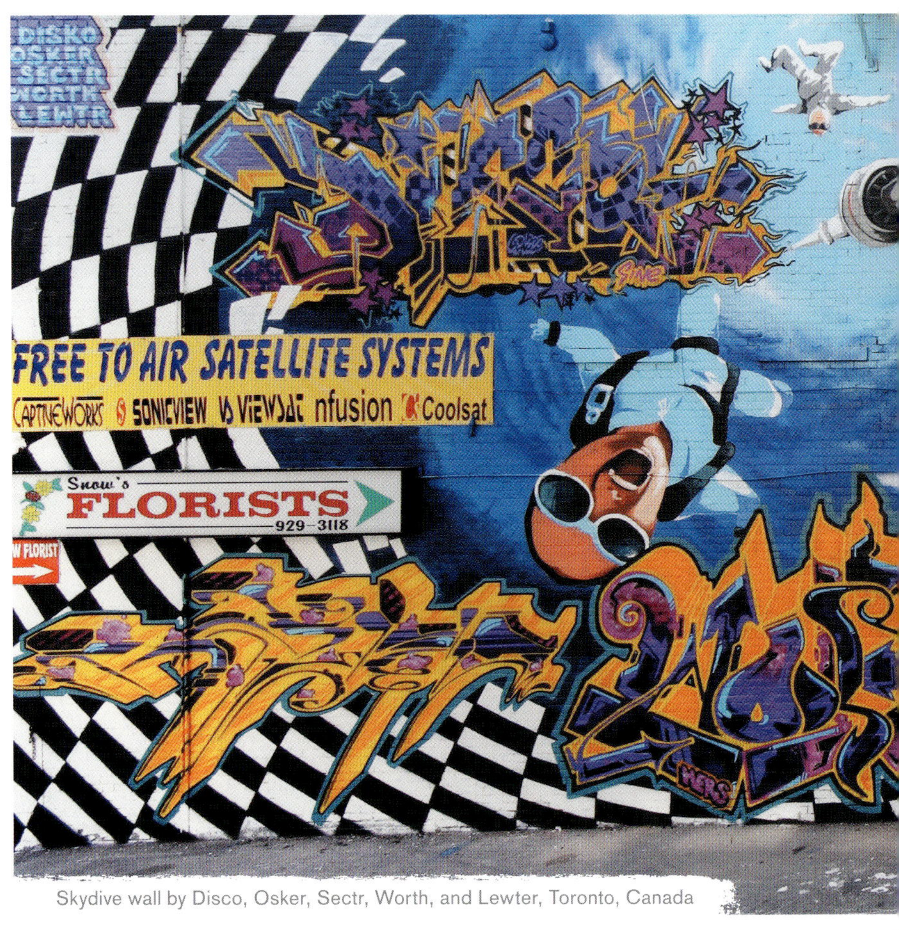

Skydive wall by Disco, Osker, Sectr, Worth, and Lewter, Toronto, Canada

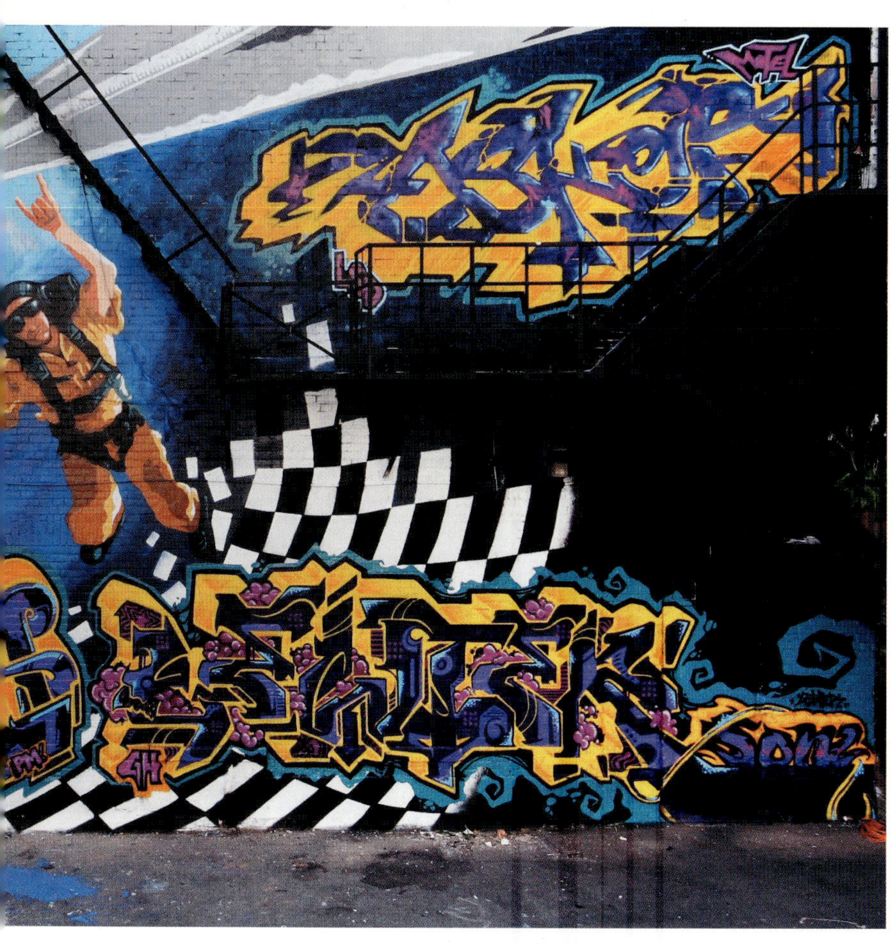

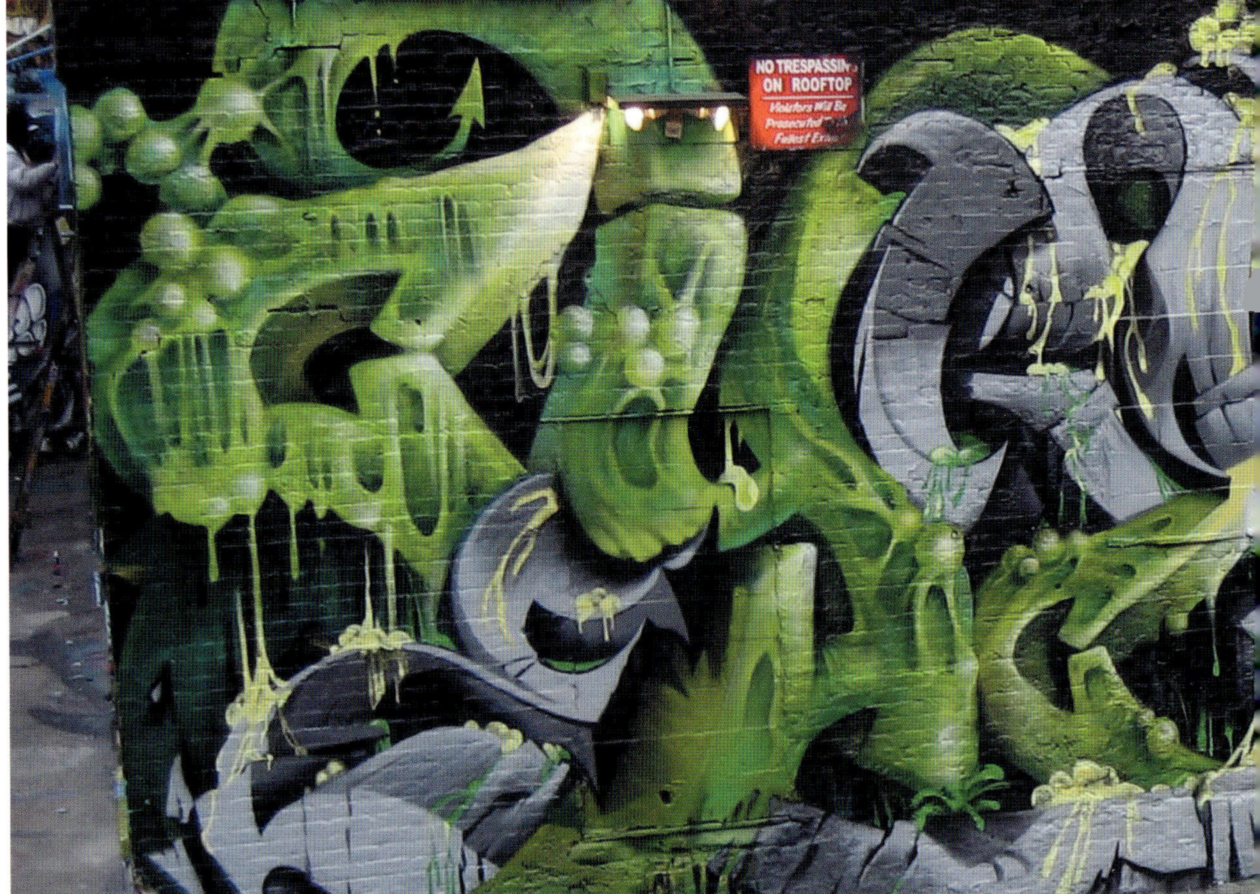
ON ROOFTOP

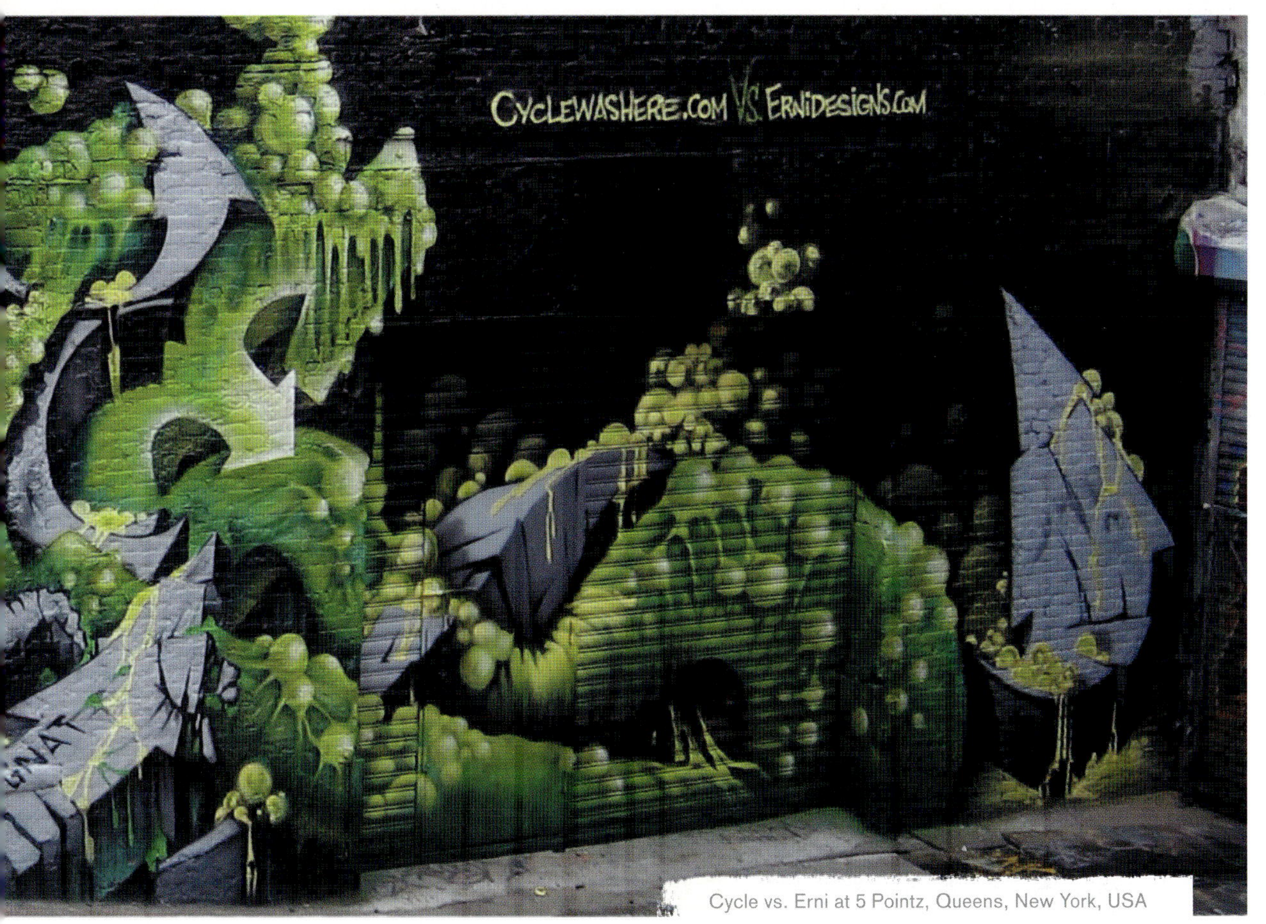

Cycle vs. Erni at 5 Pointz, Queens, New York, USA

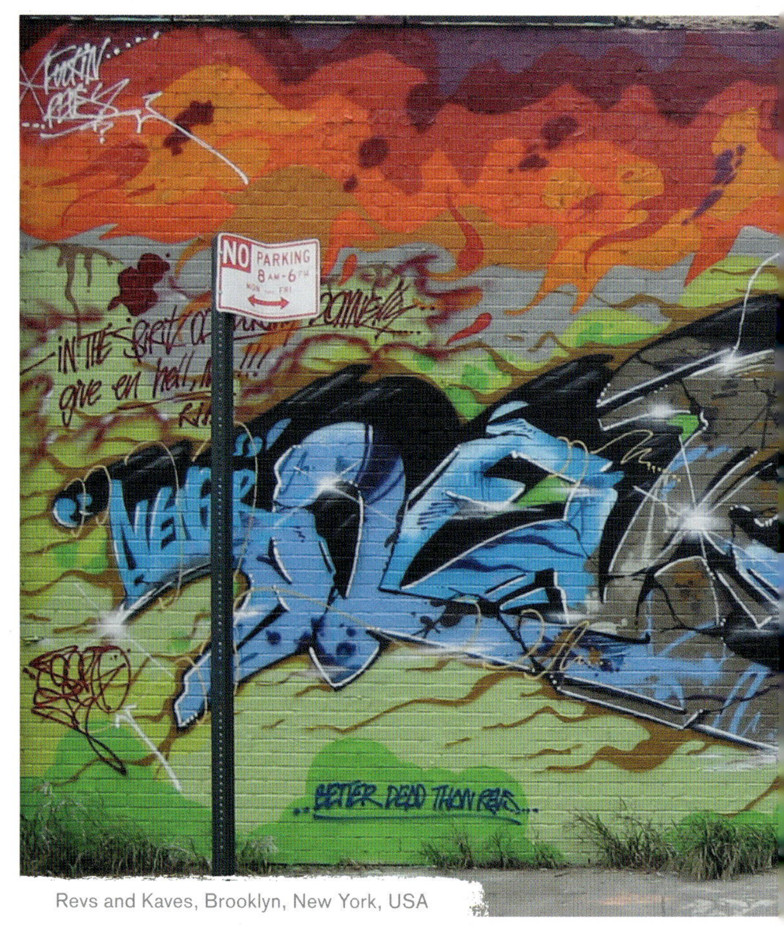

Revs and Kaves, Brooklyn, New York, USA

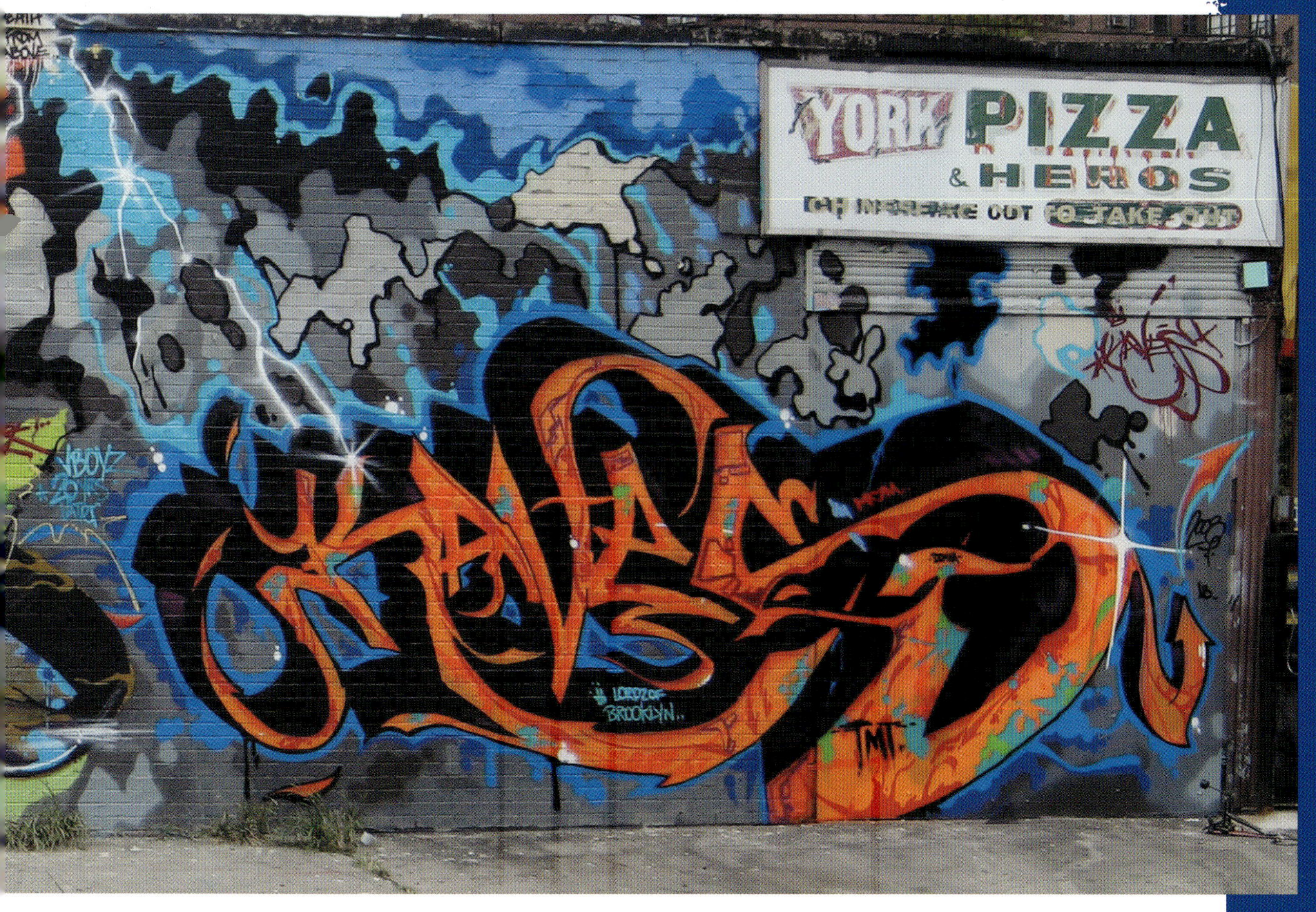
YORK PIZZA
& HEROS

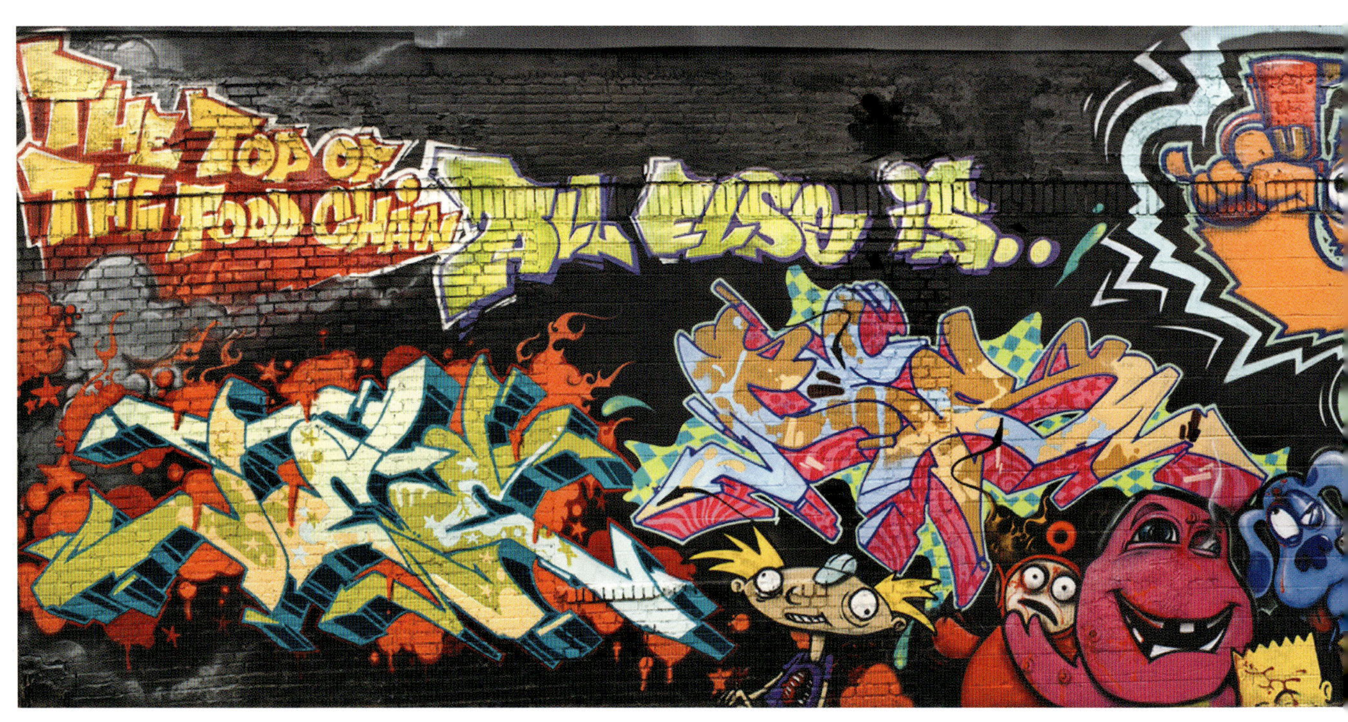
THE TOP OF THE FOOD CHAIN
ALL ELSE IS..

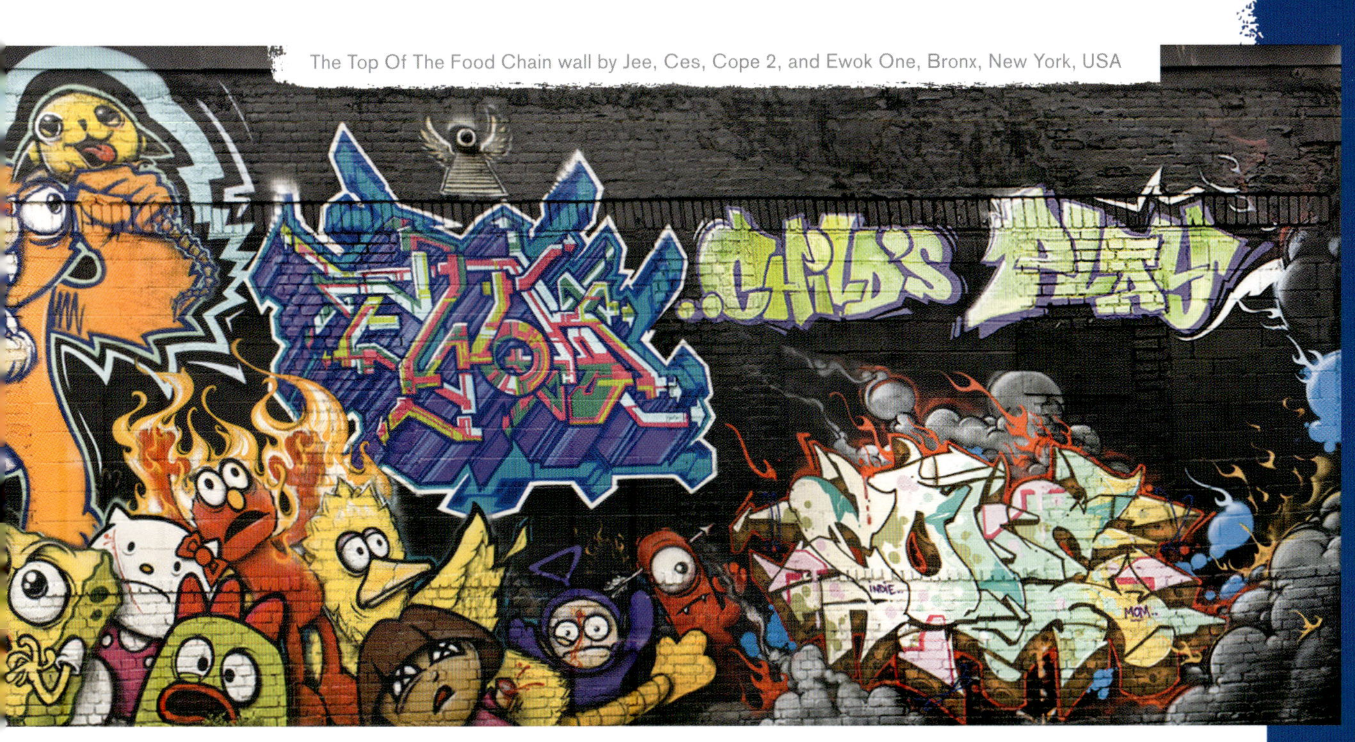

The Top Of The Food Chain wall by Jee, Ces, Cope 2, and Ewok One, Bronx, New York, USA

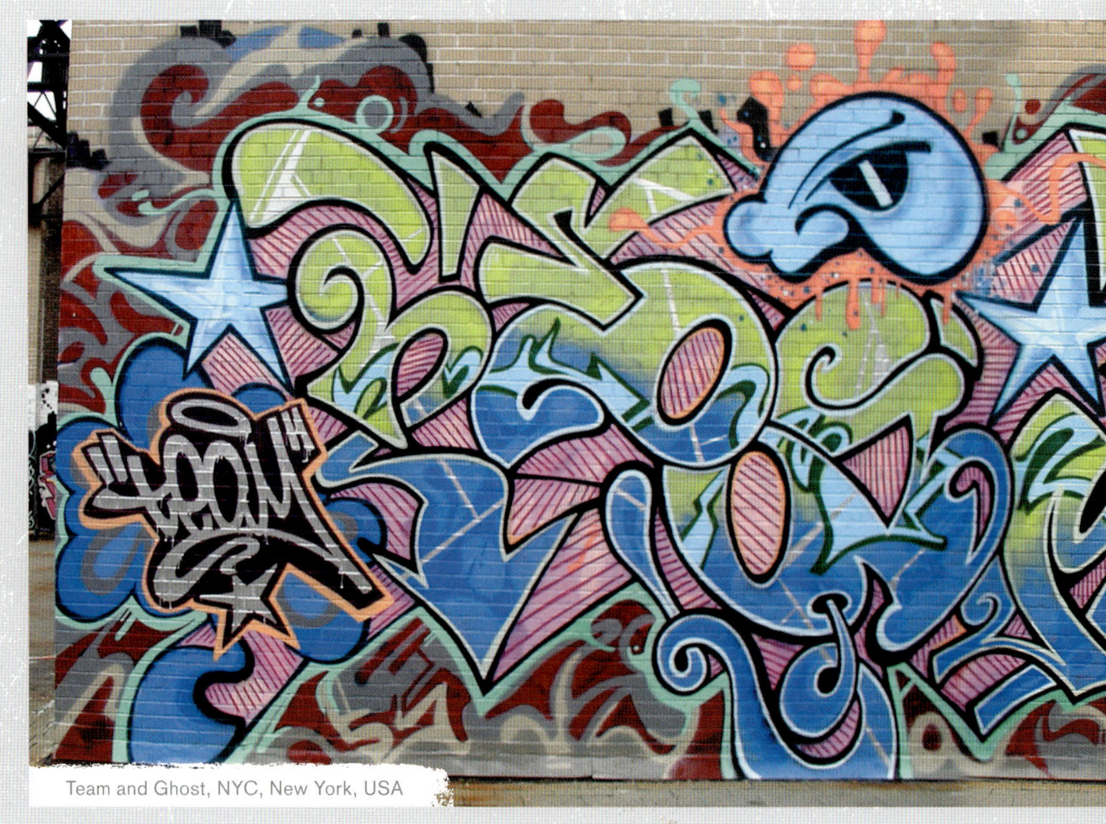

Team and Ghost, NYC, New York, USA

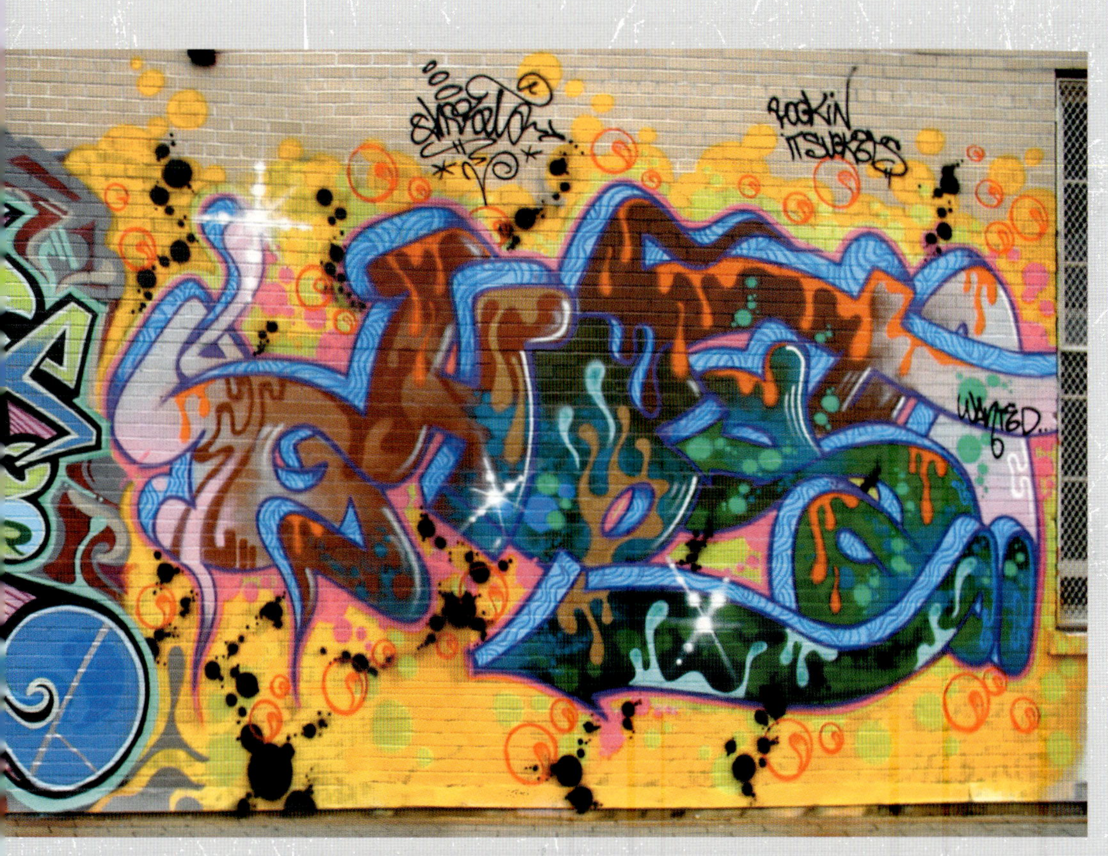
ROCKIN
WANTED...

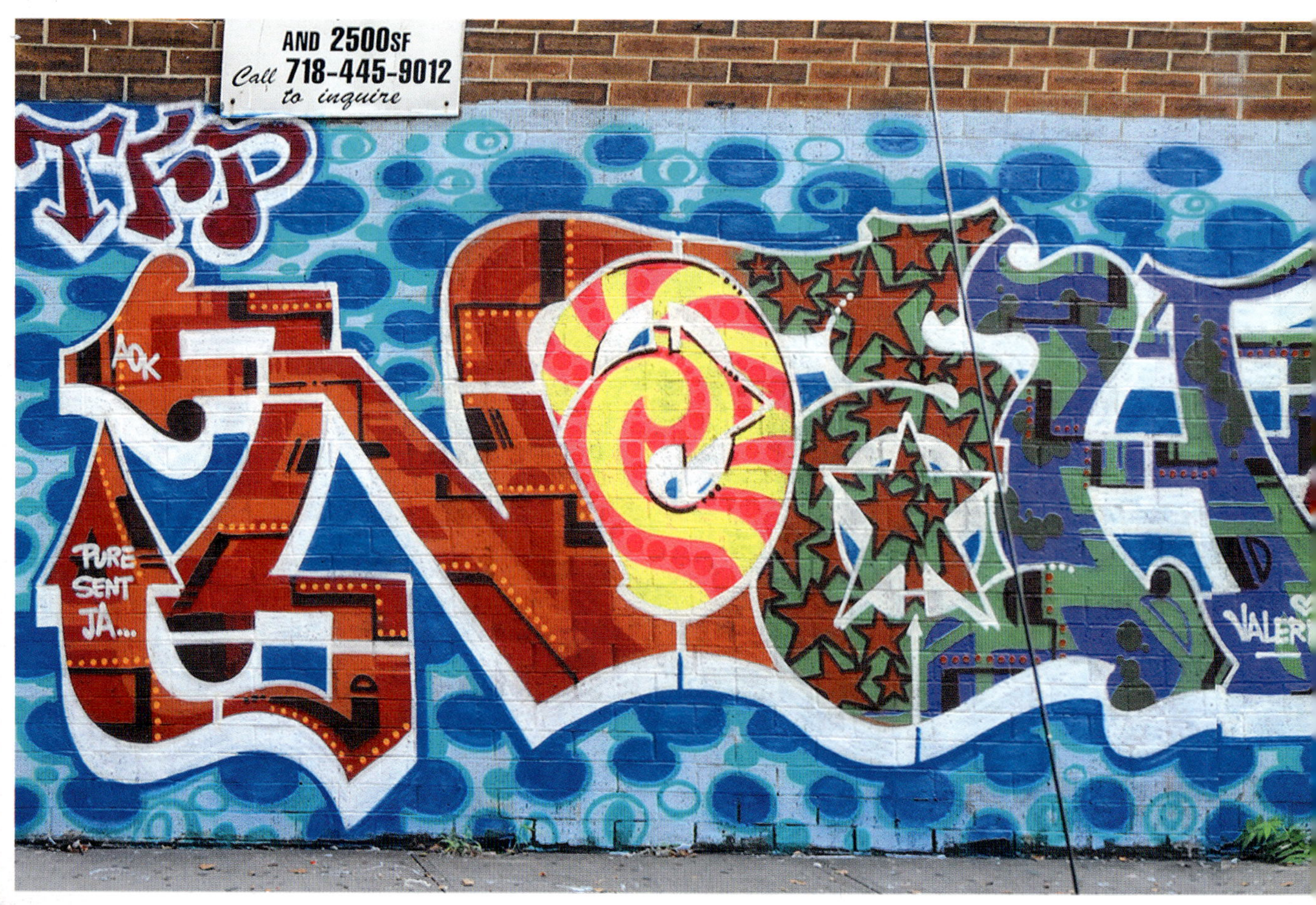
AND 2500SF
Call 718-445-9012
to inquire
PURE
SENT
JA...

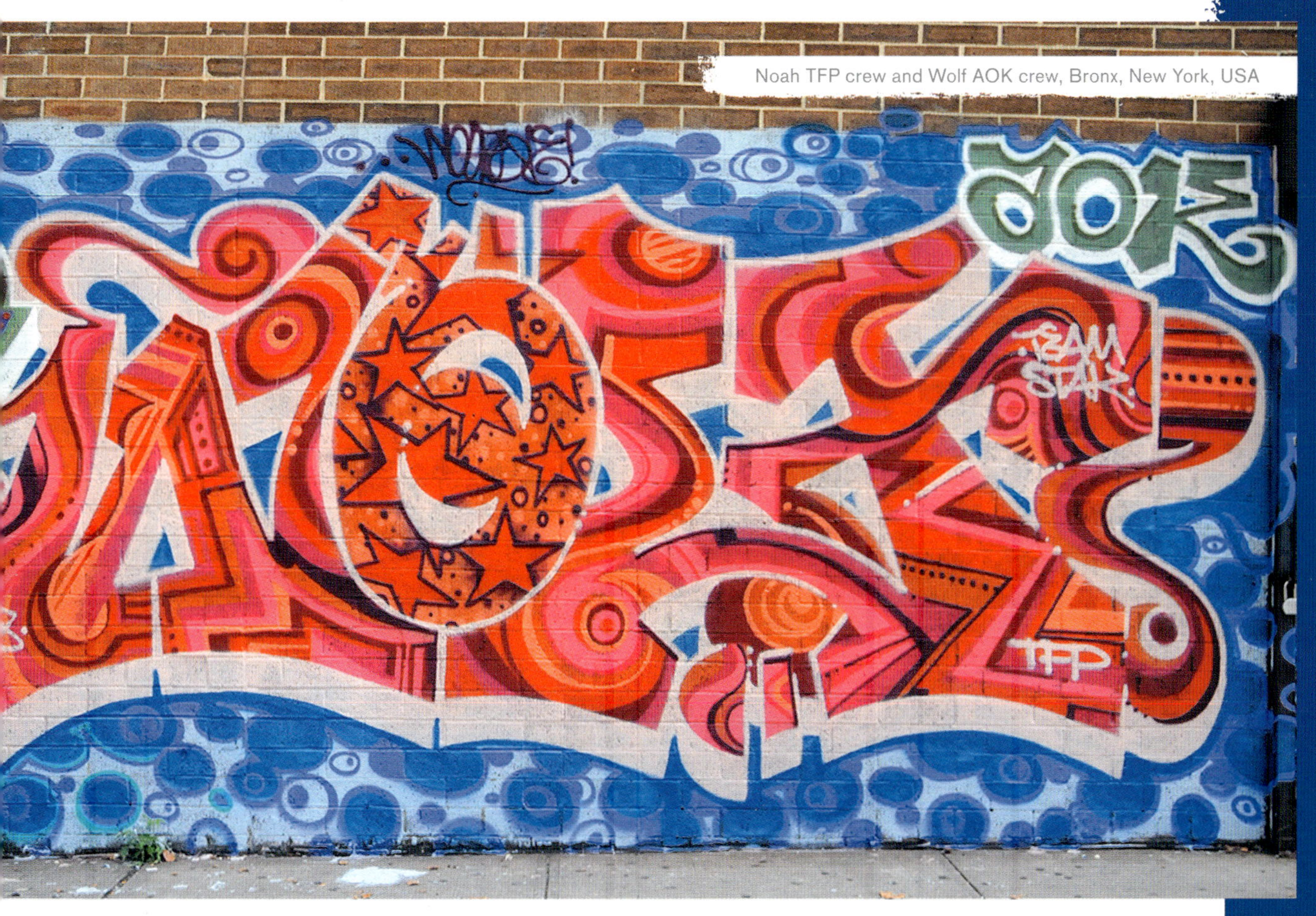

Noah TFP crew and Wolf AOK crew, Bronx, New York, USA

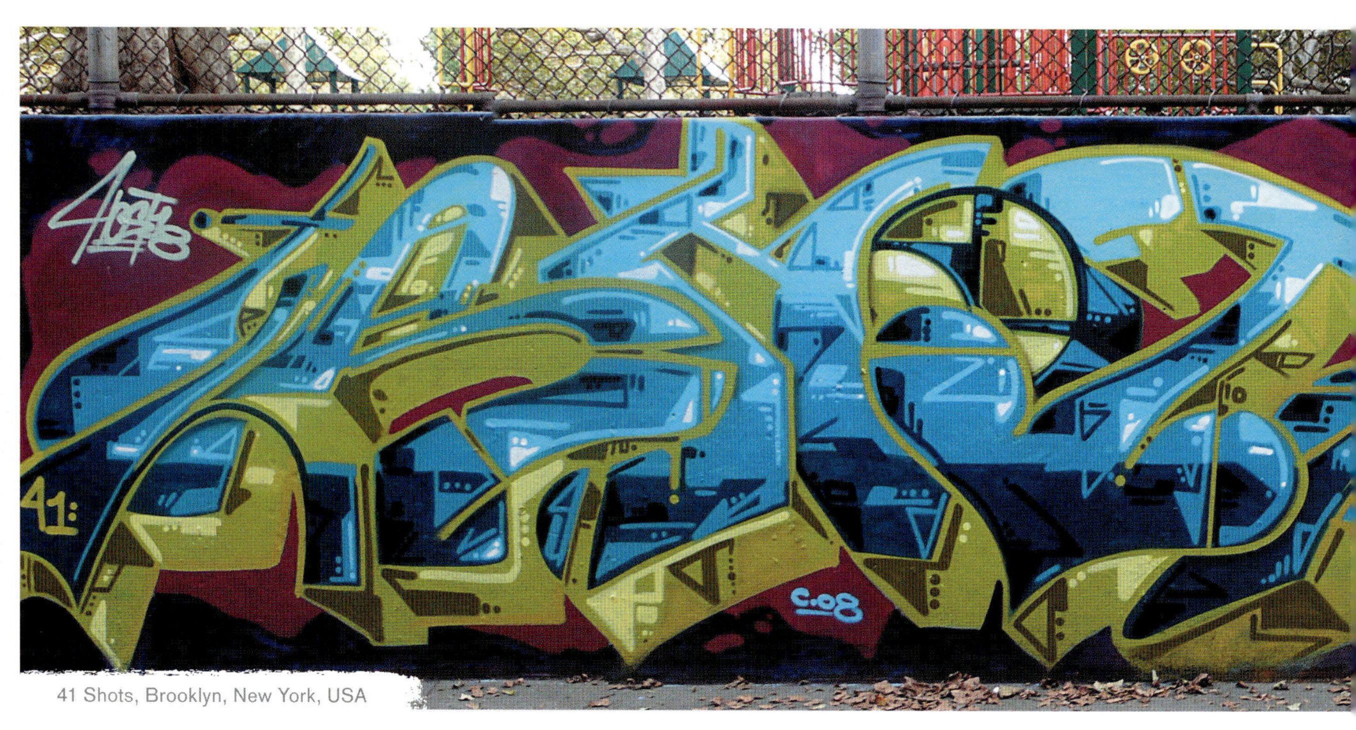

41 Shots, Brooklyn, New York, USA

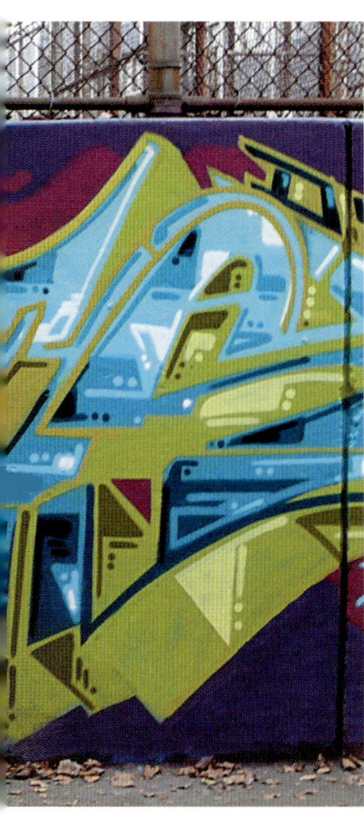

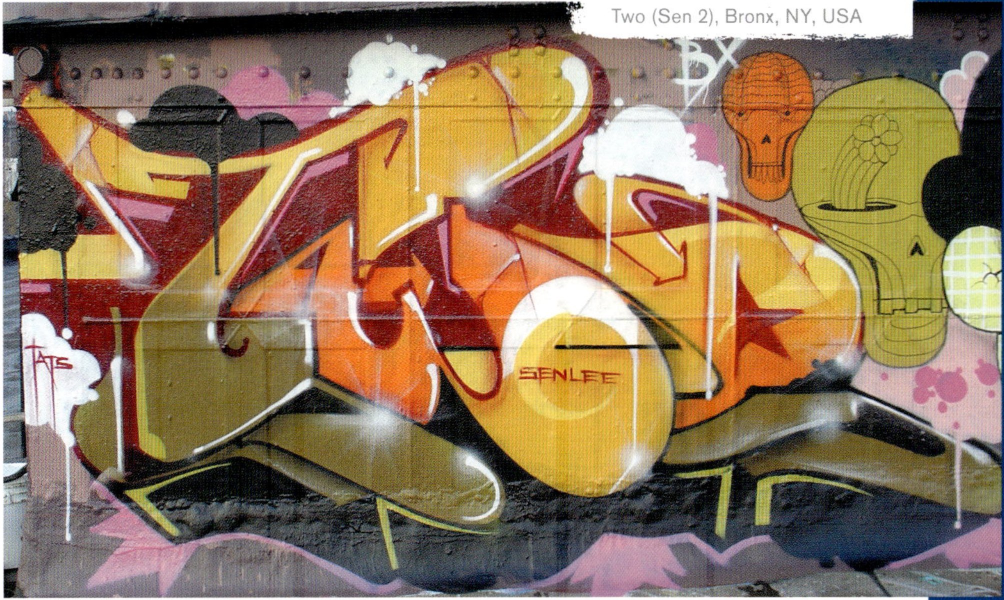

Two (Sen 2), Bronx, NY, USA

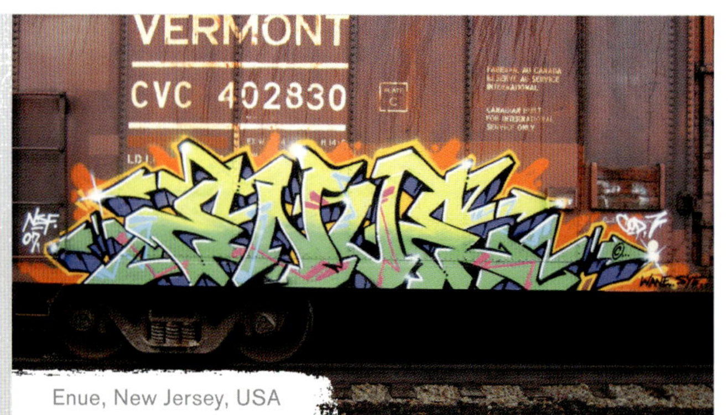

Enue, New Jersey, USA

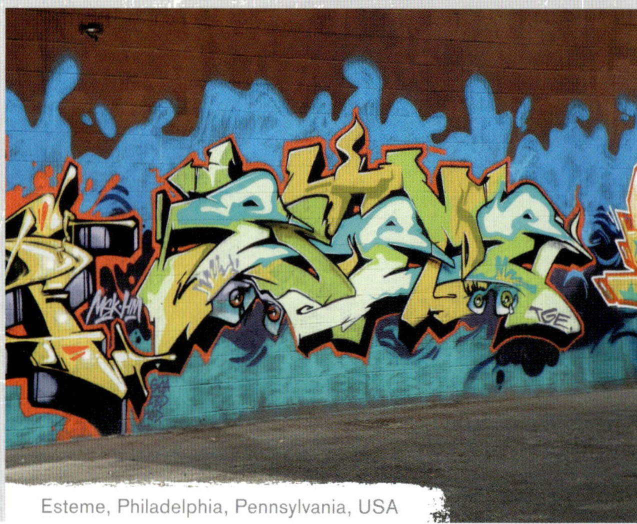

Esteme, Philadelphia, Pennsylvania, USA

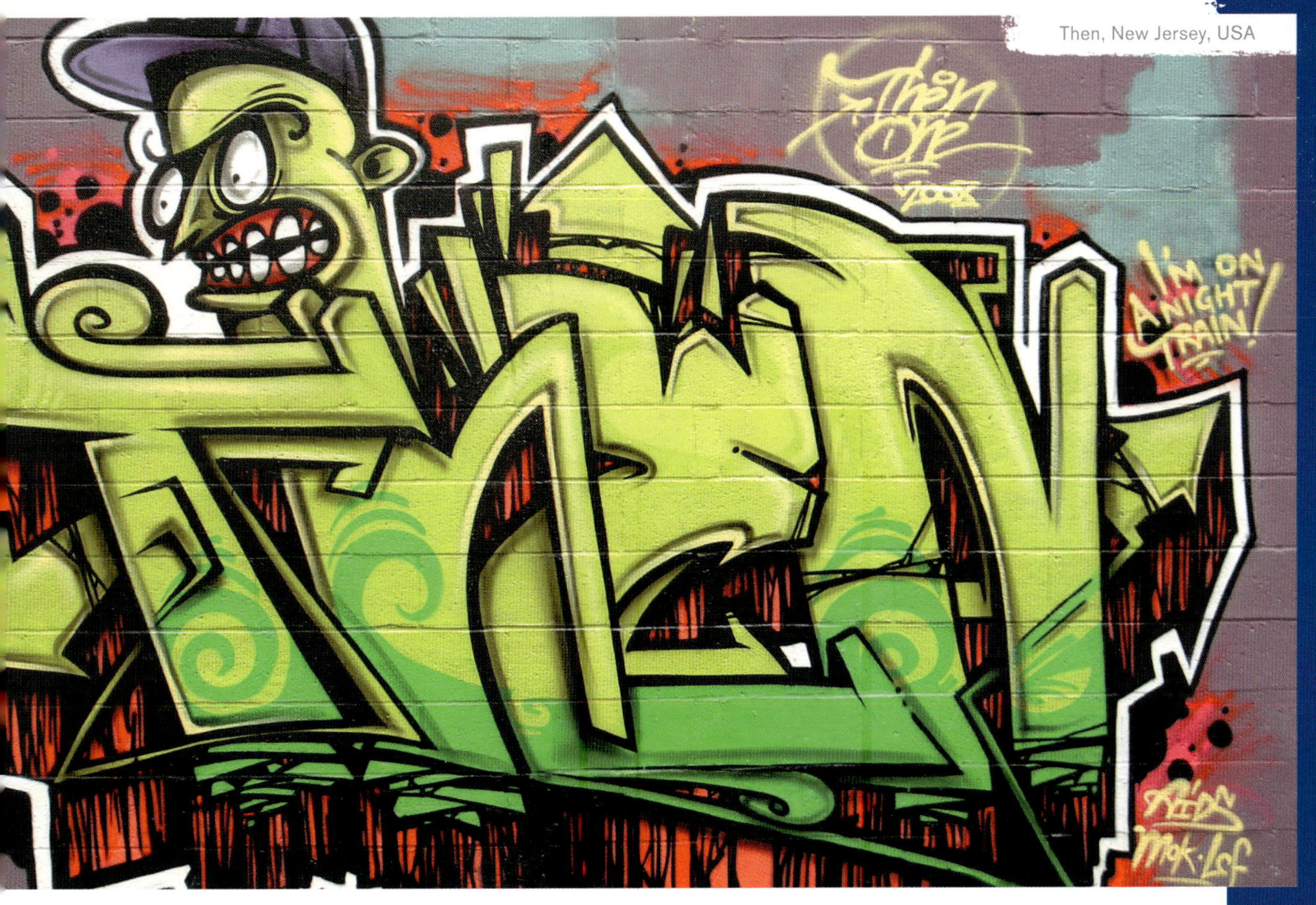

Then, New Jersey, USA

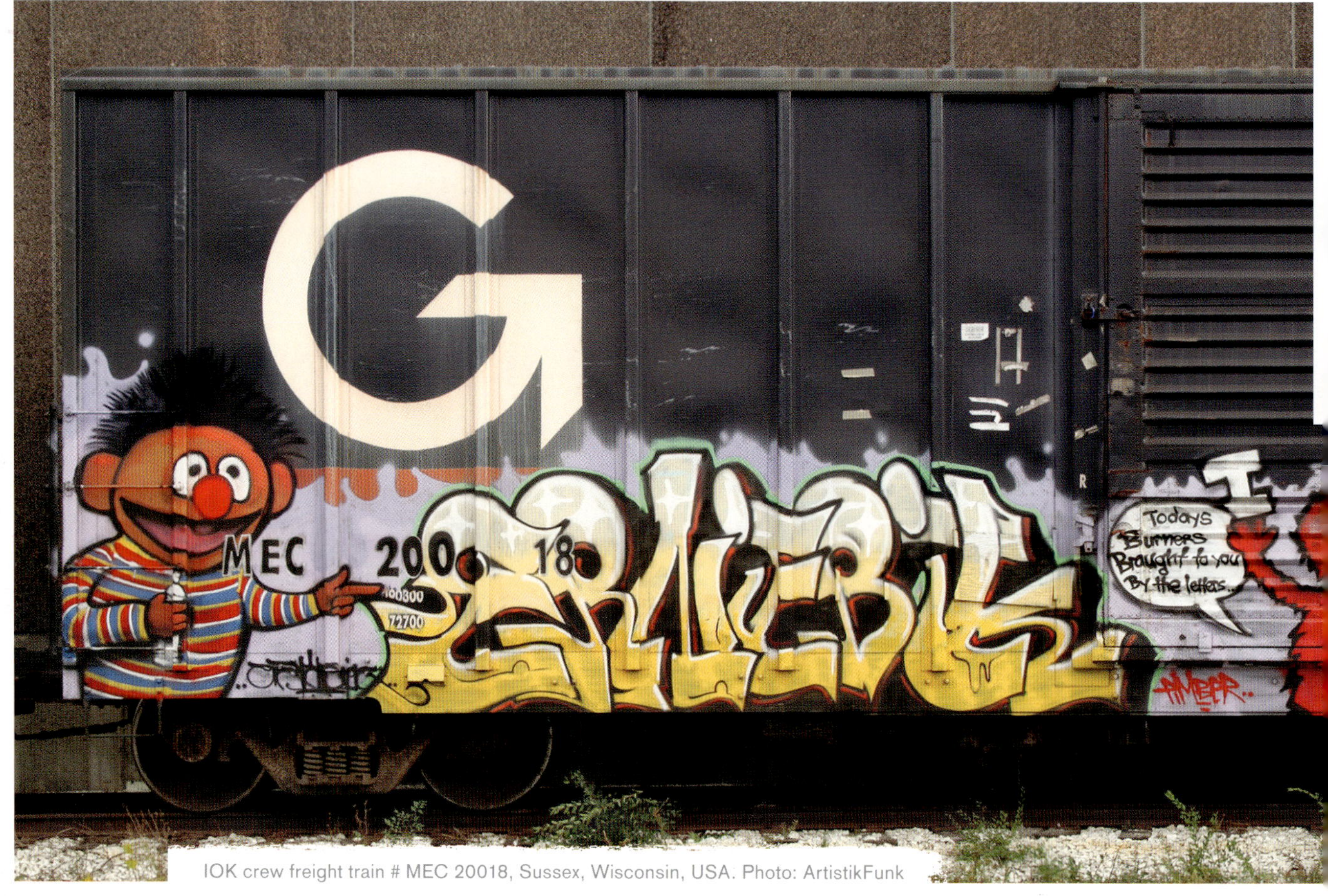

IOK crew freight train # MEC 20018, Sussex, Wisconsin, USA. Photo: ArtistikFunk

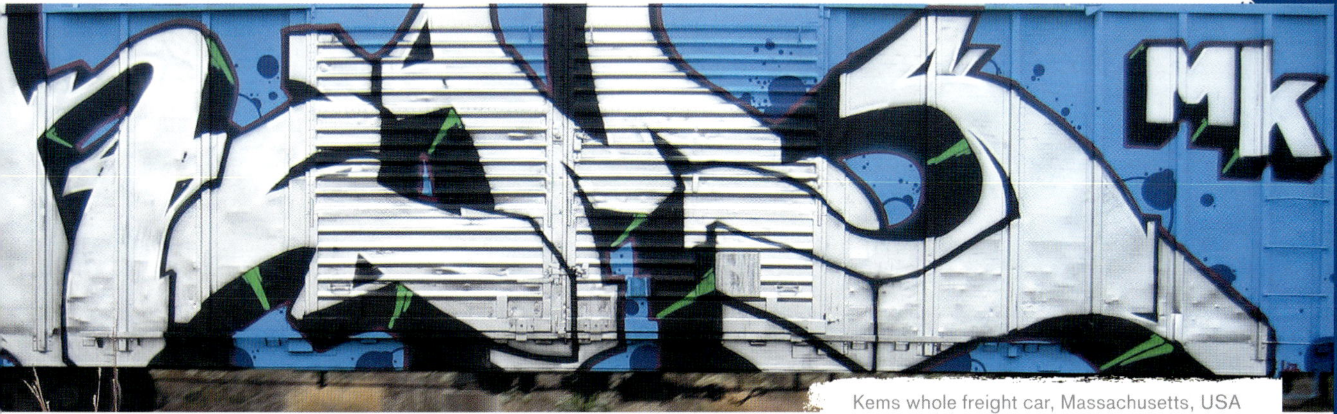

Kems whole freight car, Massachusetts, USA

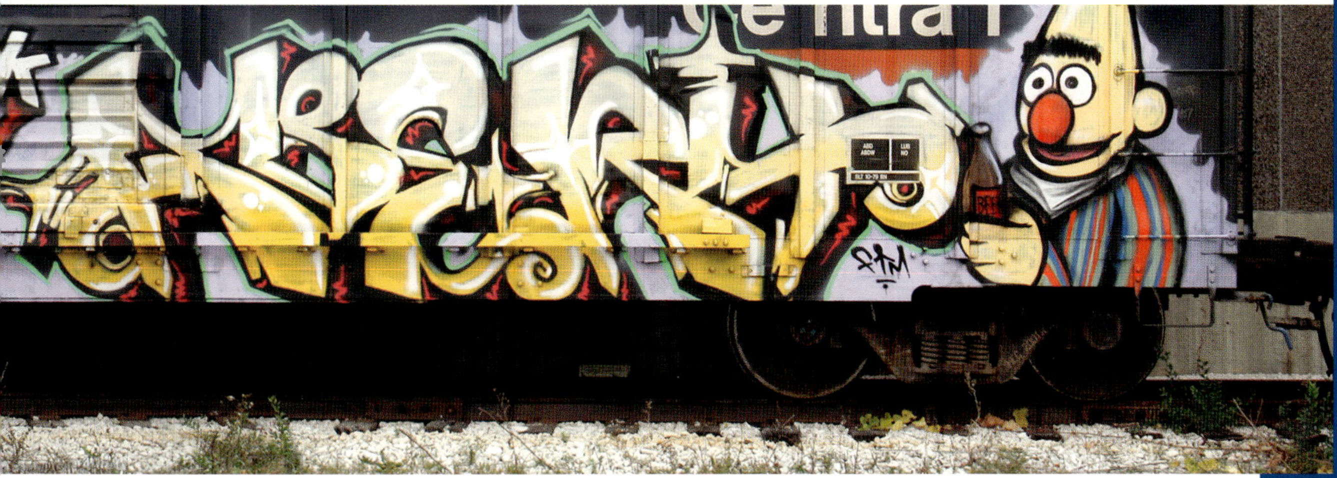

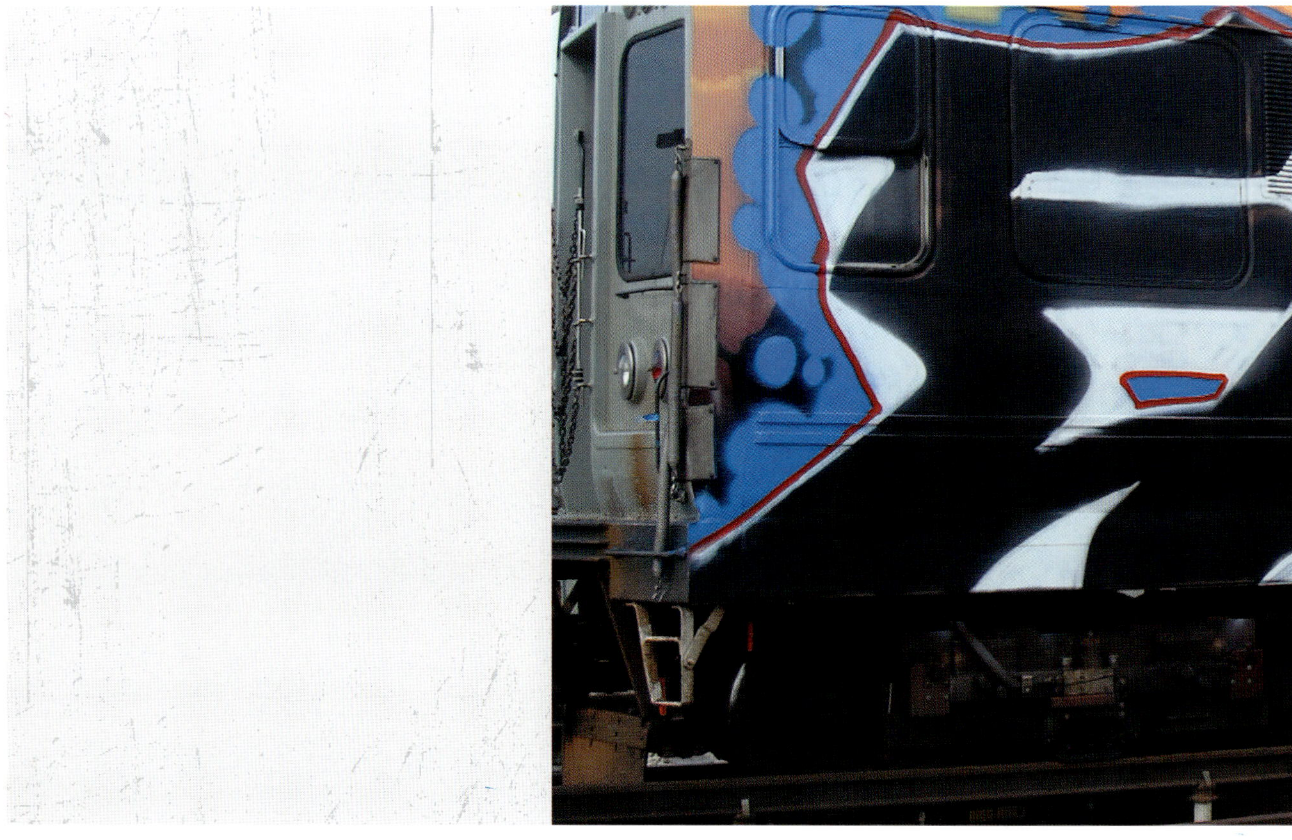

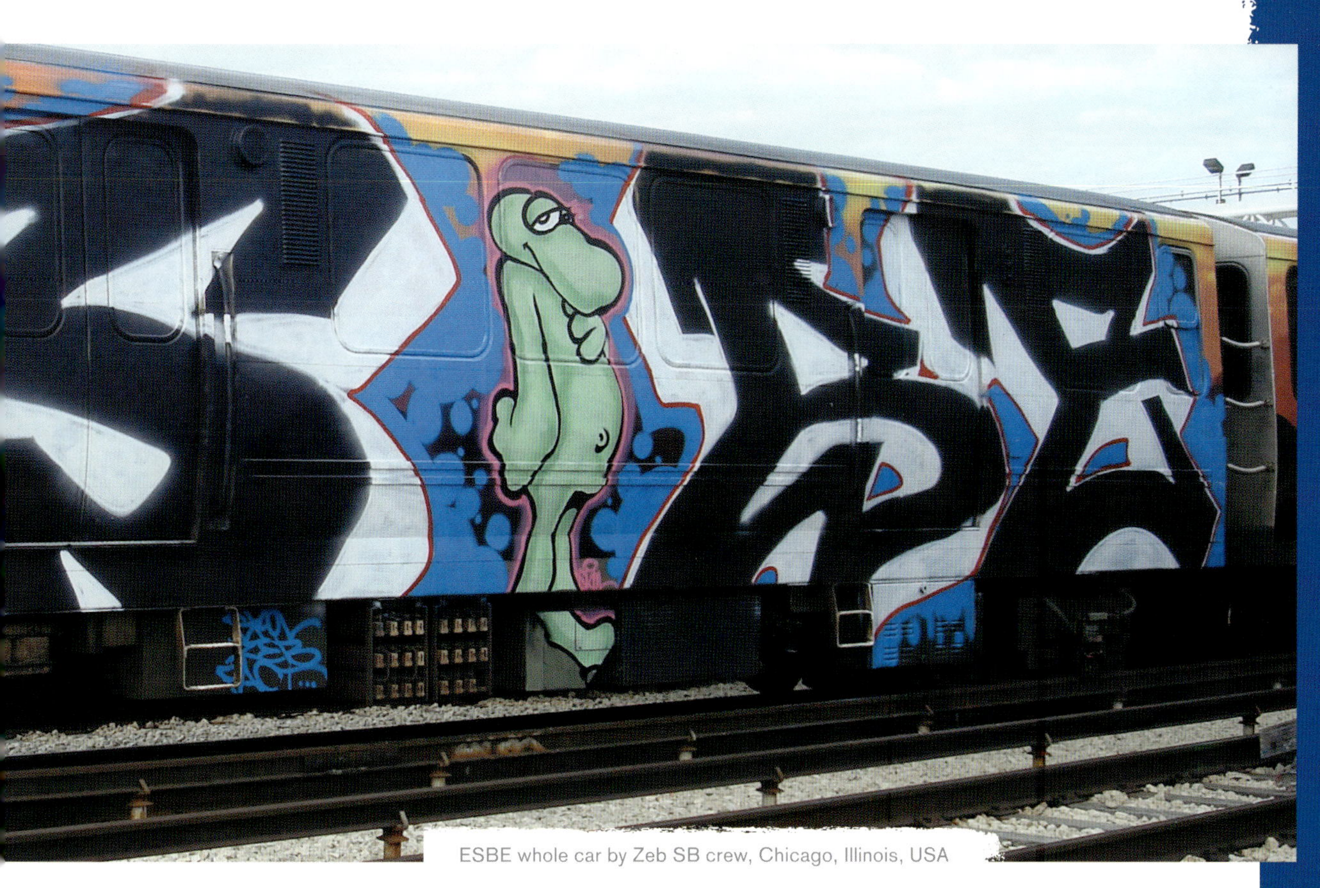

ESBE whole car by Zeb SB crew, Chicago, Illinois, USA

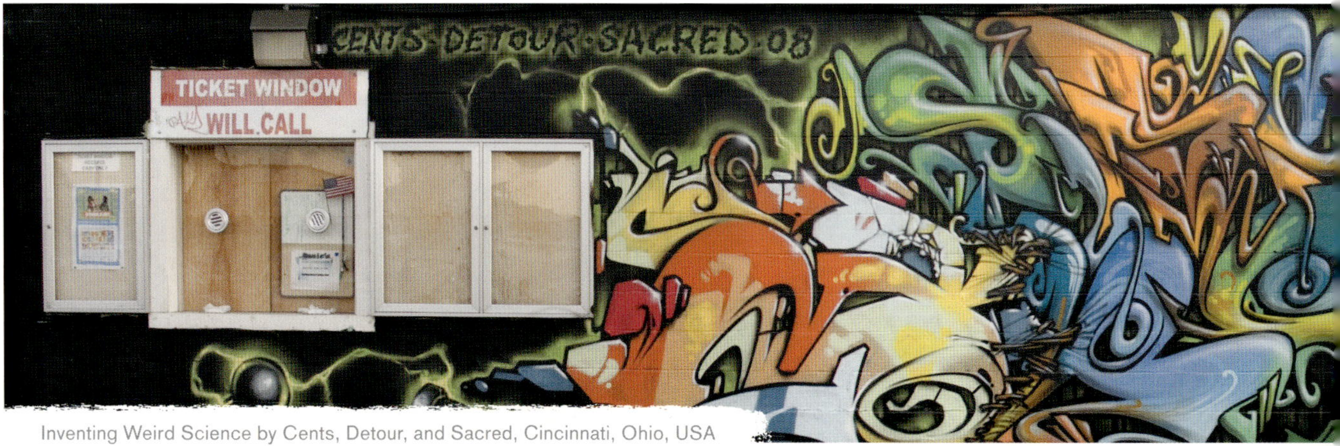

Inventing Weird Science by Cents, Detour, and Sacred, Cincinnati, Ohio, USA

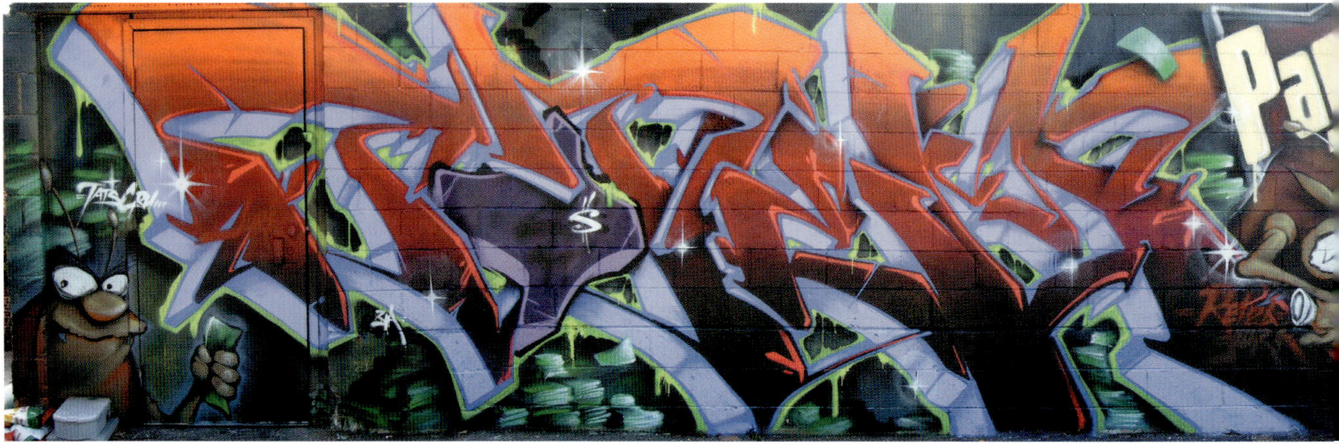

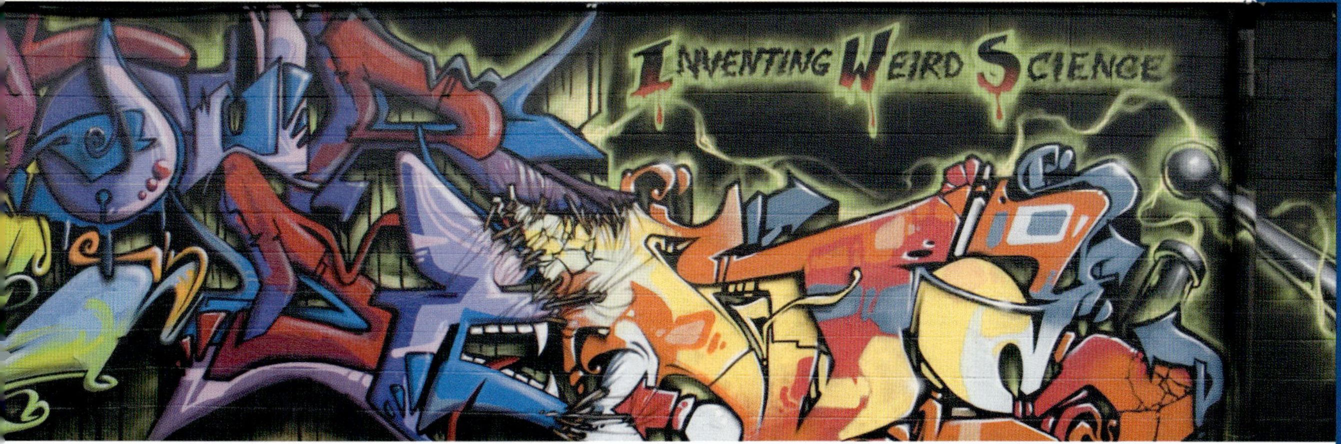

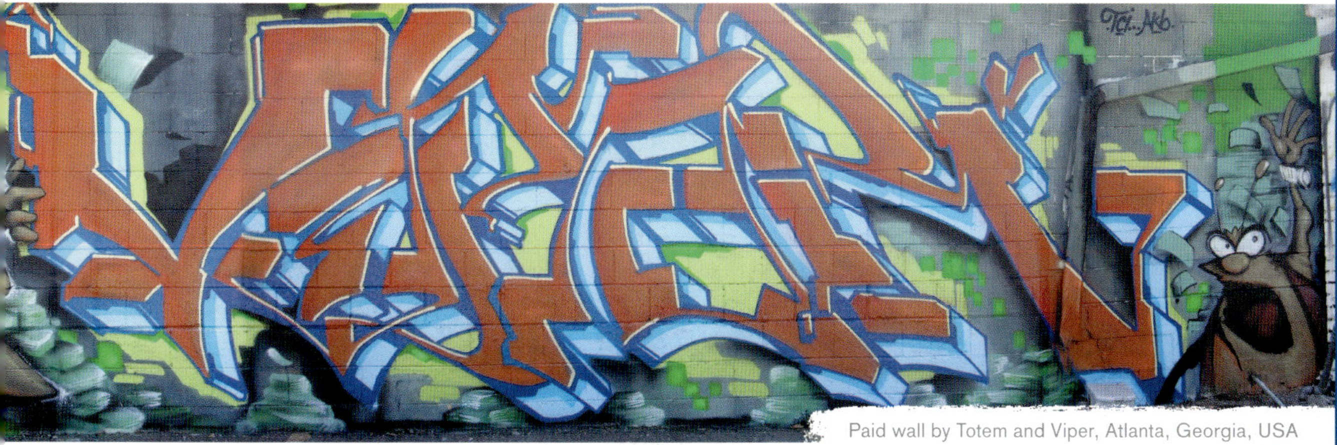

Paid wall by Totem and Viper, Atlanta, Georgia, USA

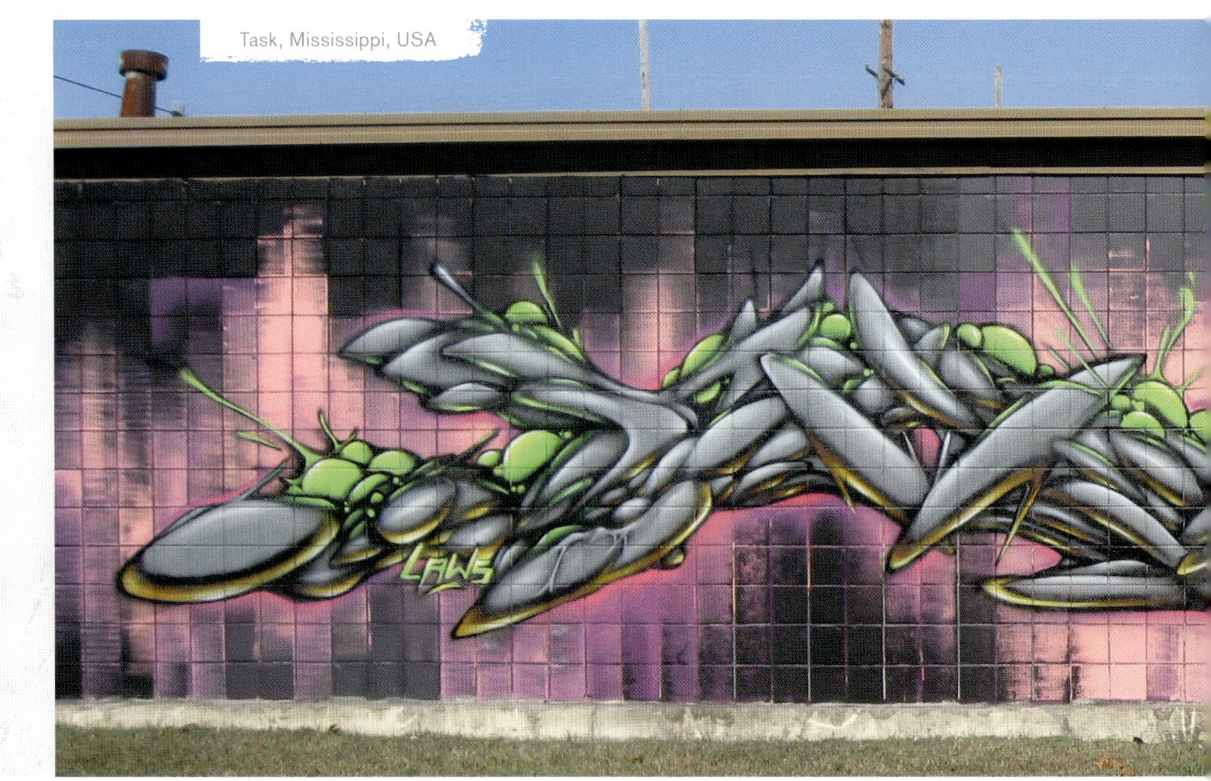

Task, Mississippi, USA

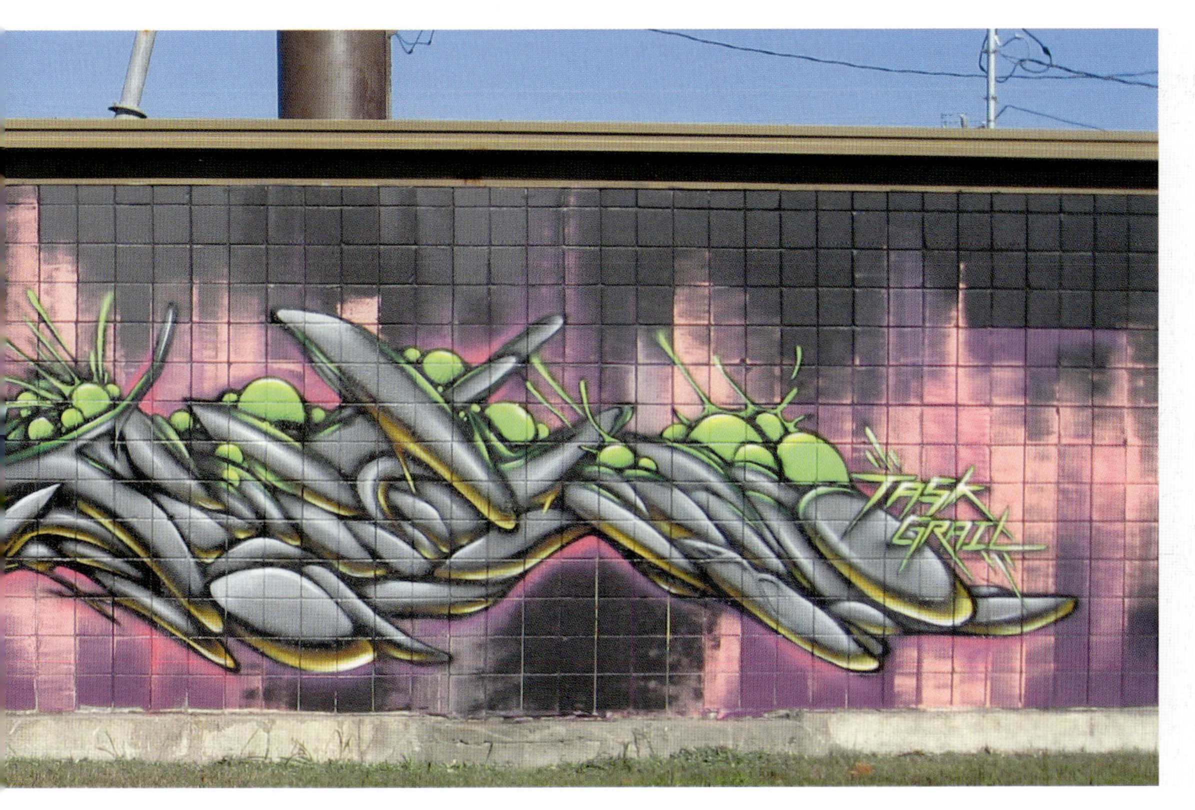

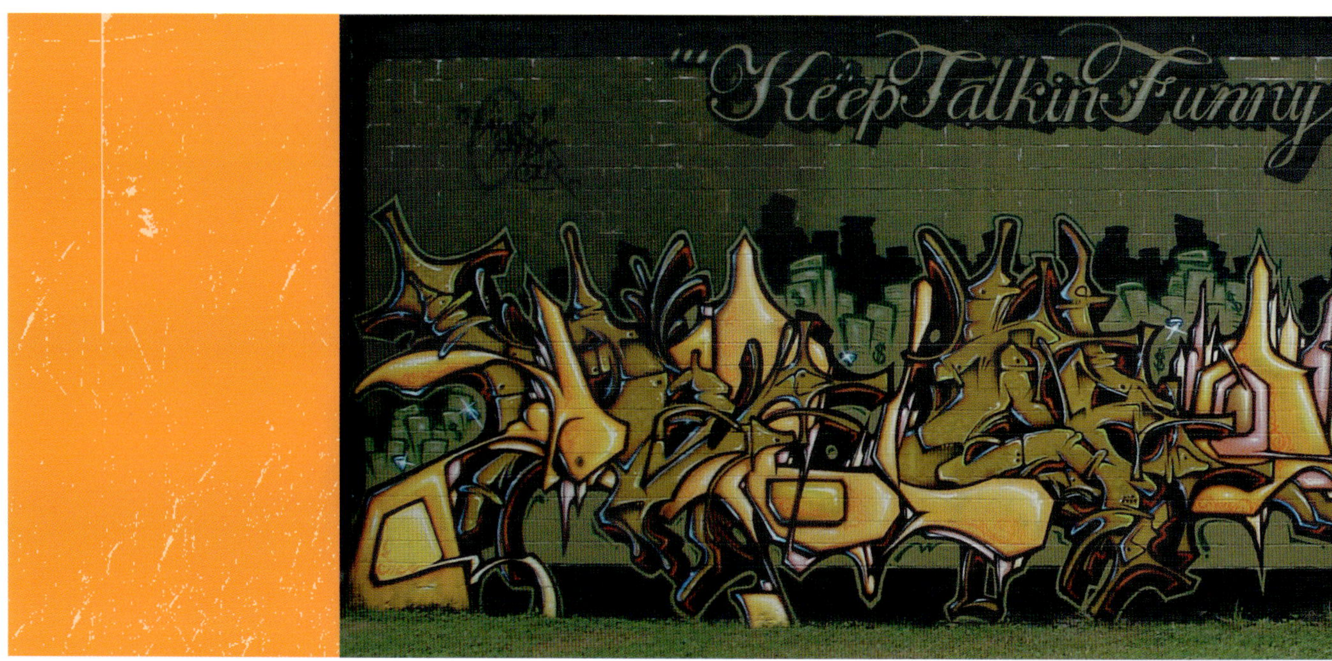
"Keep Talkin Funny

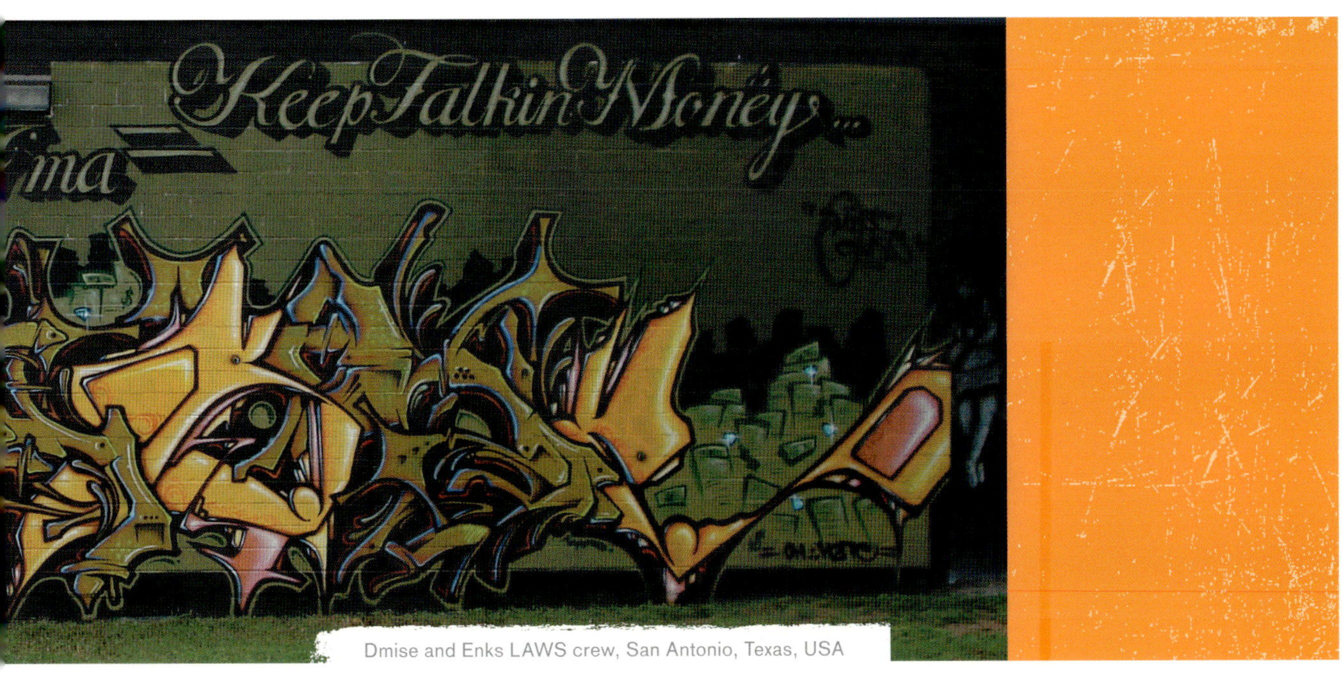

Dmise and Enks LAWS crew, San Antonio, Texas, USA

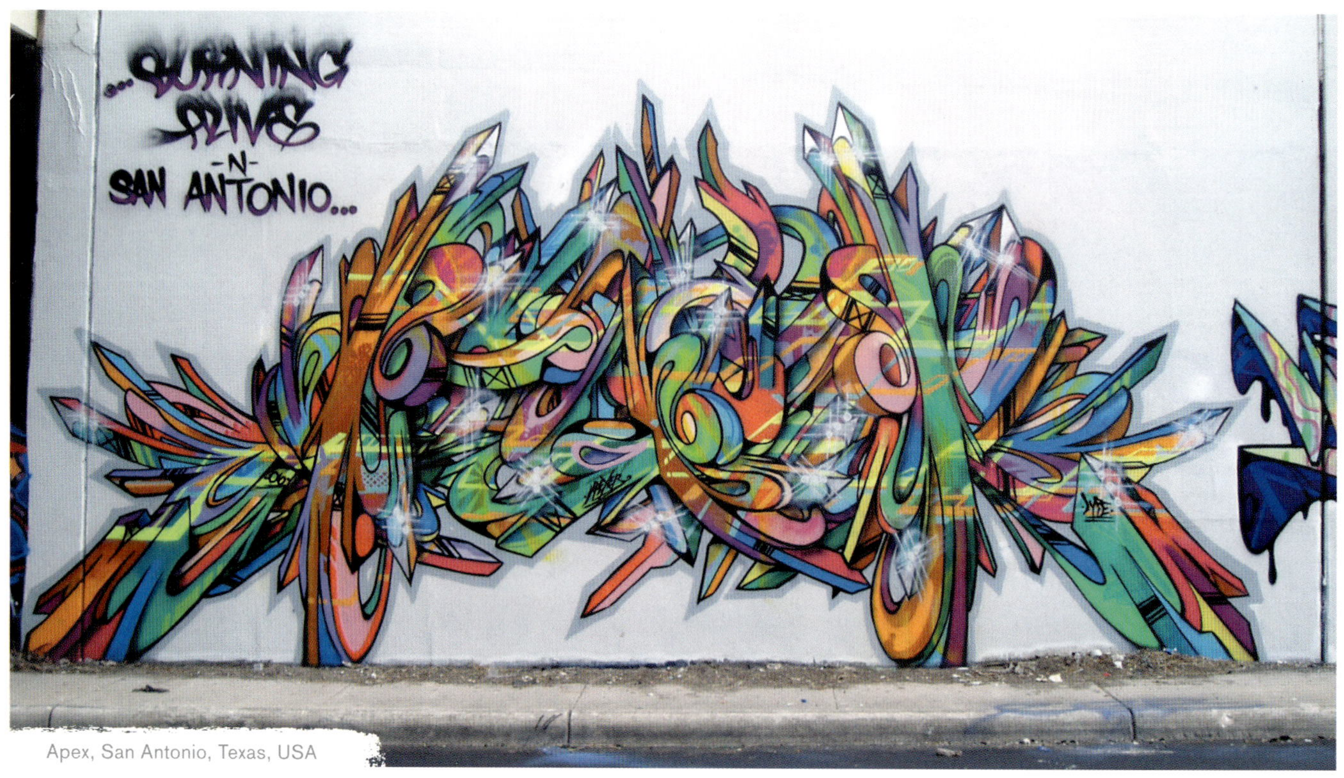

Apex, San Antonio, Texas, USA

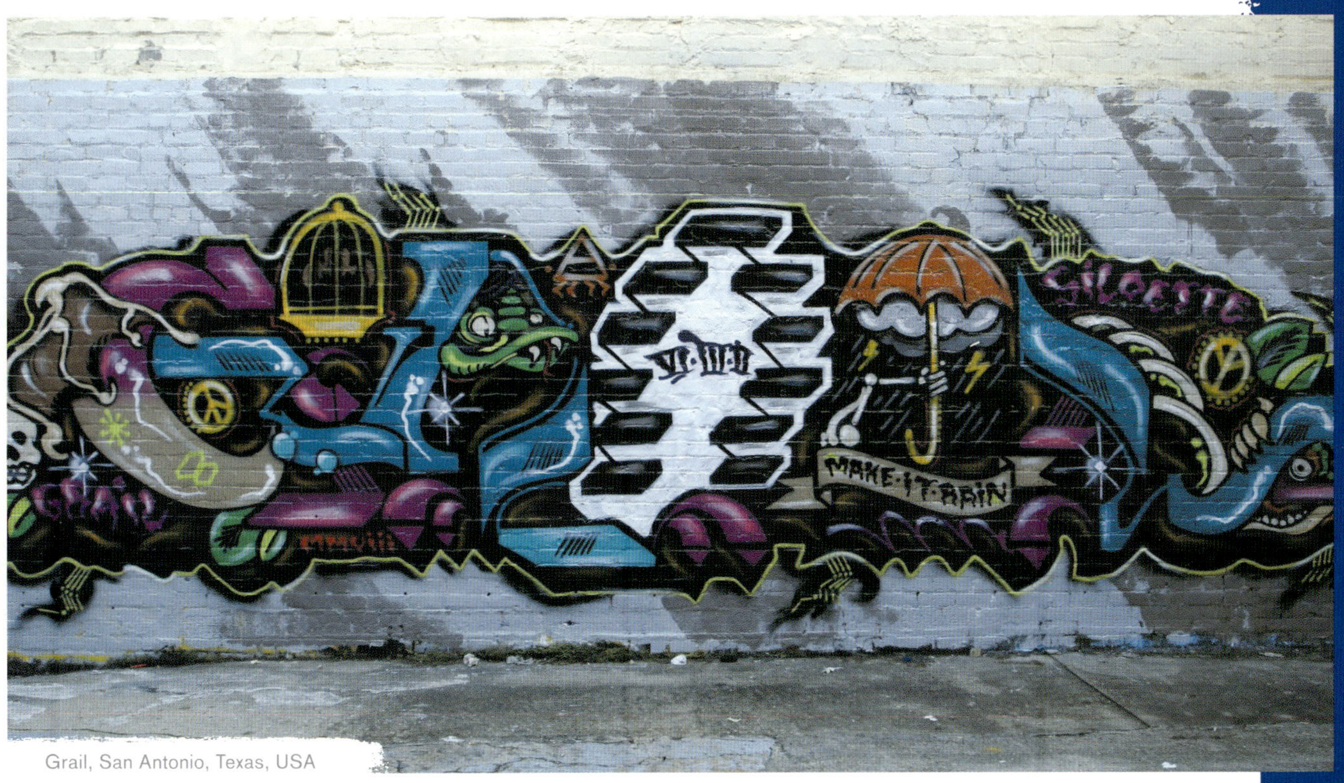

Grail, San Antonio, Texas, USA

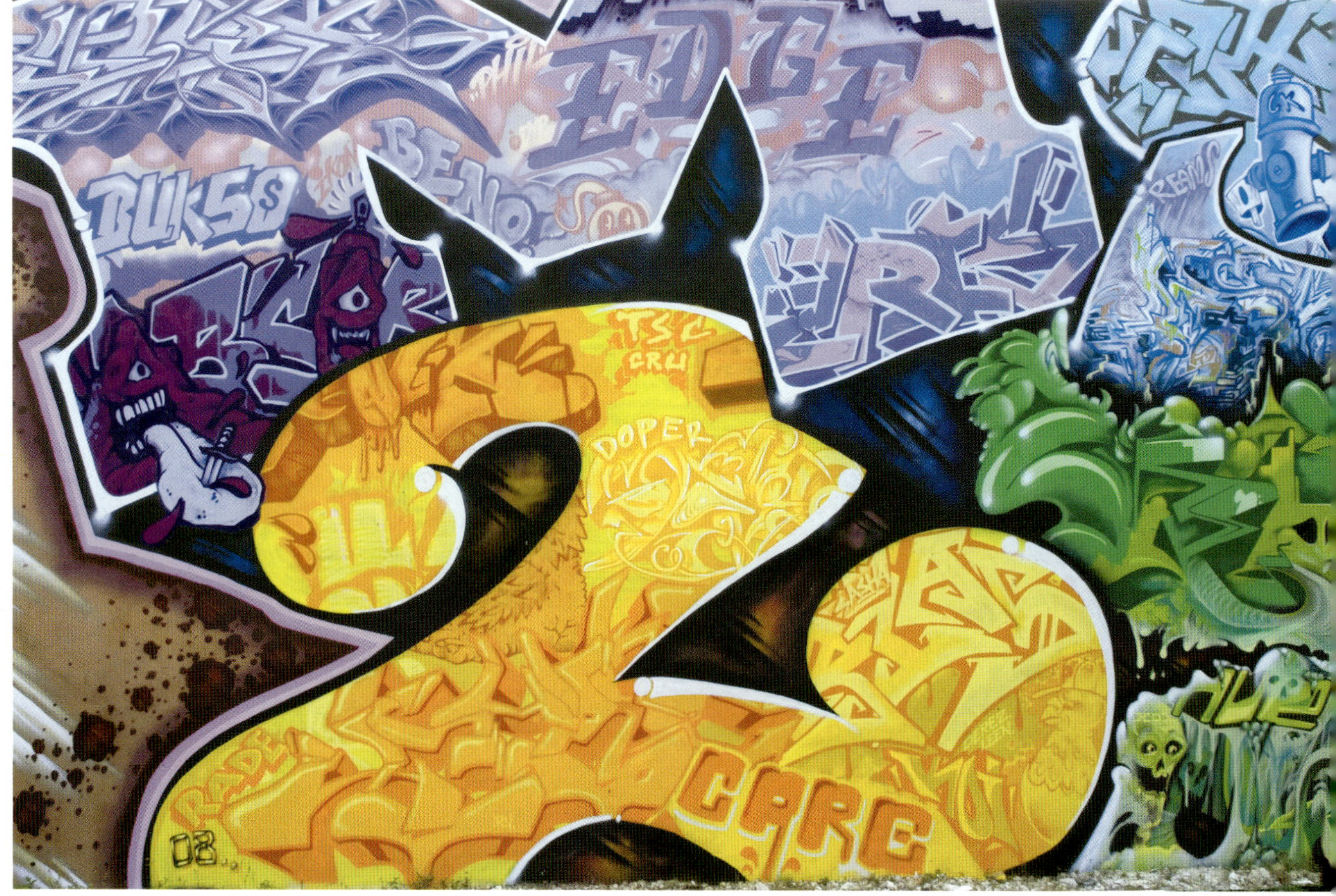
BENO
TSC
CRU
DOPER
CARC
08

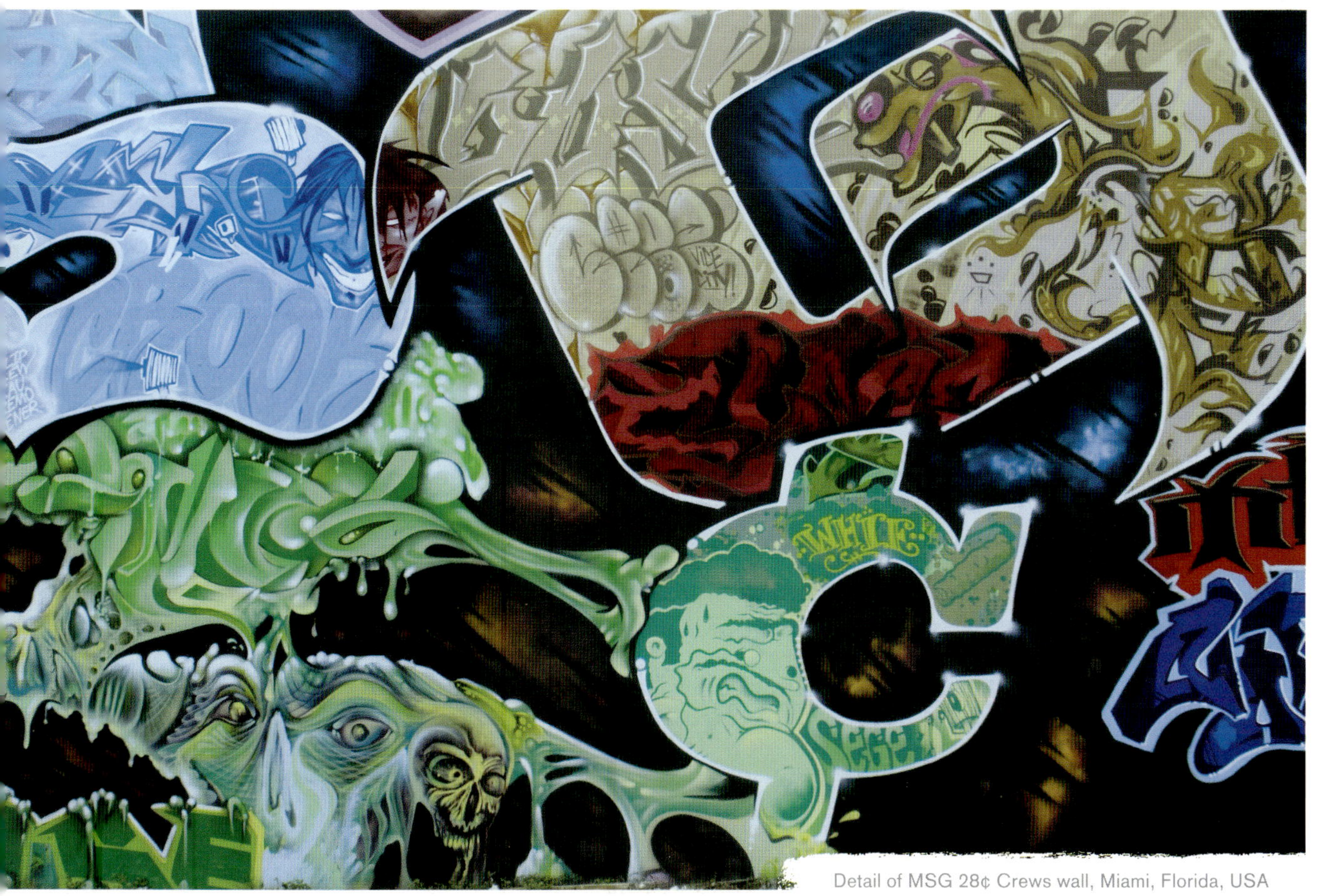

Detail of MSG 28¢ Crews wall, Miami, Florida, USA

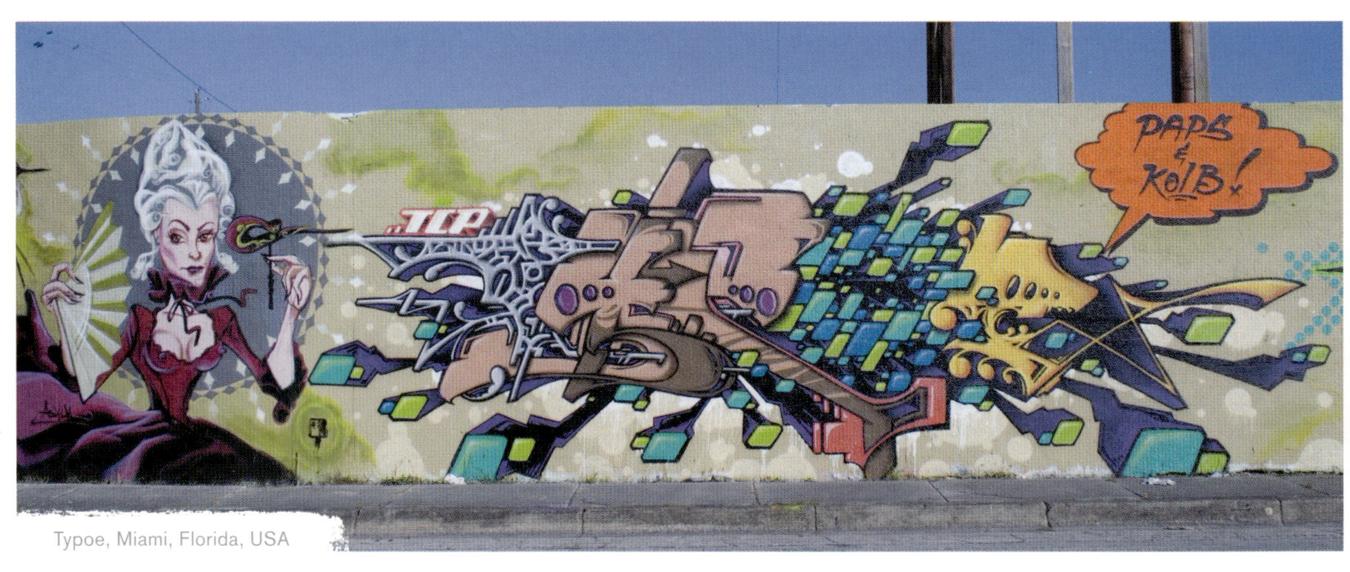

Typoe, Miami, Florida, USA

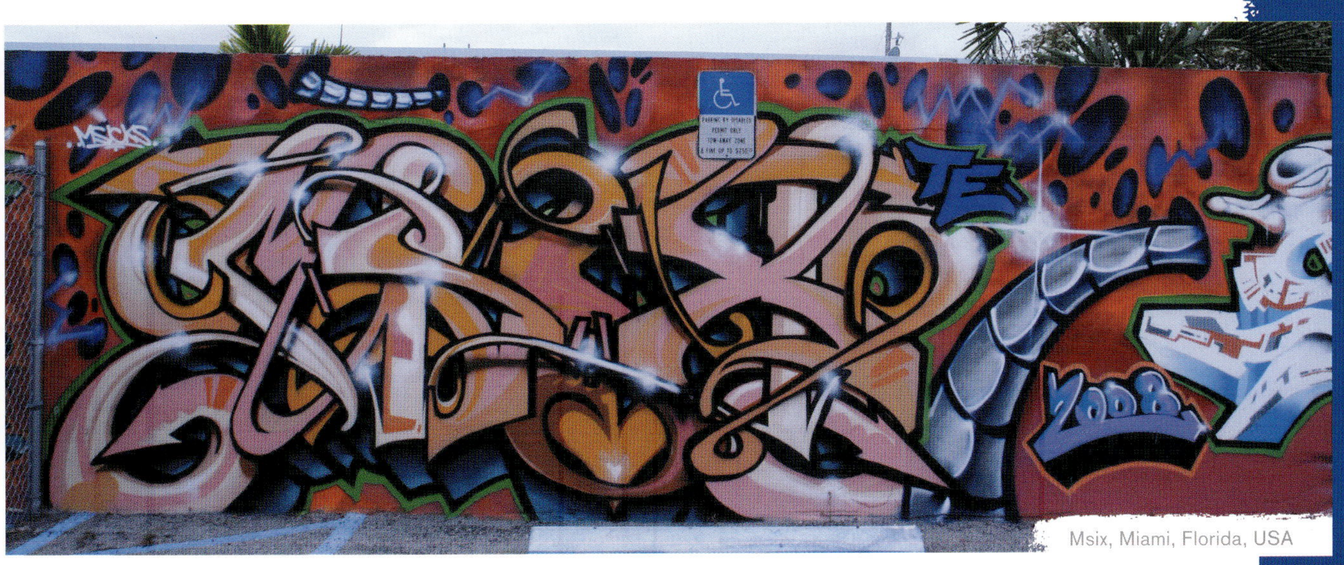

Msix, Miami, Florida, USA

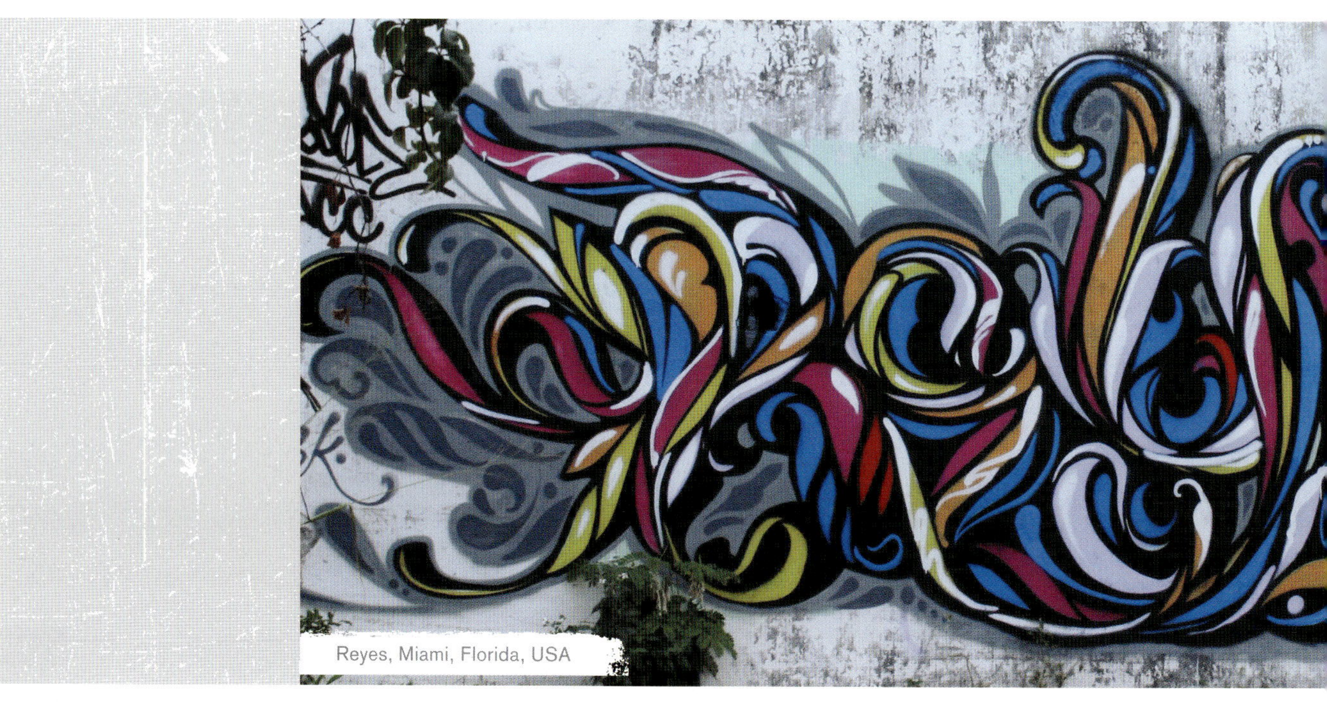
Reyes, Miami, Florida, USA

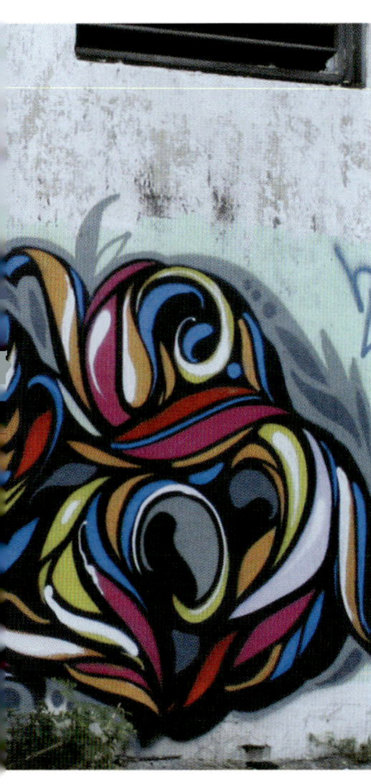

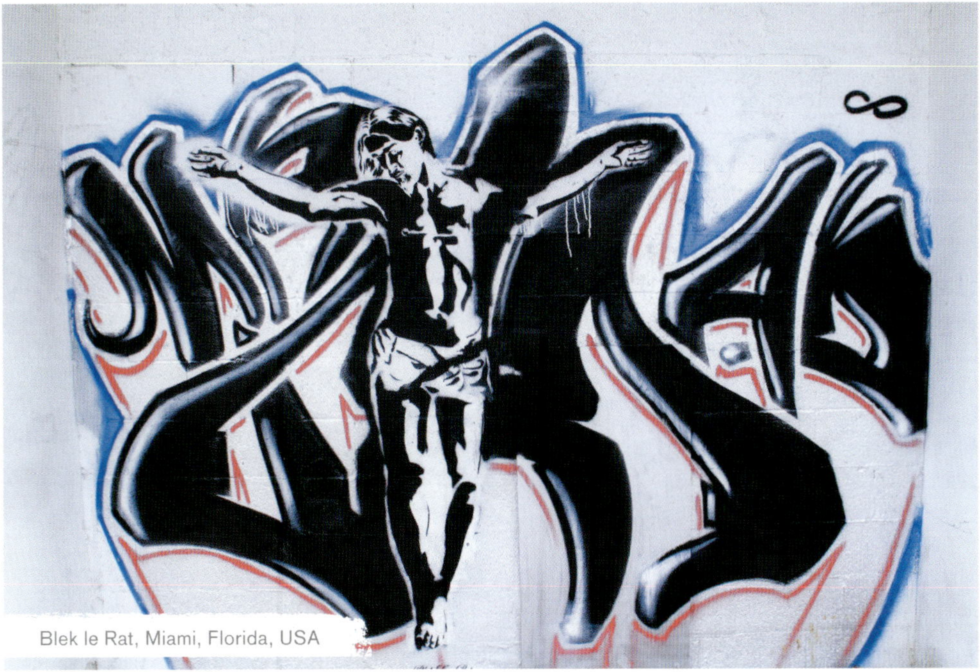

Blek le Rat, Miami, Florida, USA

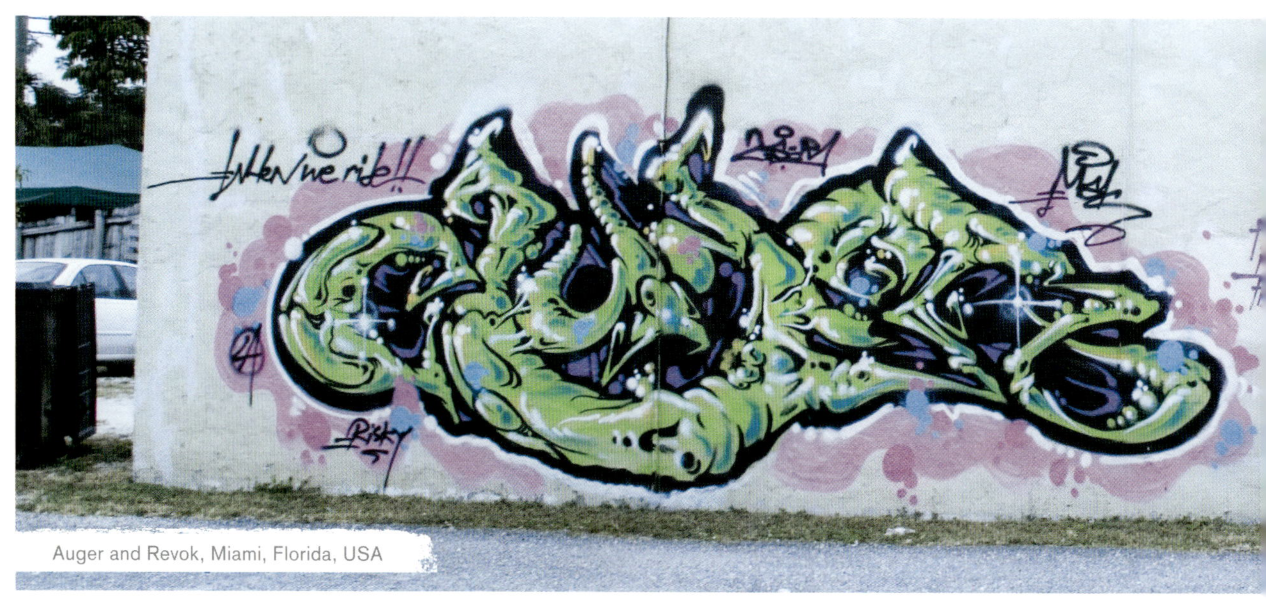

Auger and Revok, Miami, Florida, USA

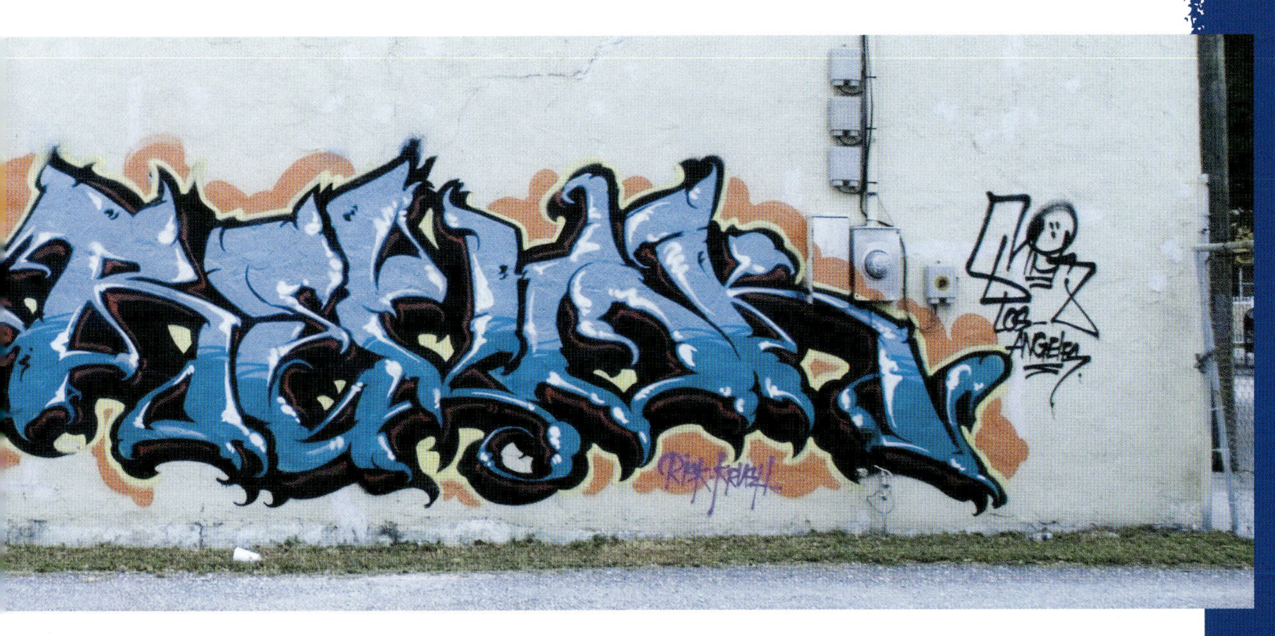
LOS ANGELES

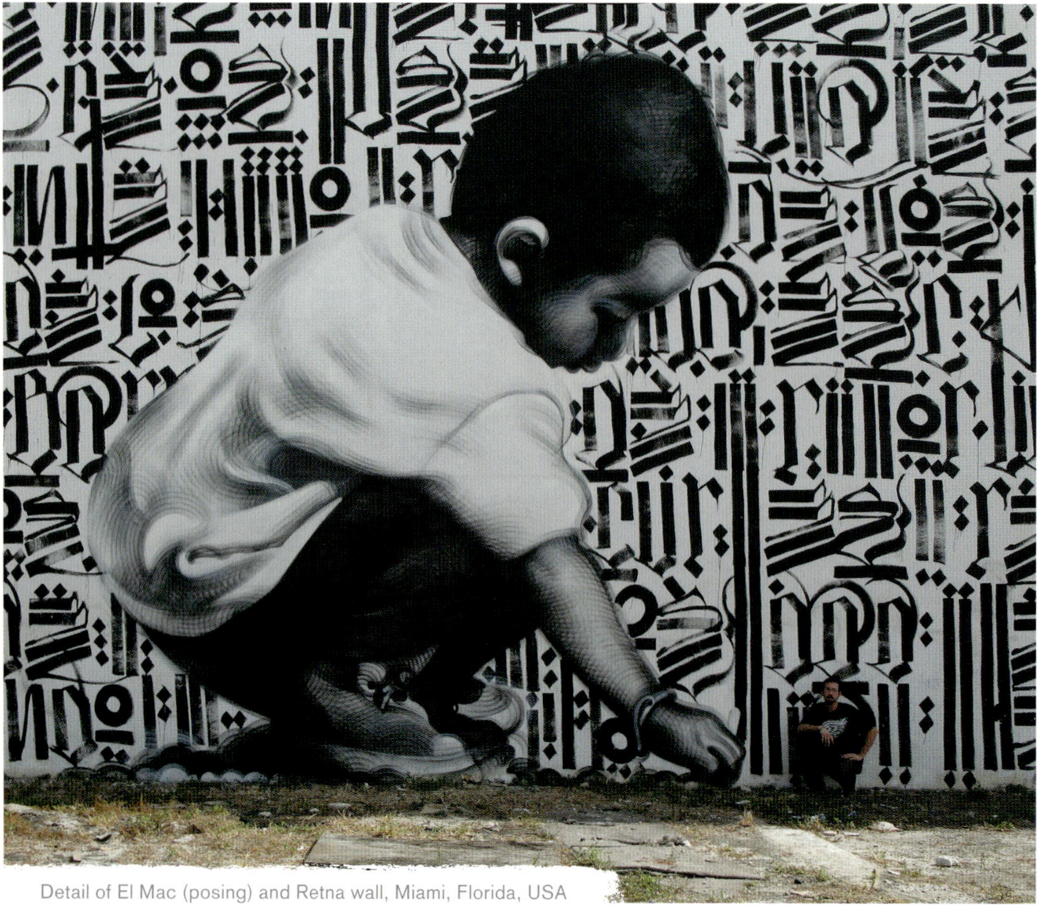

Detail of El Mac (posing) and Retna wall, Miami, Florida, USA

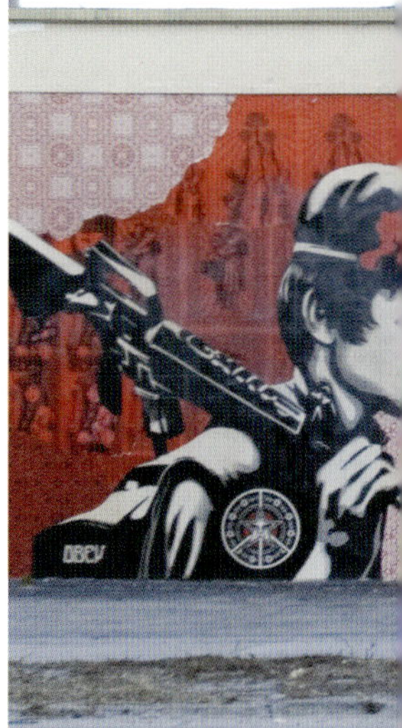

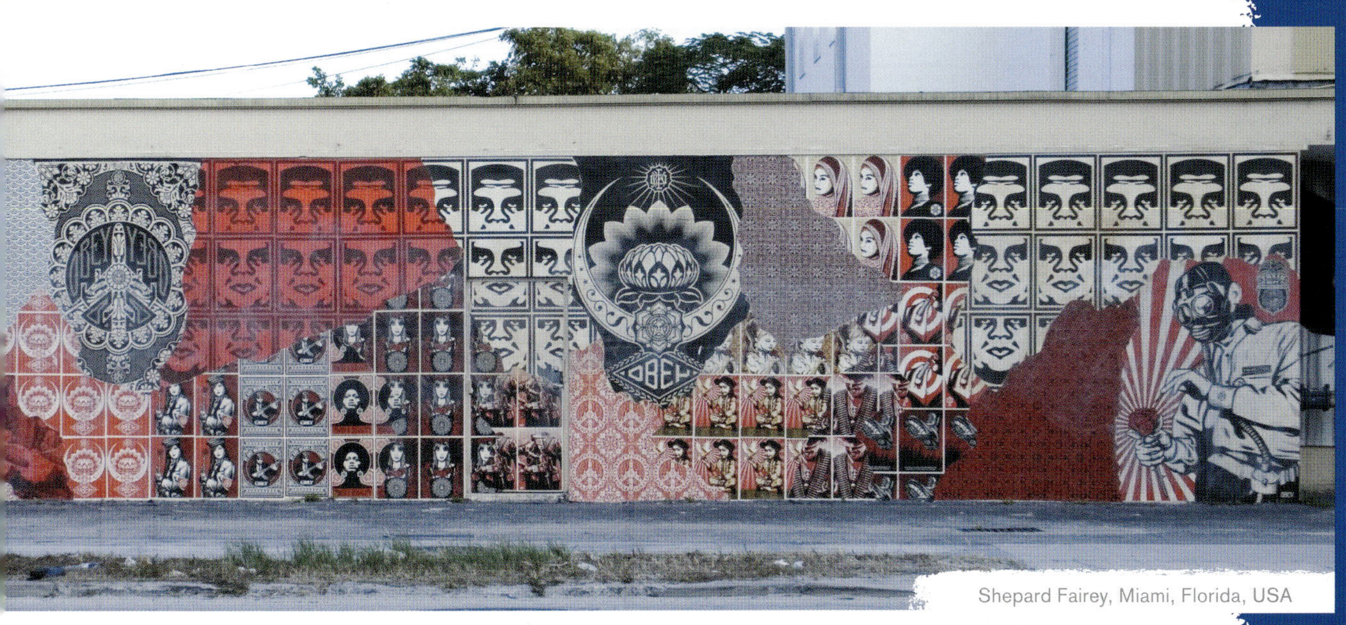

Shepard Fairey, Miami, Florida, USA

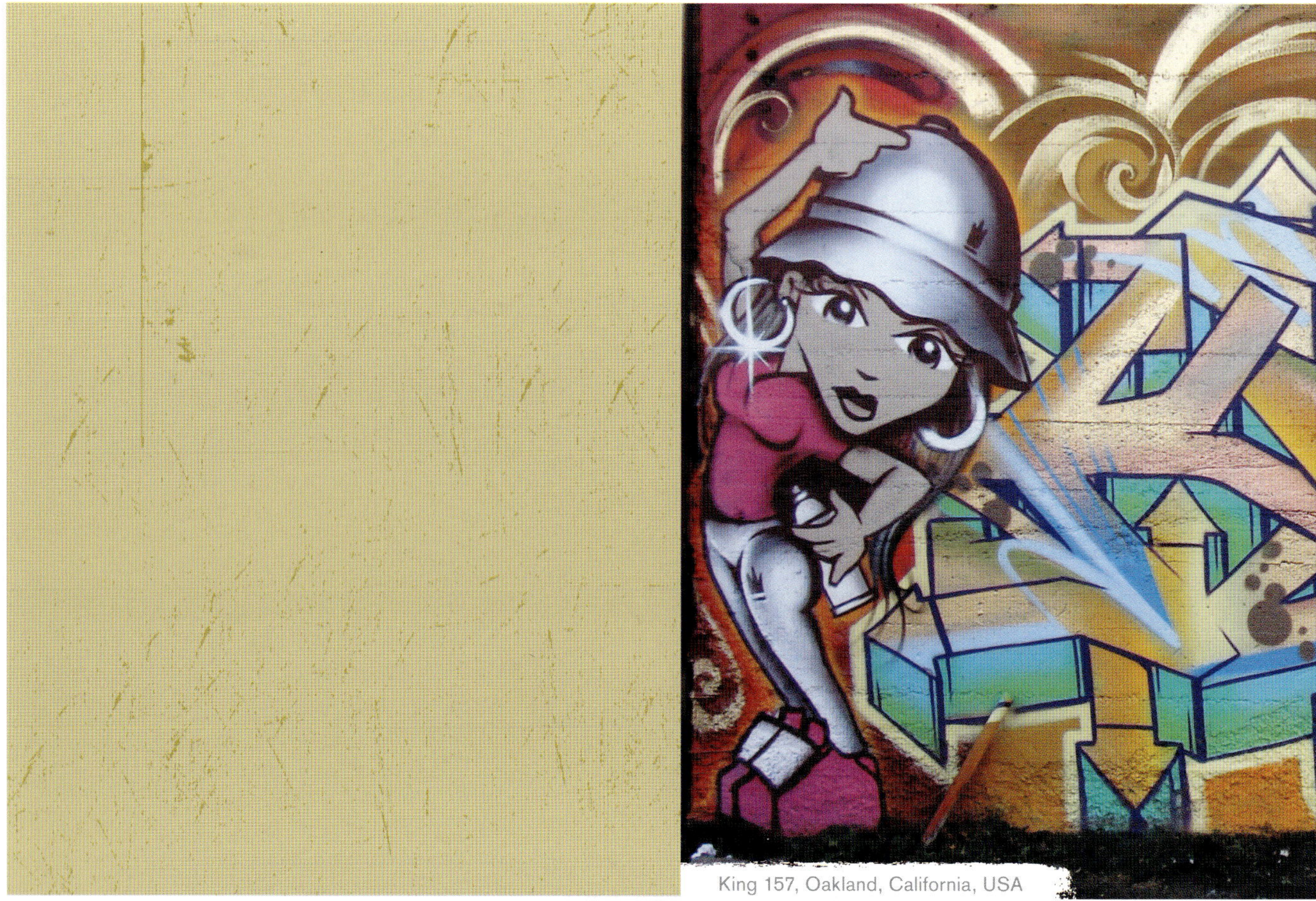

King 157, Oakland, California, USA

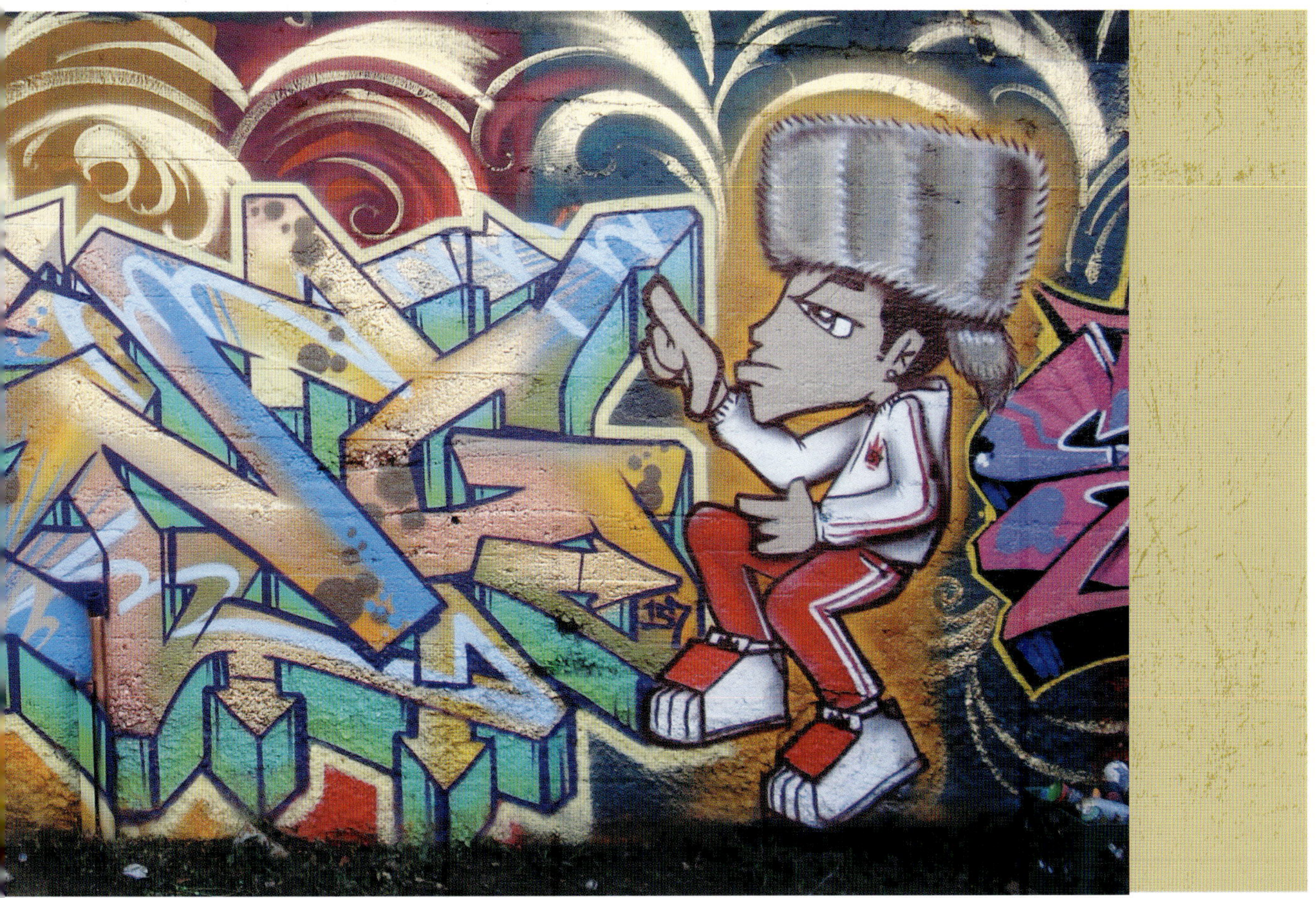

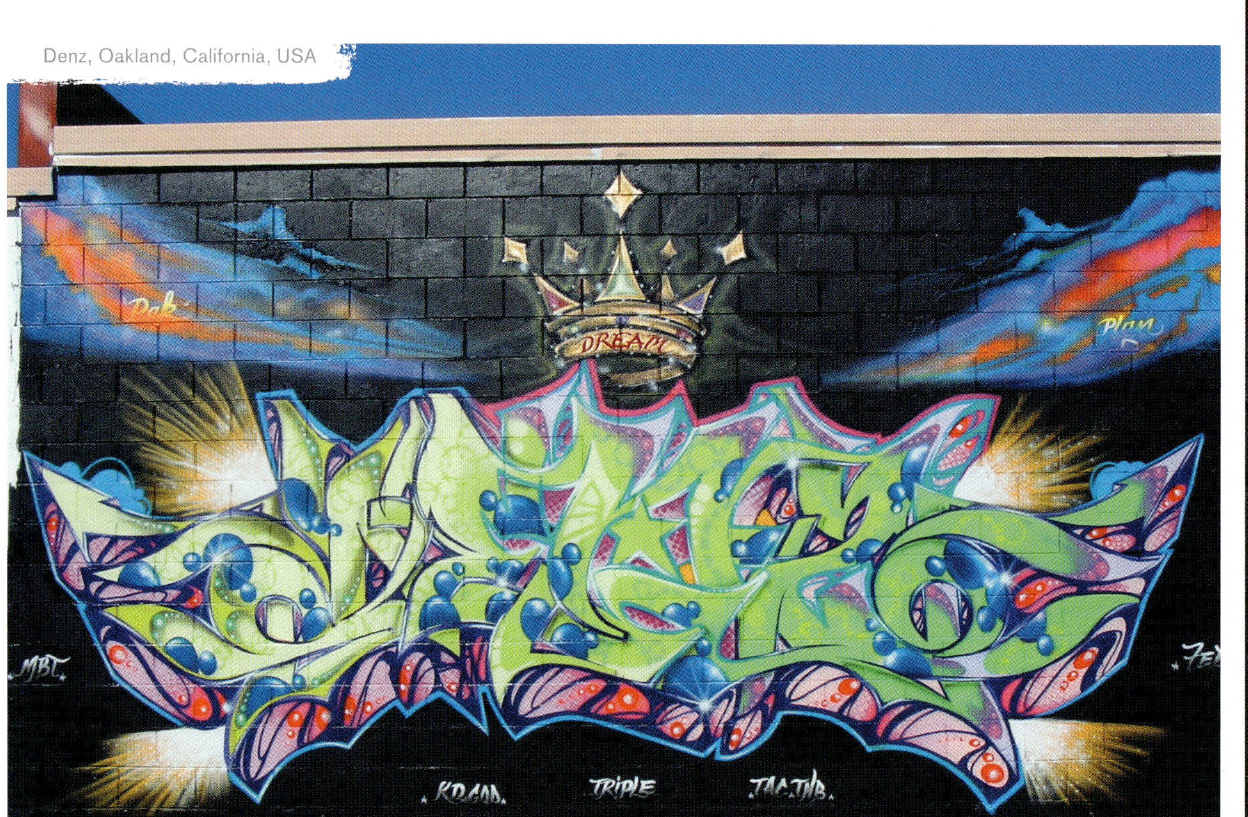

Denz, Oakland, California, USA

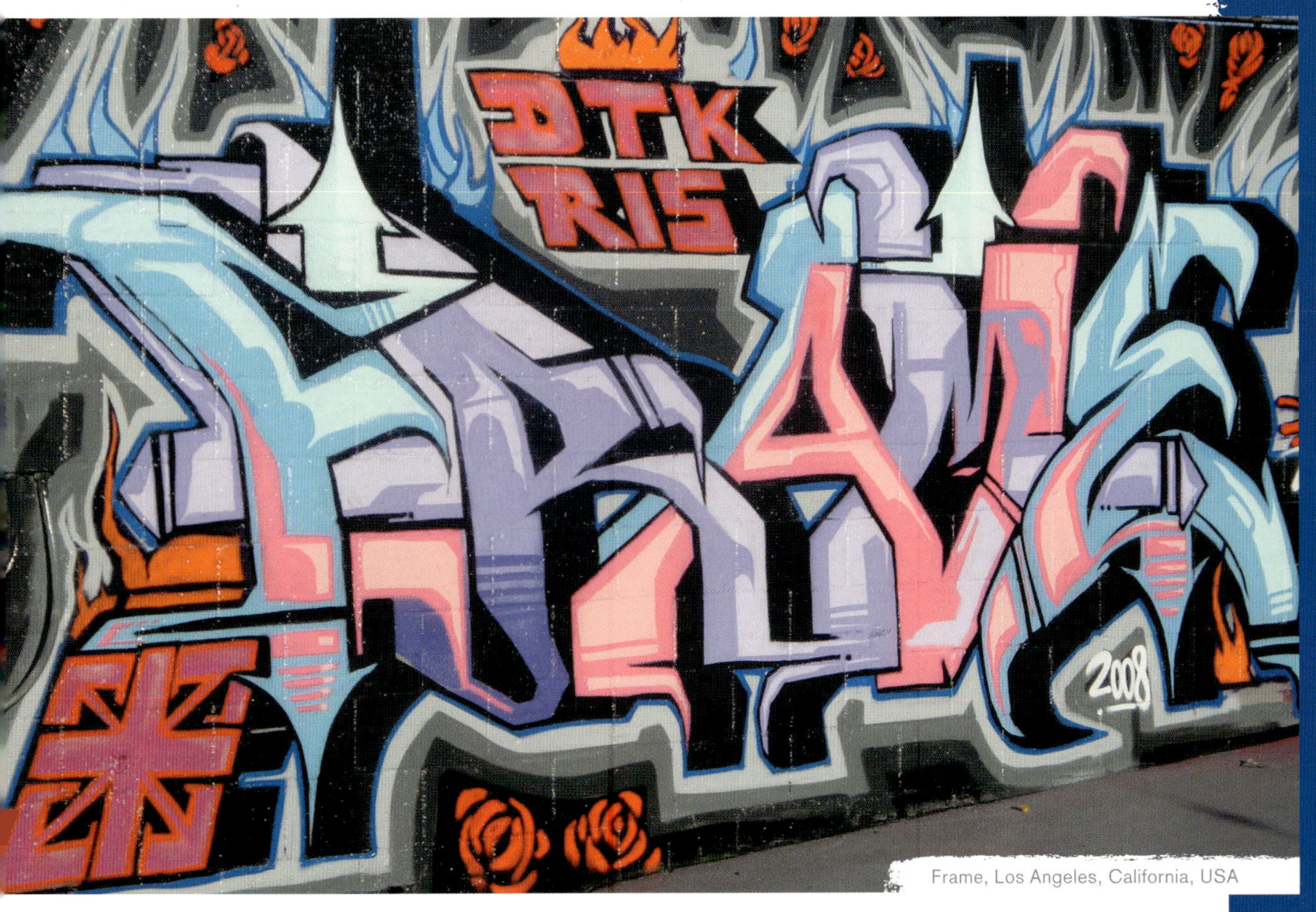

Frame, Los Angeles, California, USA

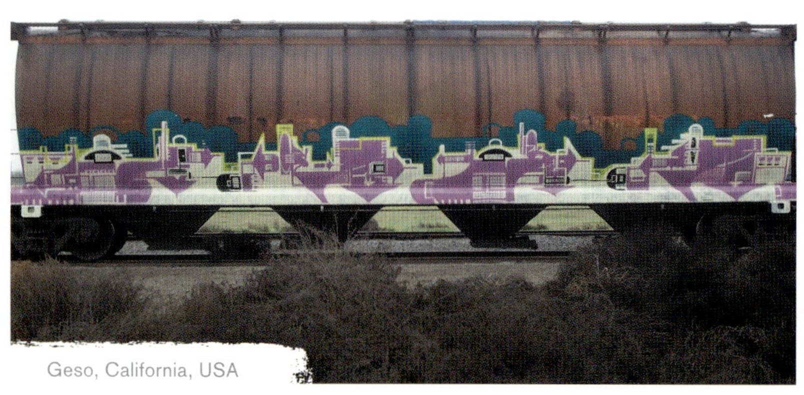

Geso, California, USA

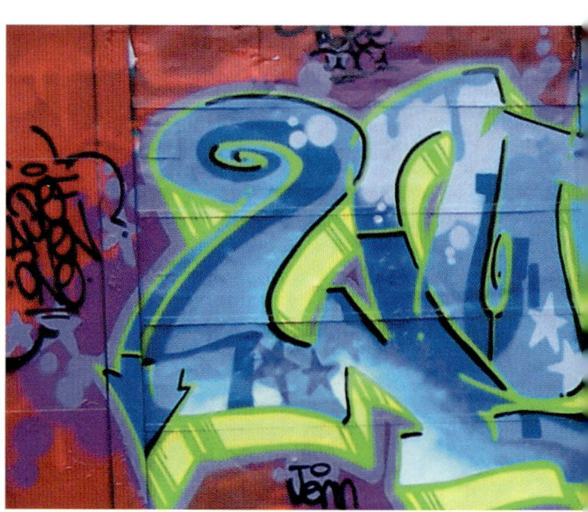

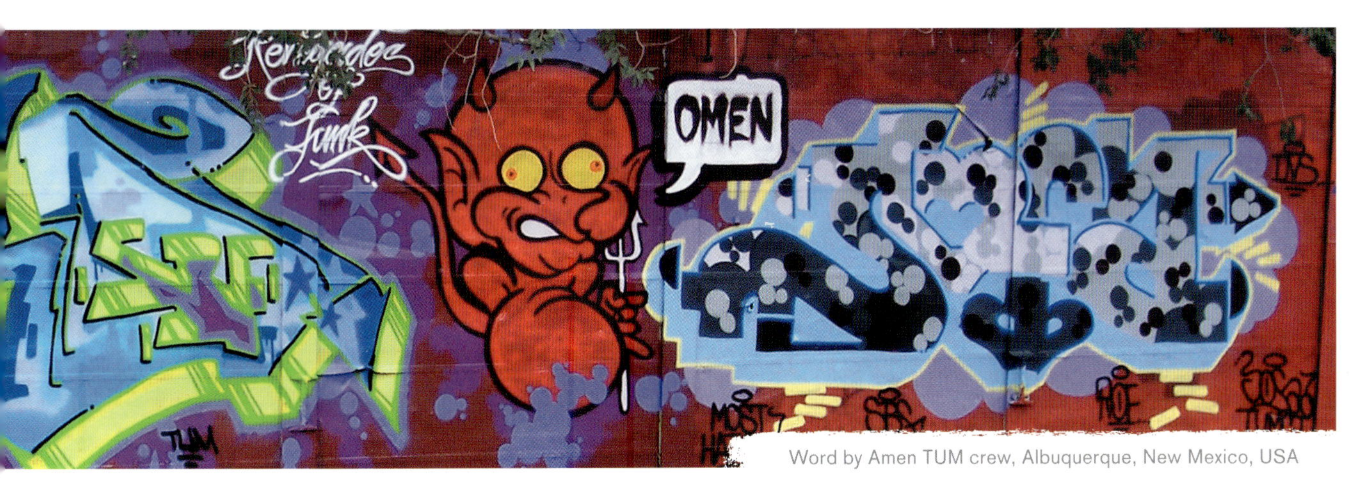

Word by Amen TUM crew, Albuquerque, New Mexico, USA

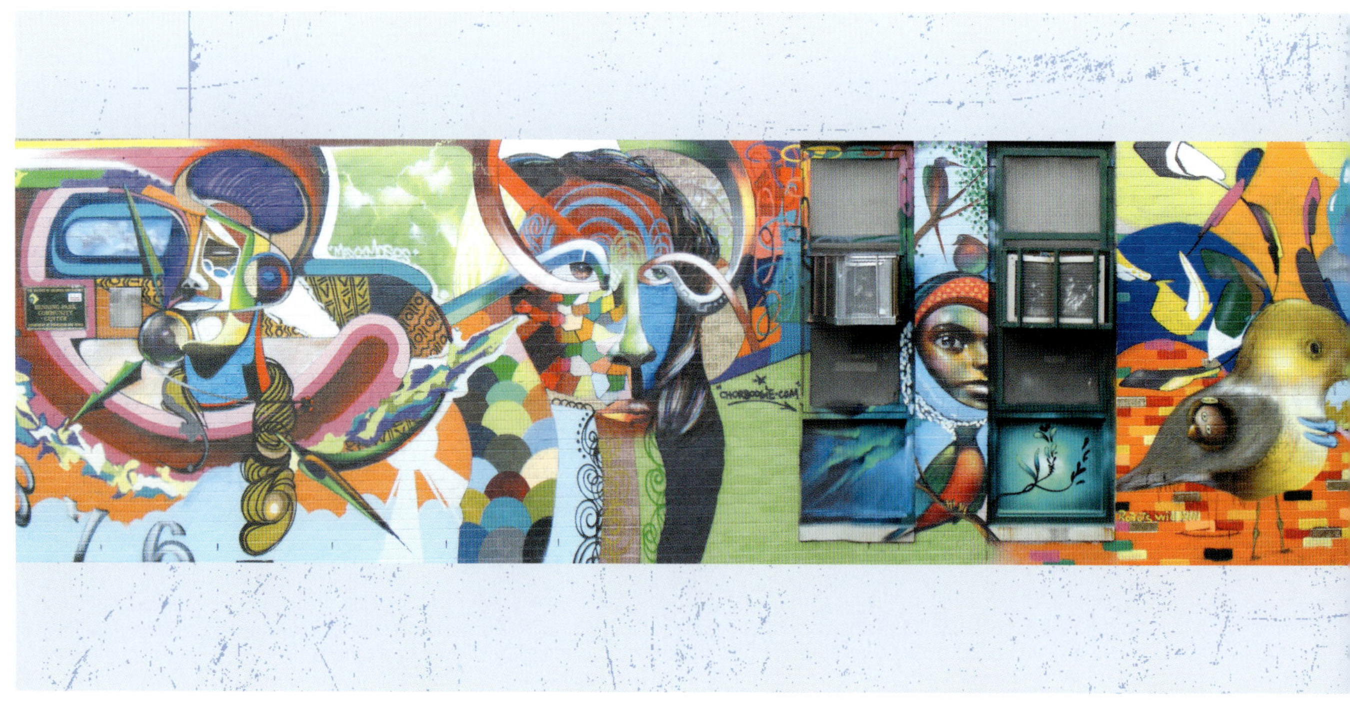
CHORBOOGIE.COM

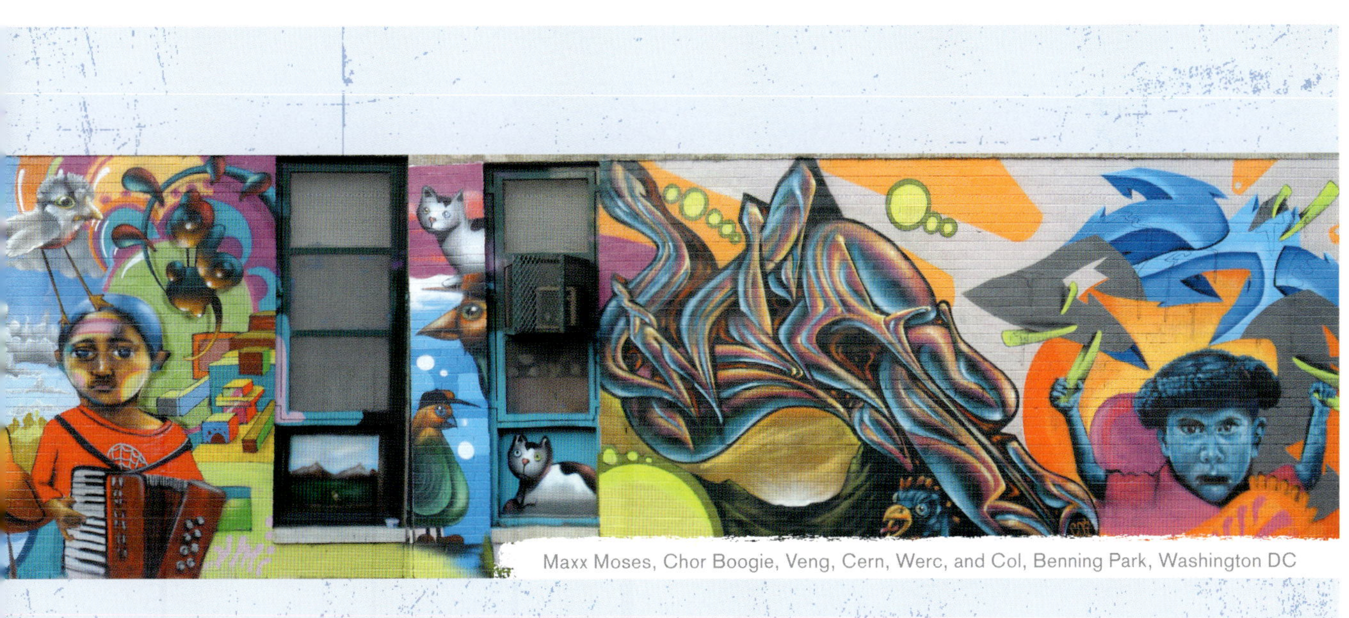

Maxx Moses, Chor Boogie, Veng, Cern, Werc, and Col, Benning Park, Washington DC

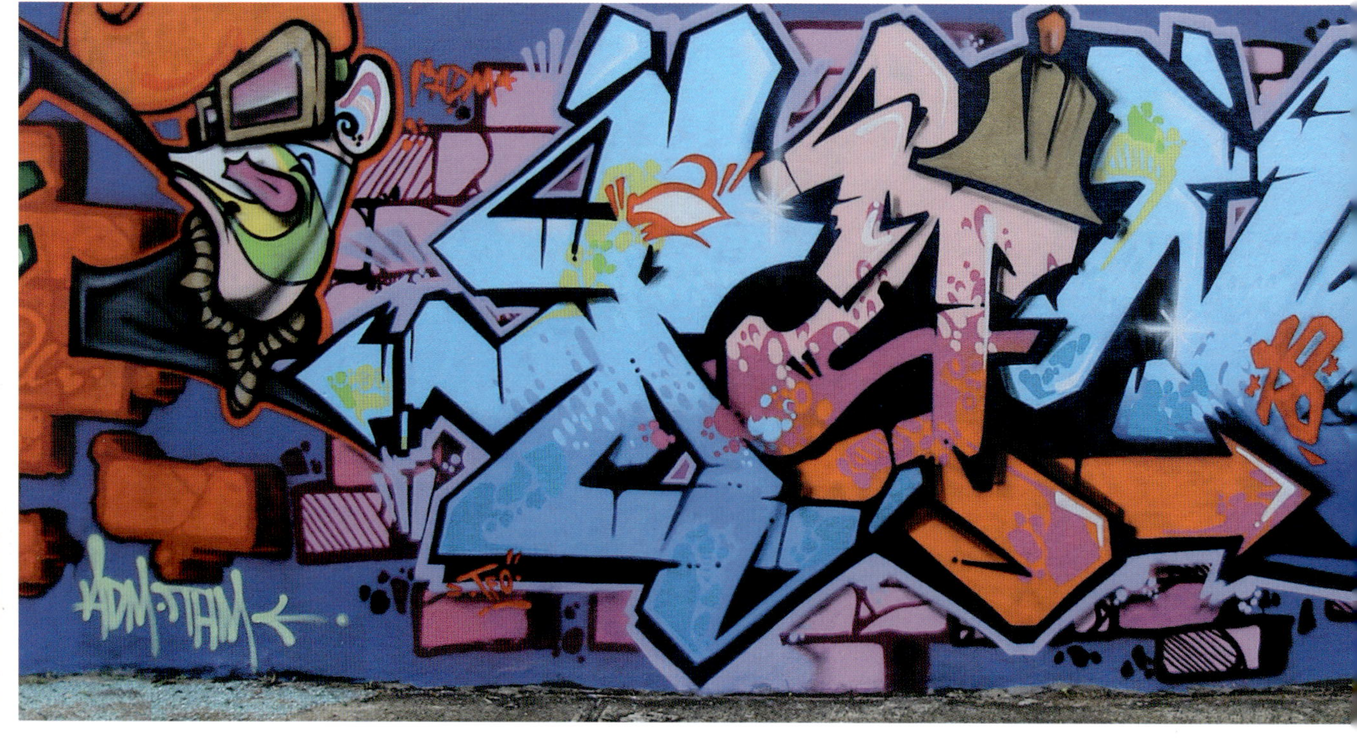

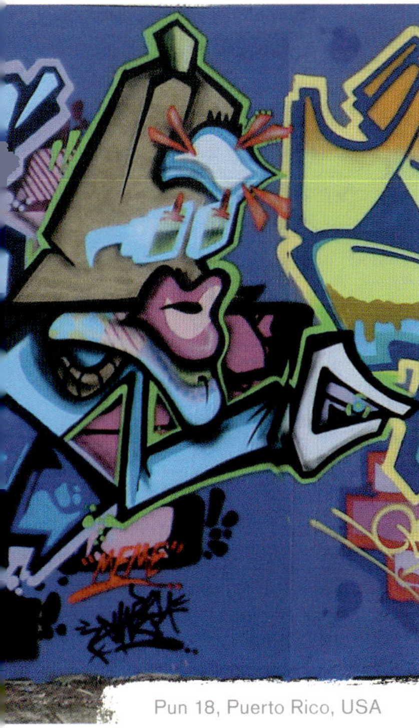

Pun 18, Puerto Rico, USA

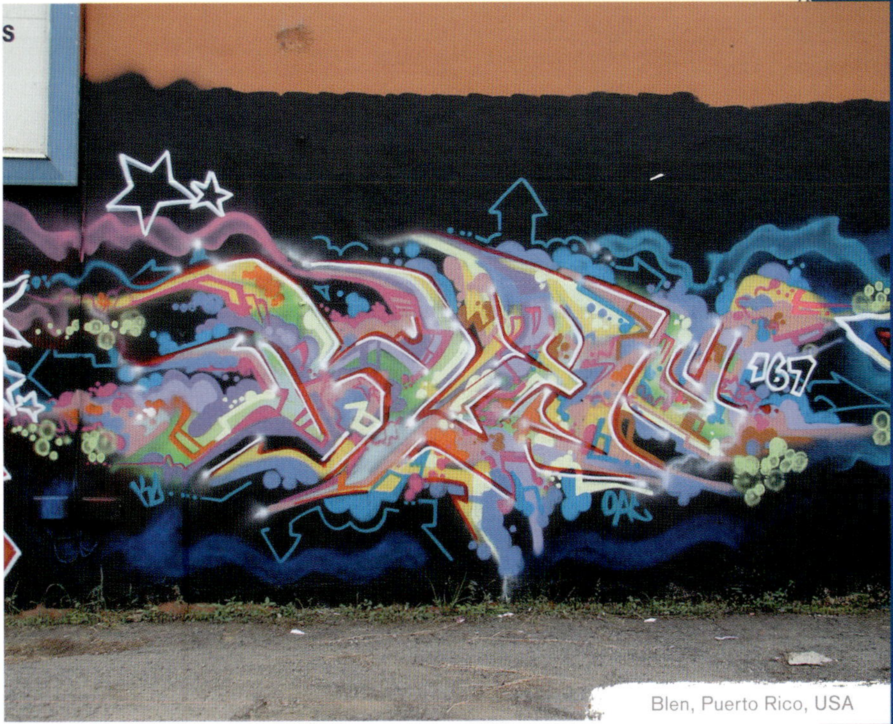

Blen, Puerto Rico, USA

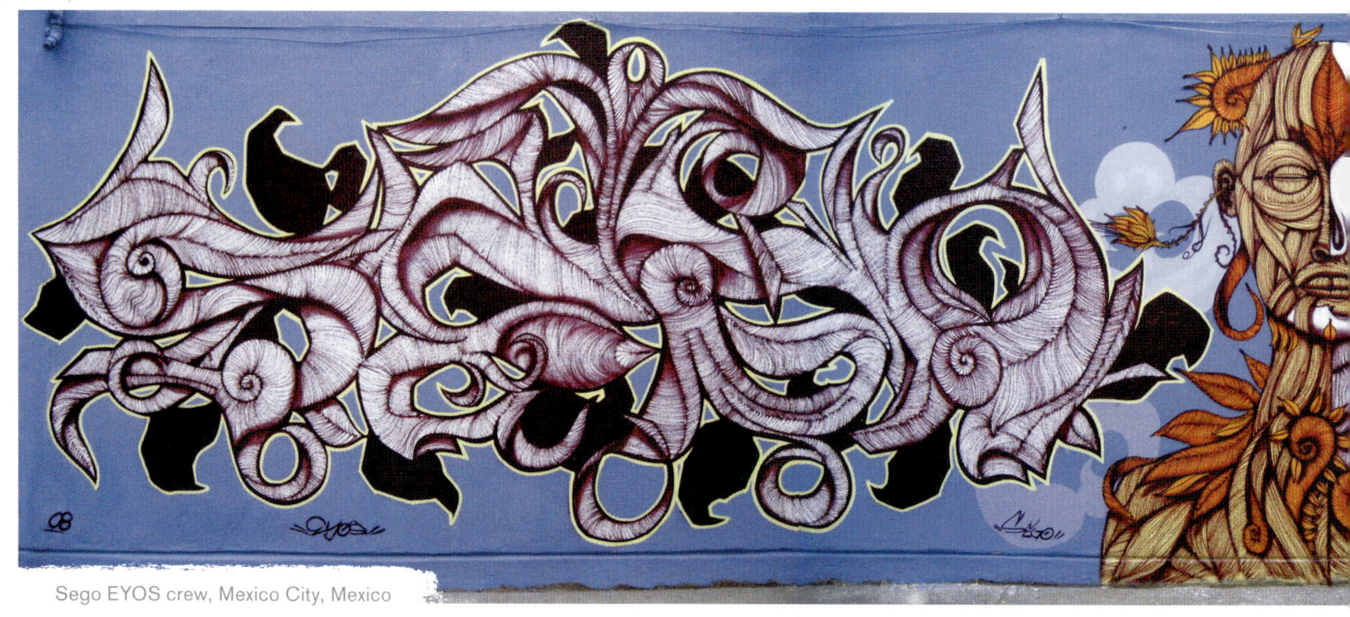

Sego EYOS crew, Mexico City, Mexico

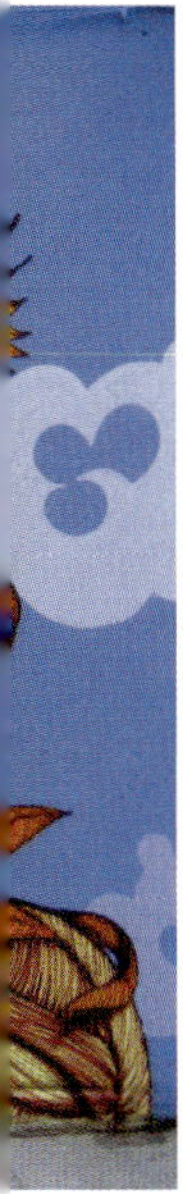

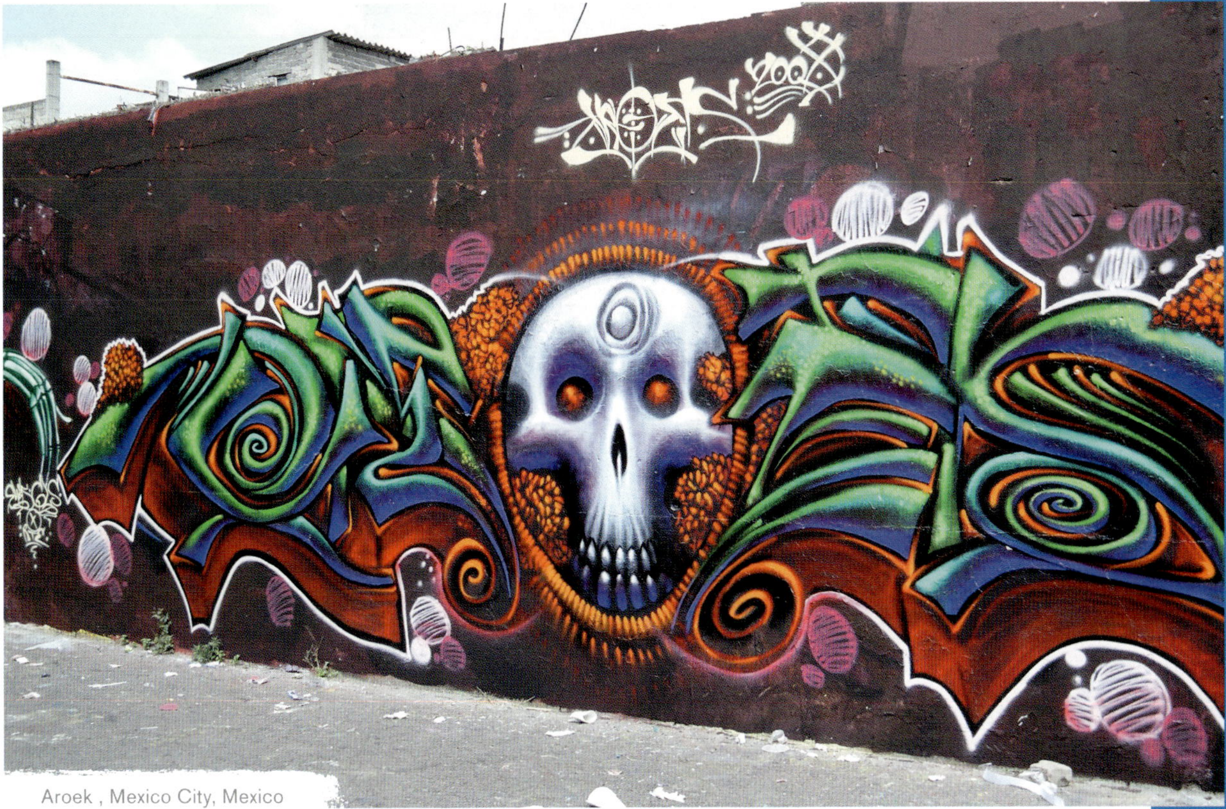

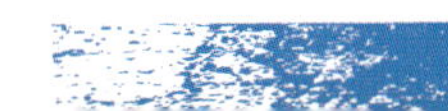

Aroek , Mexico City, Mexico

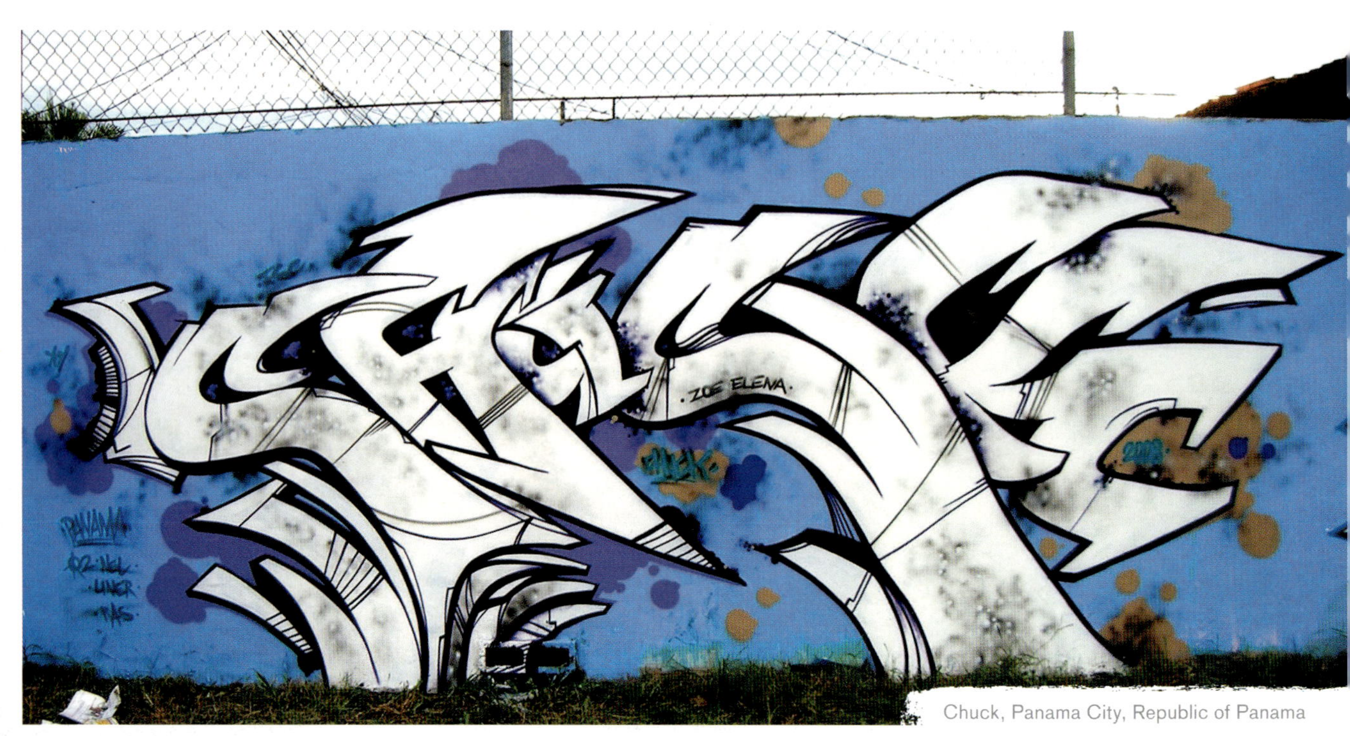

Chuck, Panama City, Republic of Panama

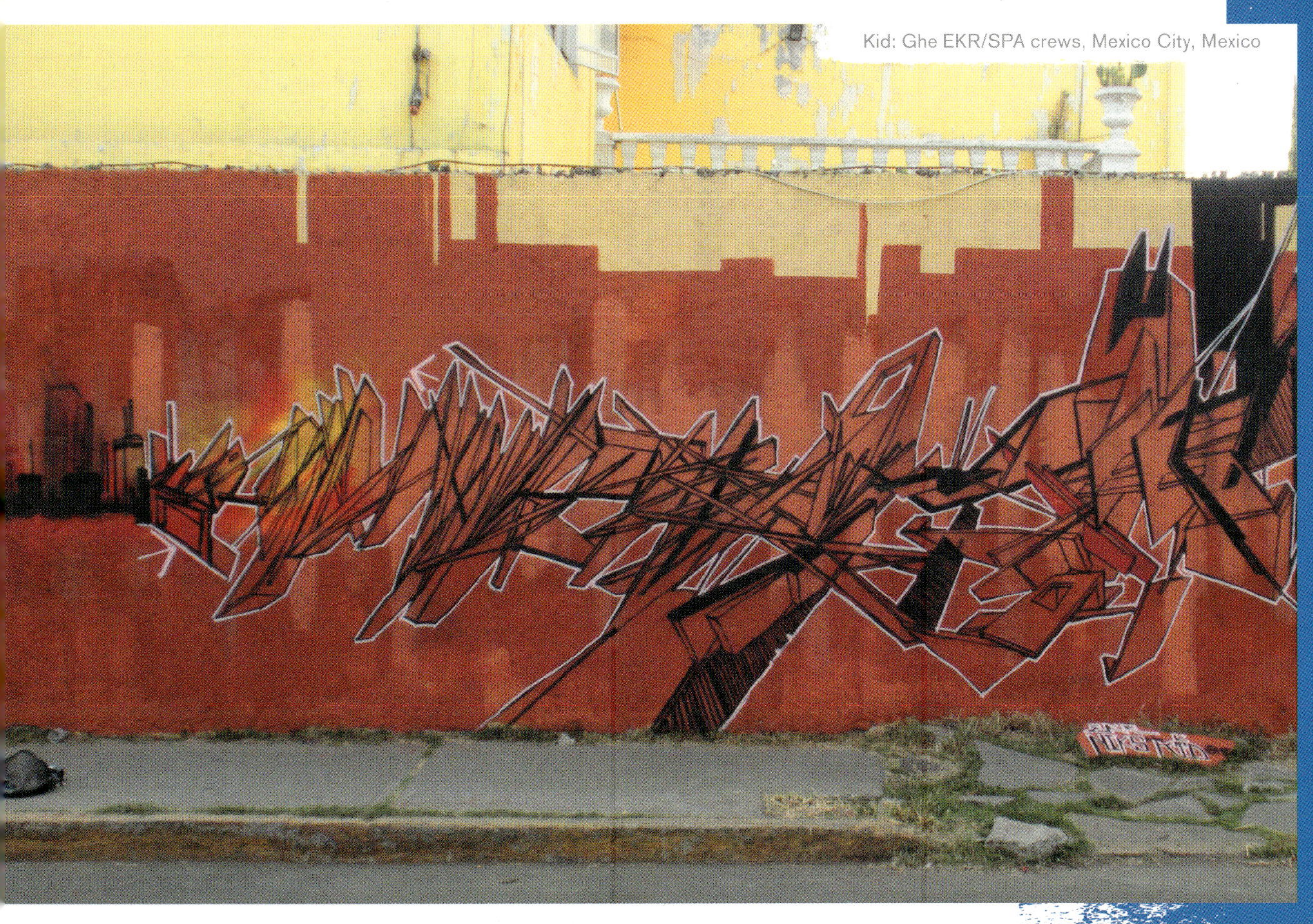

Kid: Ghe EKR/SPA crews, Mexico City, Mexico

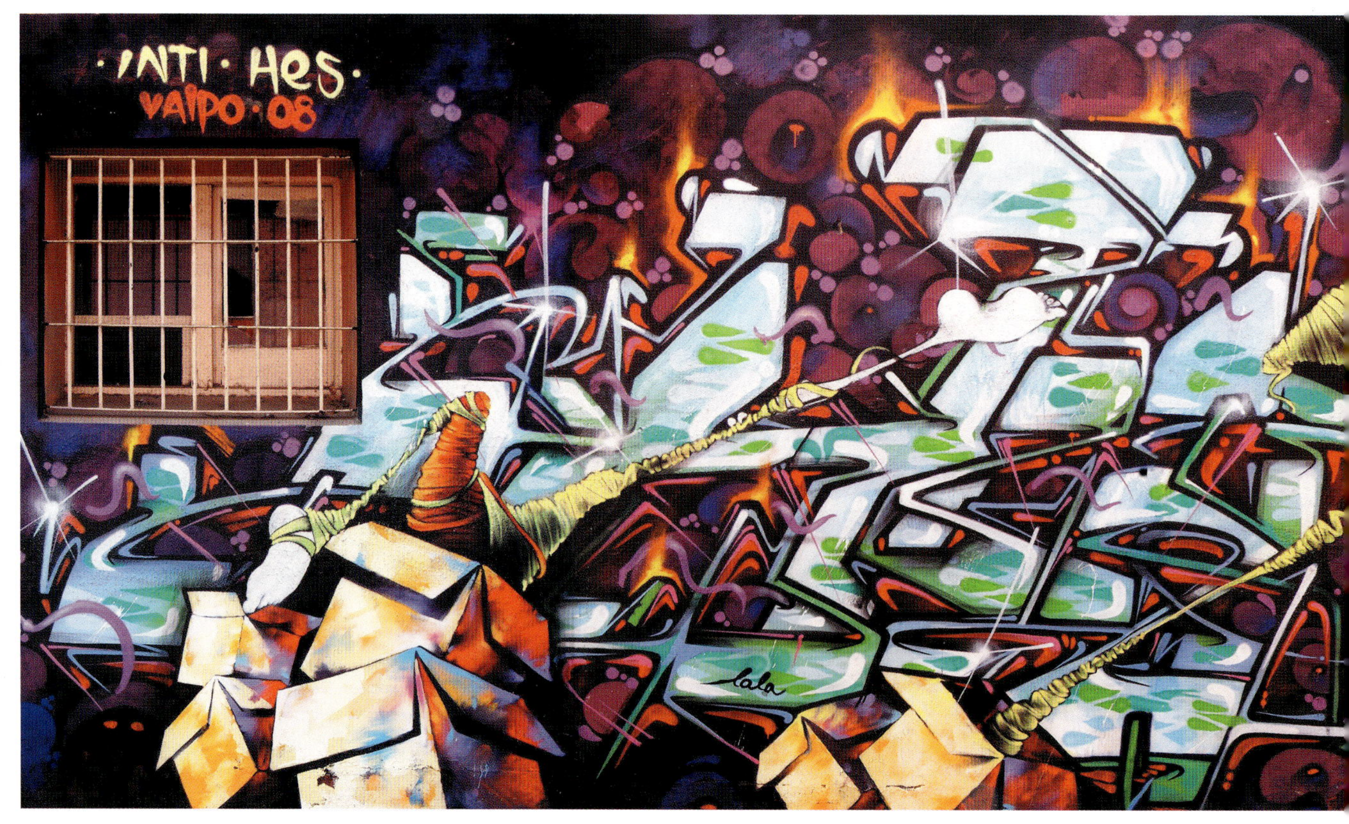

·INTI·HES·
VALPO·08

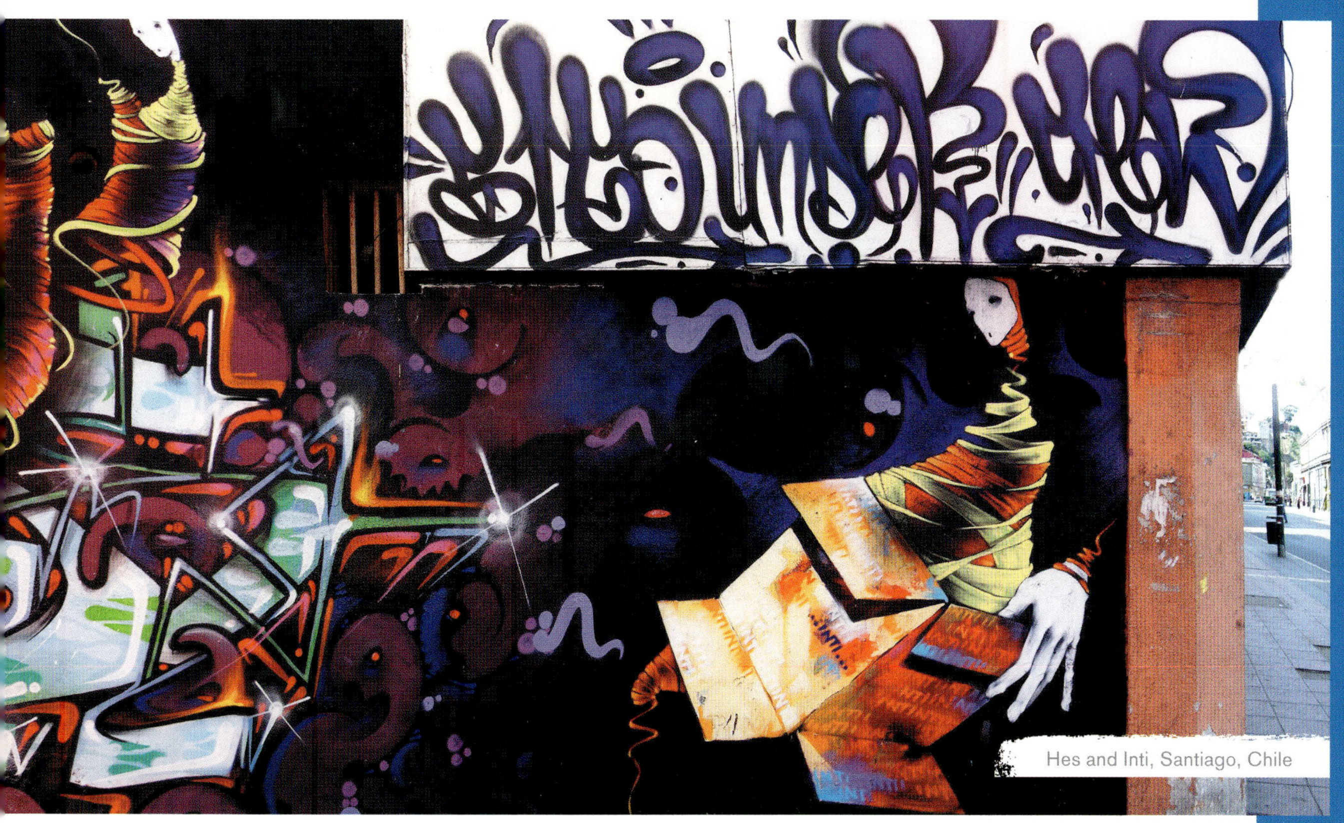

Hes and Inti, Santiago, Chile

Inti, Saile, and Hes,
Santiago, Chile

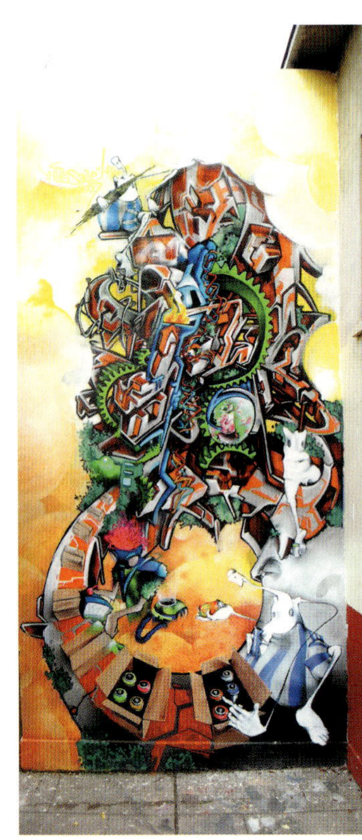

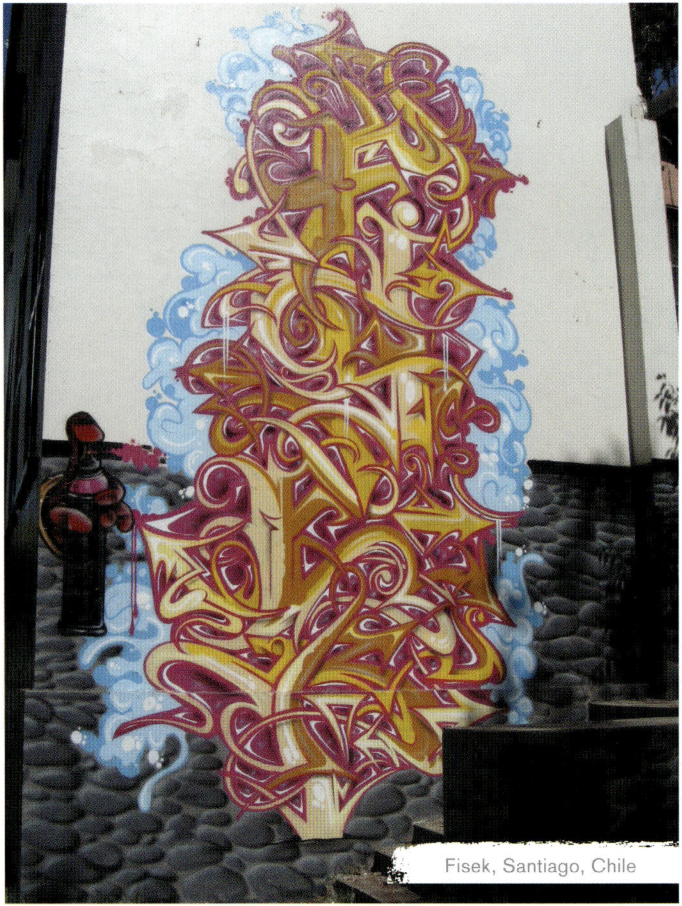

Fisek, Santiago, Chile

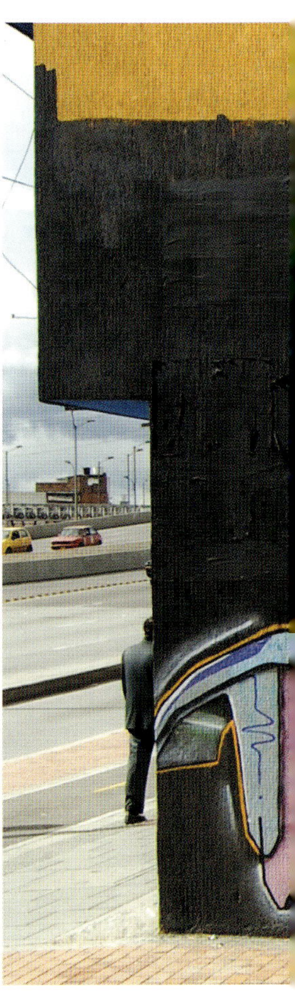

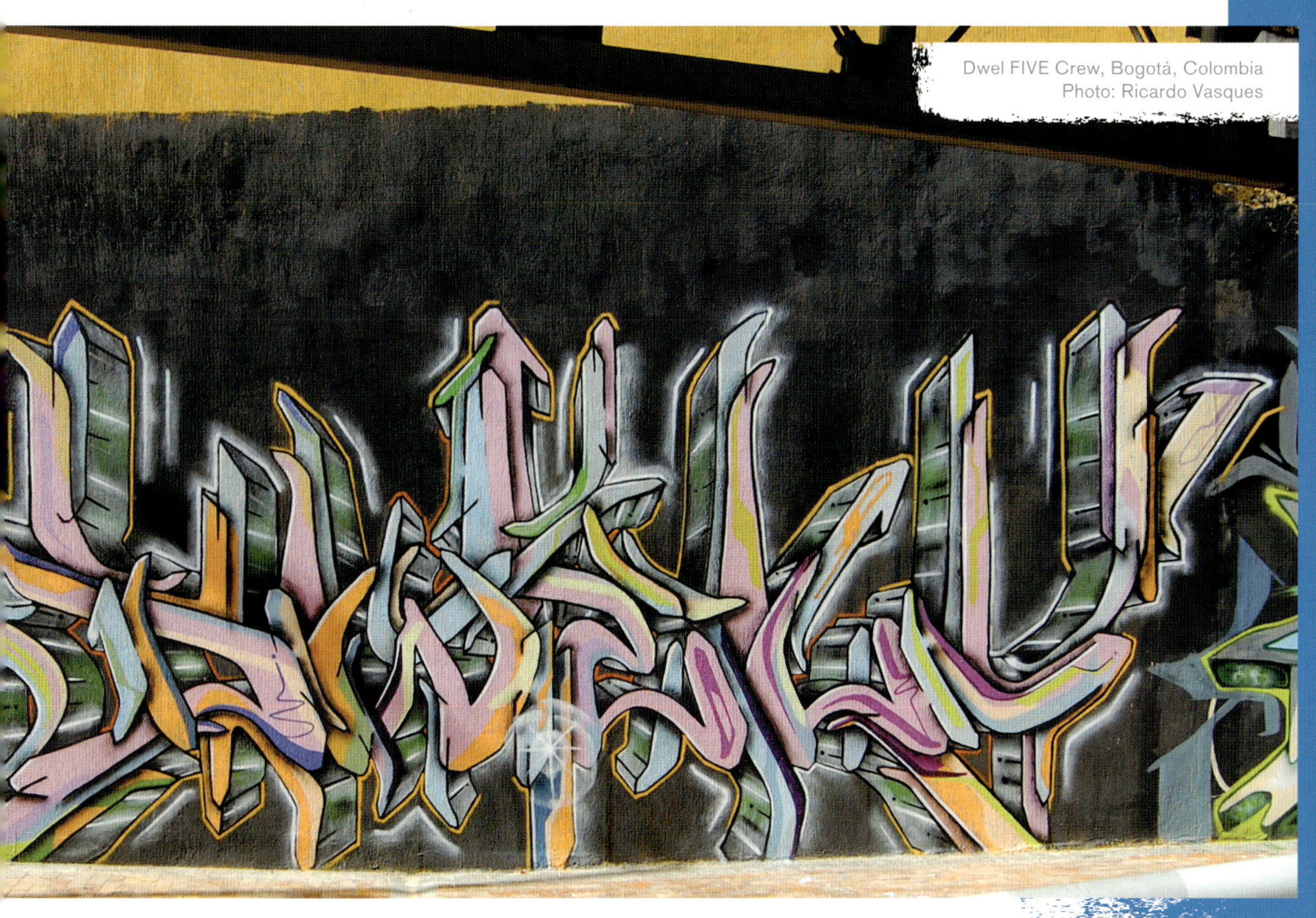

Dwel FIVE Crew, Bogotá, Colombia
Photo: Ricardo Vasques

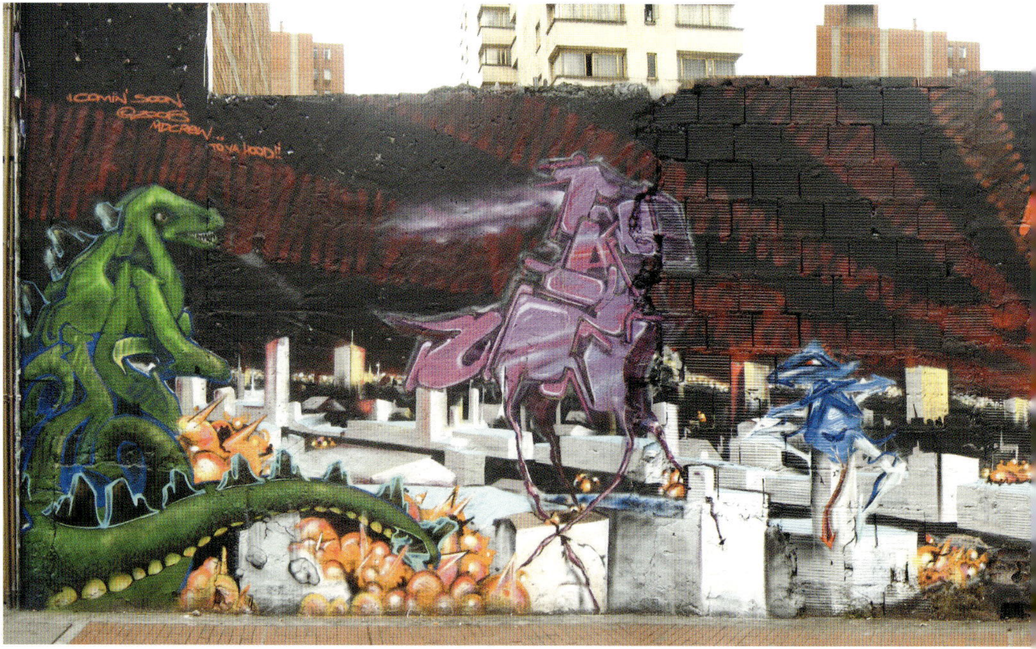

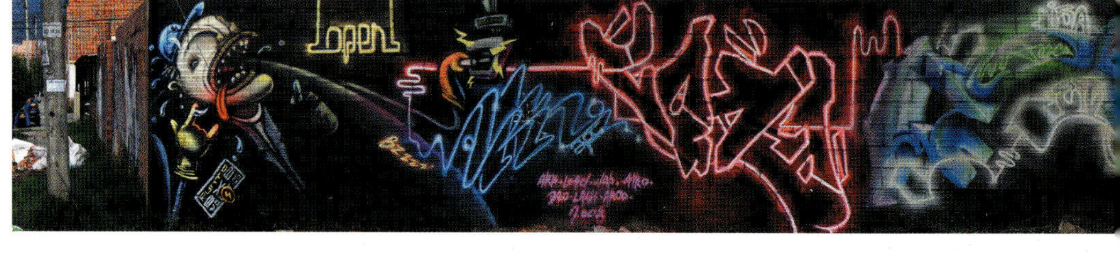
open

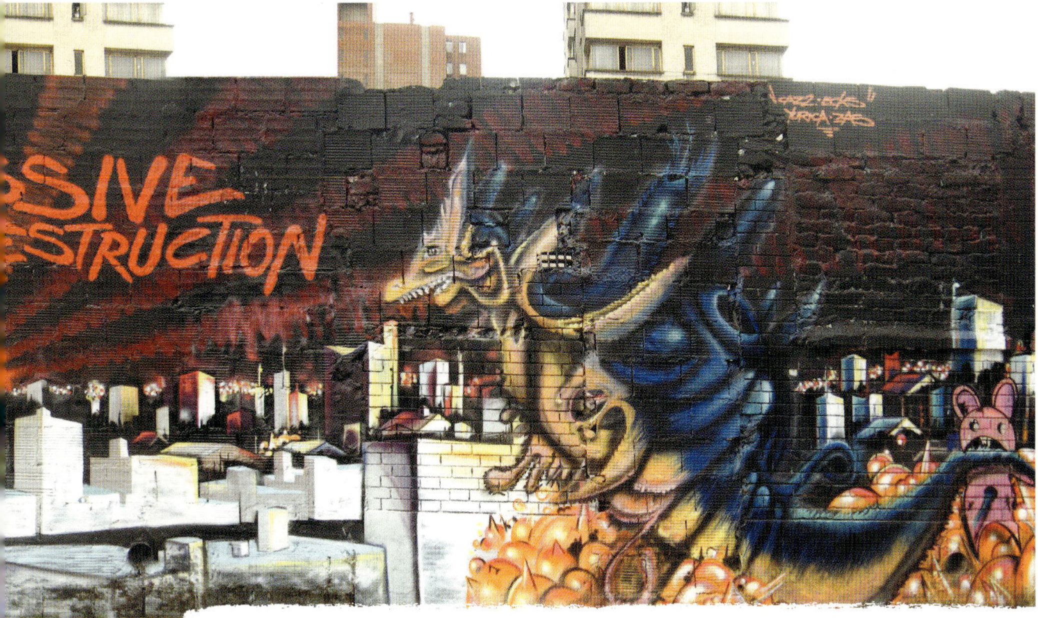

Massive Destruction by Eckso, Zas, Cazdos, and Yurika MDC crew, Bogotá, Colombia

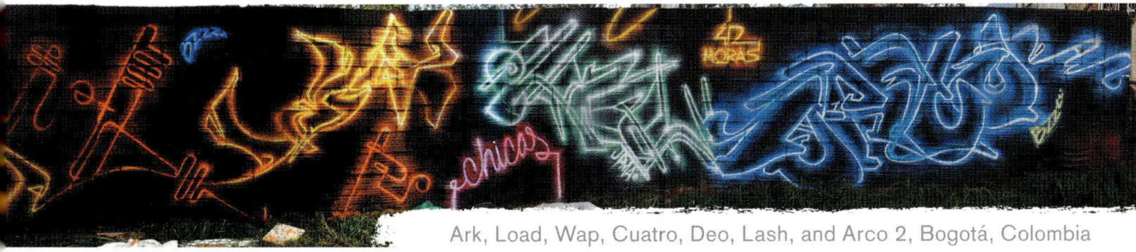

Ark, Load, Wap, Cuatro, Deo, Lash, and Arco 2, Bogotá, Colombia

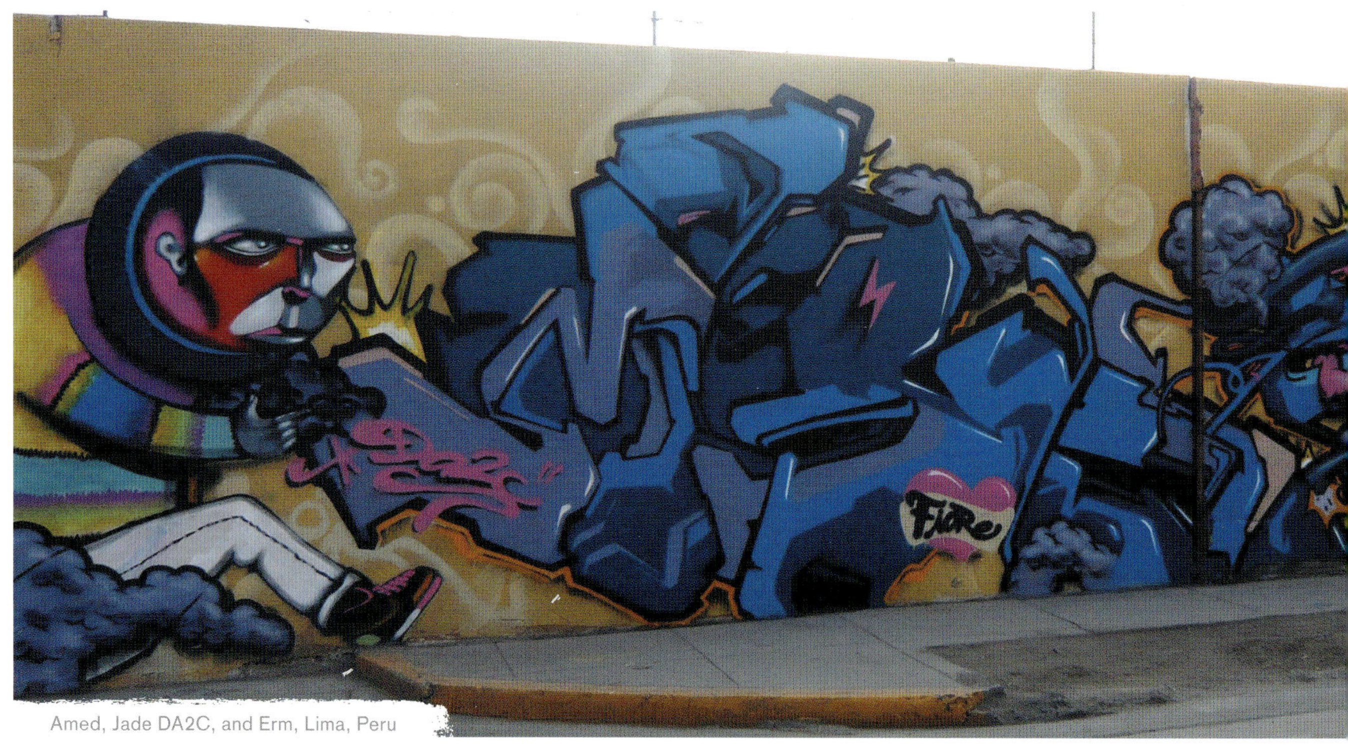

Amed, Jade DA2C, and Erm, Lima, Peru

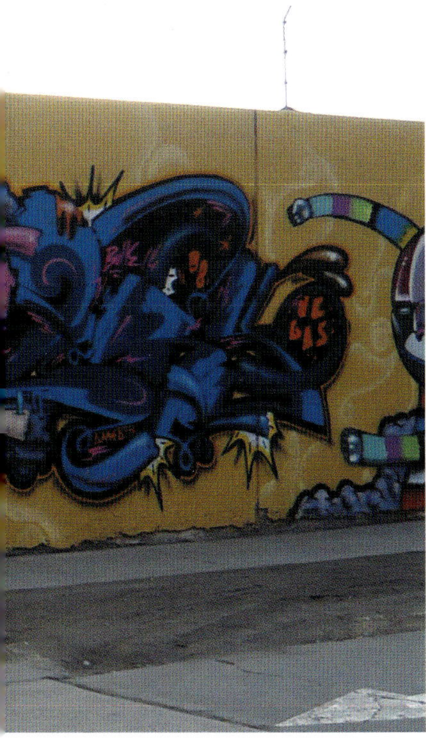

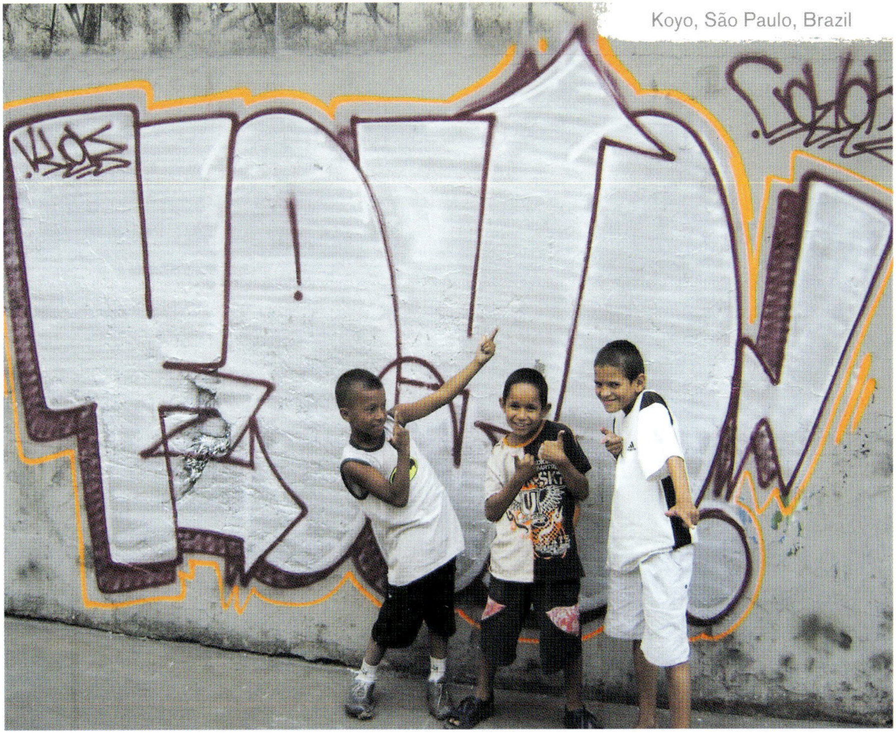

Koyo, São Paulo, Brazil

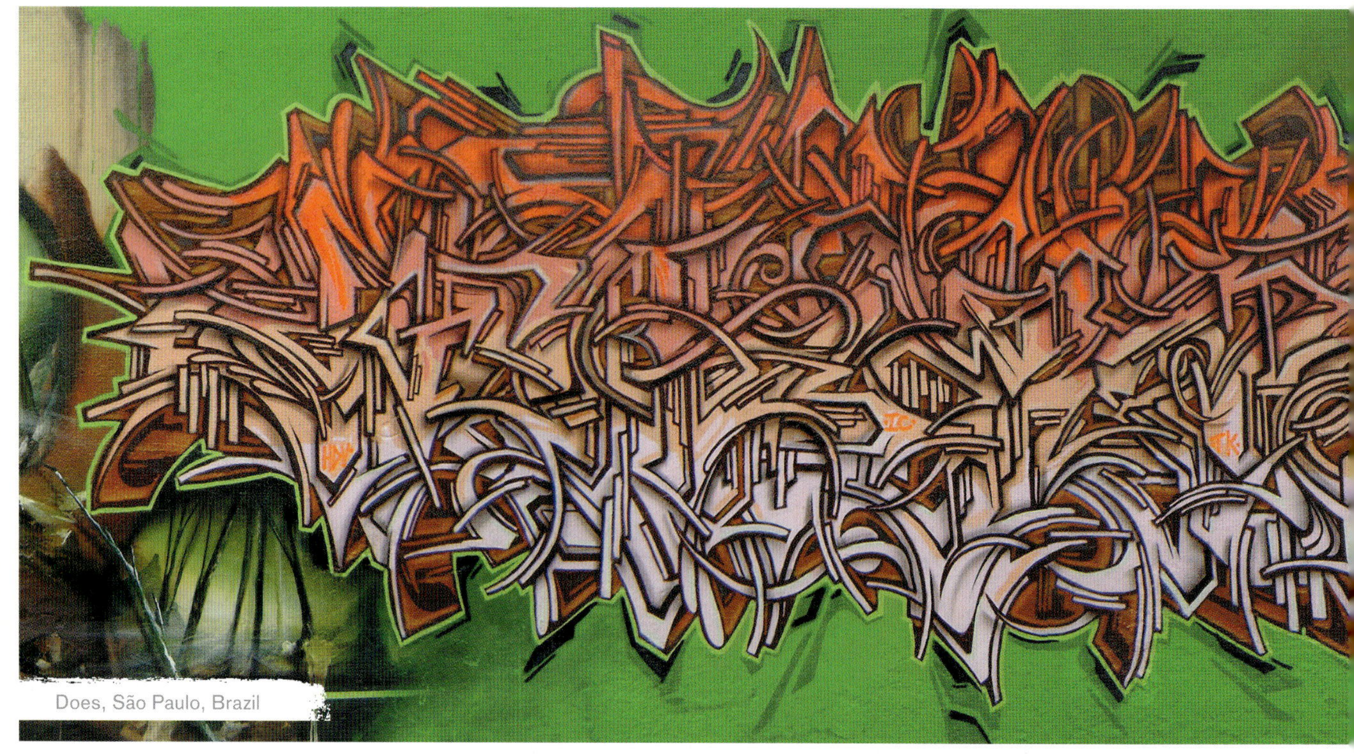

Does, São Paulo, Brazil

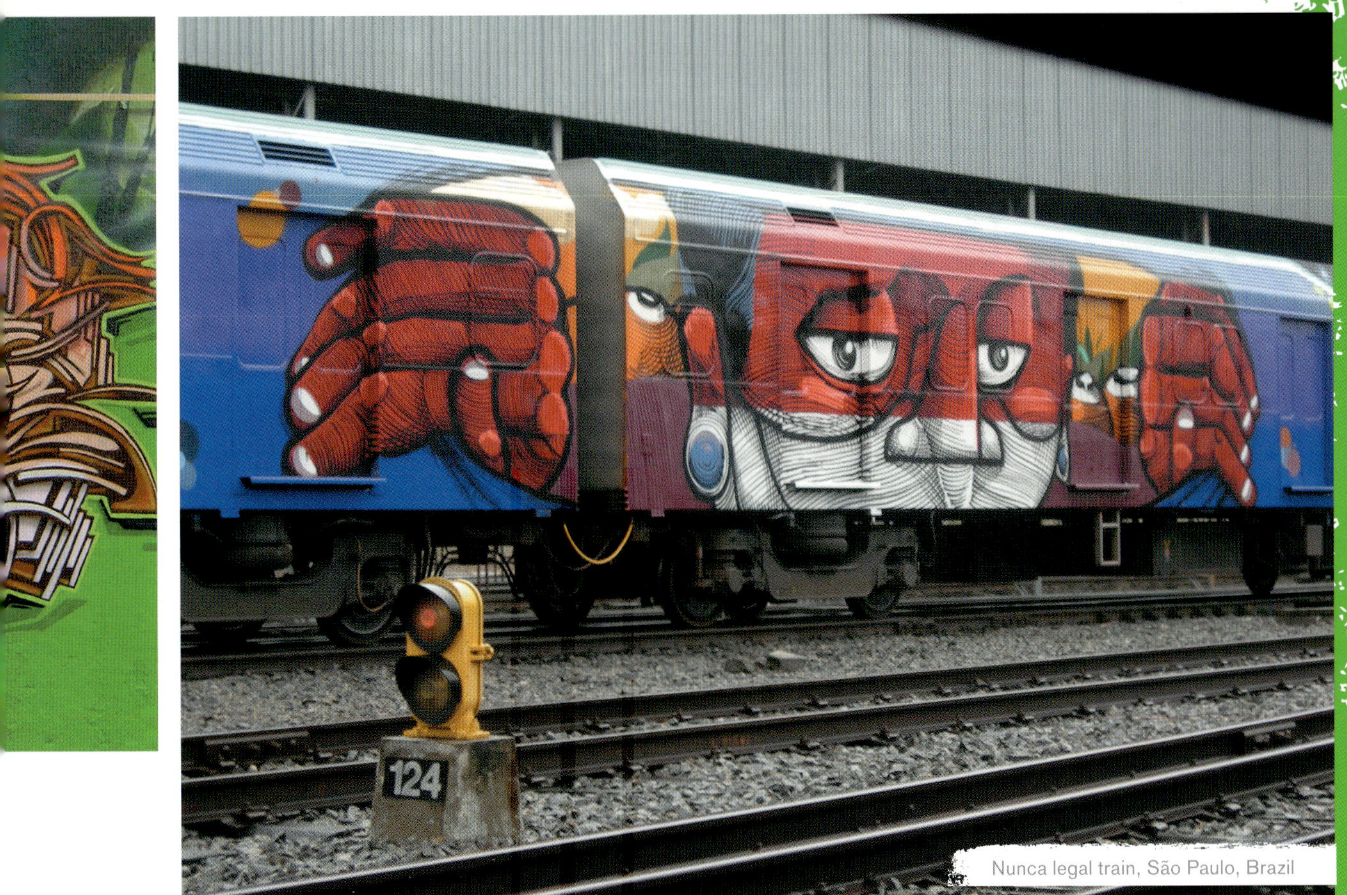

Nunca legal train, São Paulo, Brazil

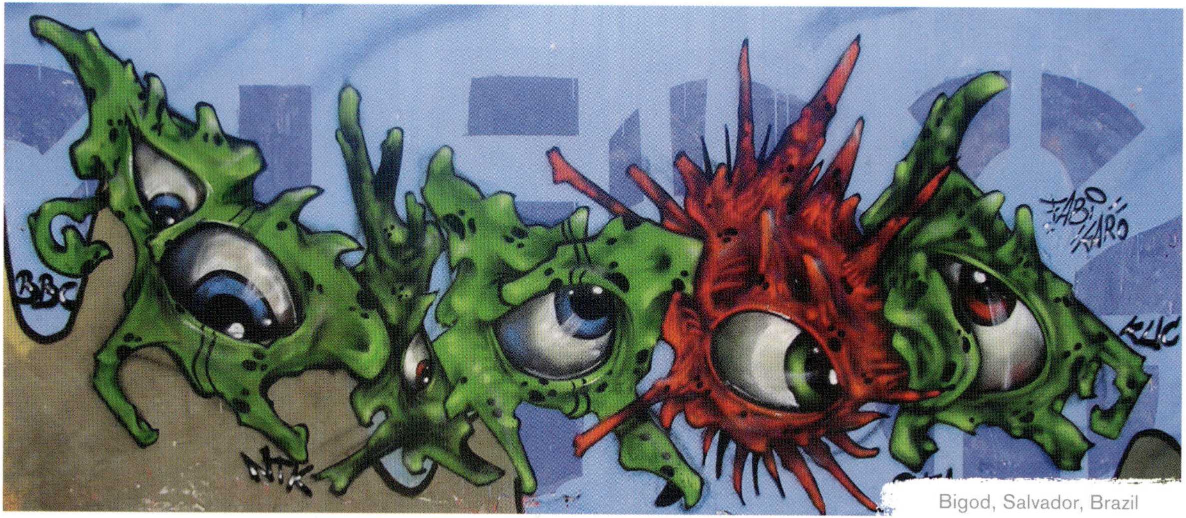

Bigod, Salvador, Brazil

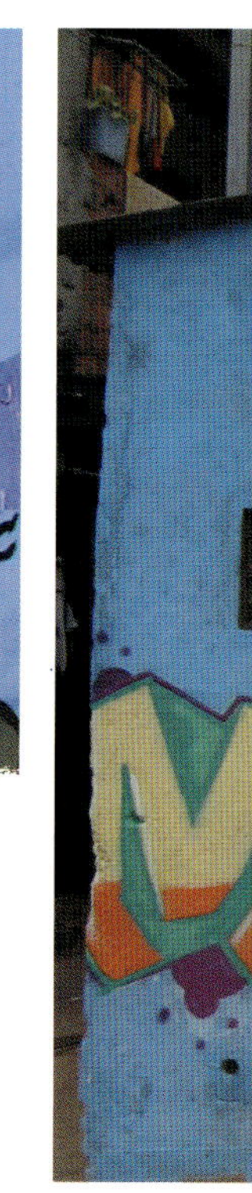

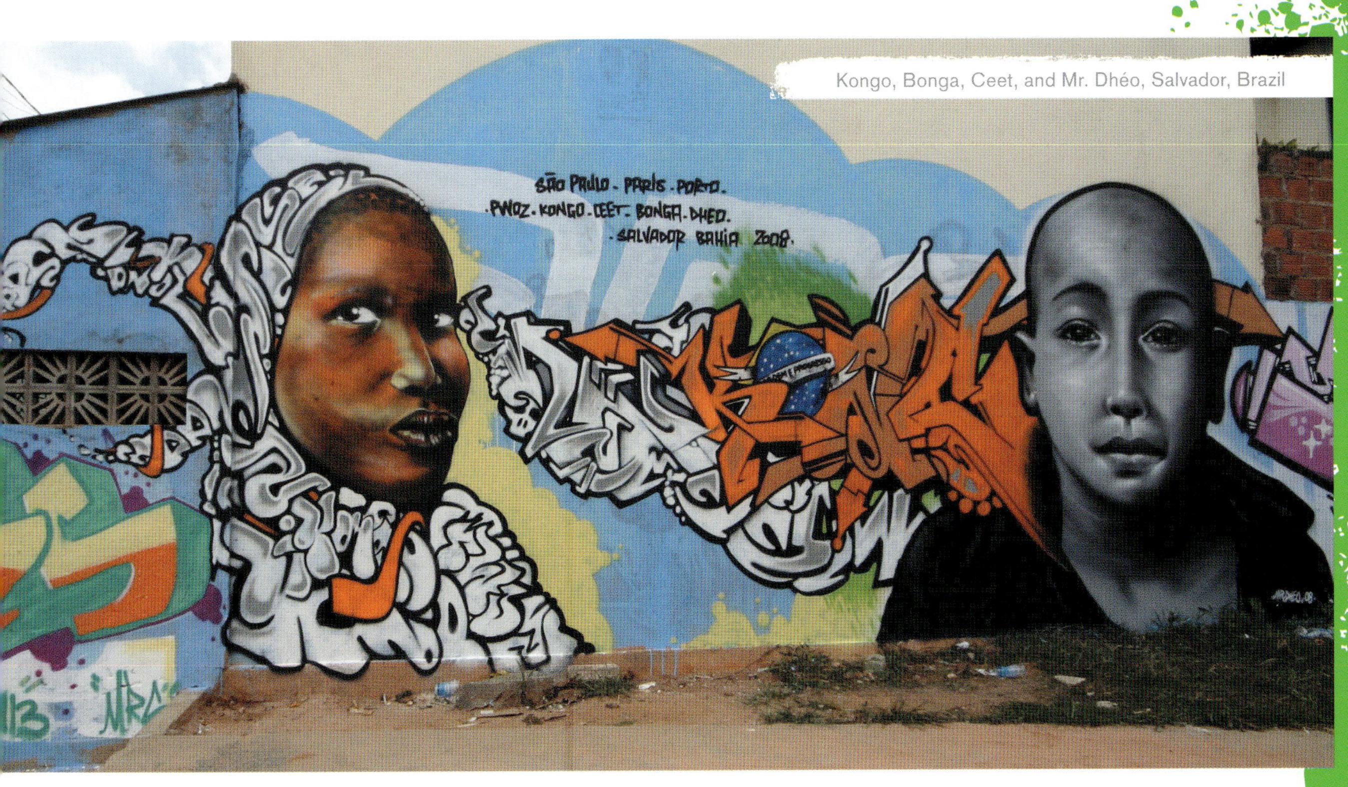

Kongo, Bonga, Ceet, and Mr. Dhéo, Salvador, Brazil

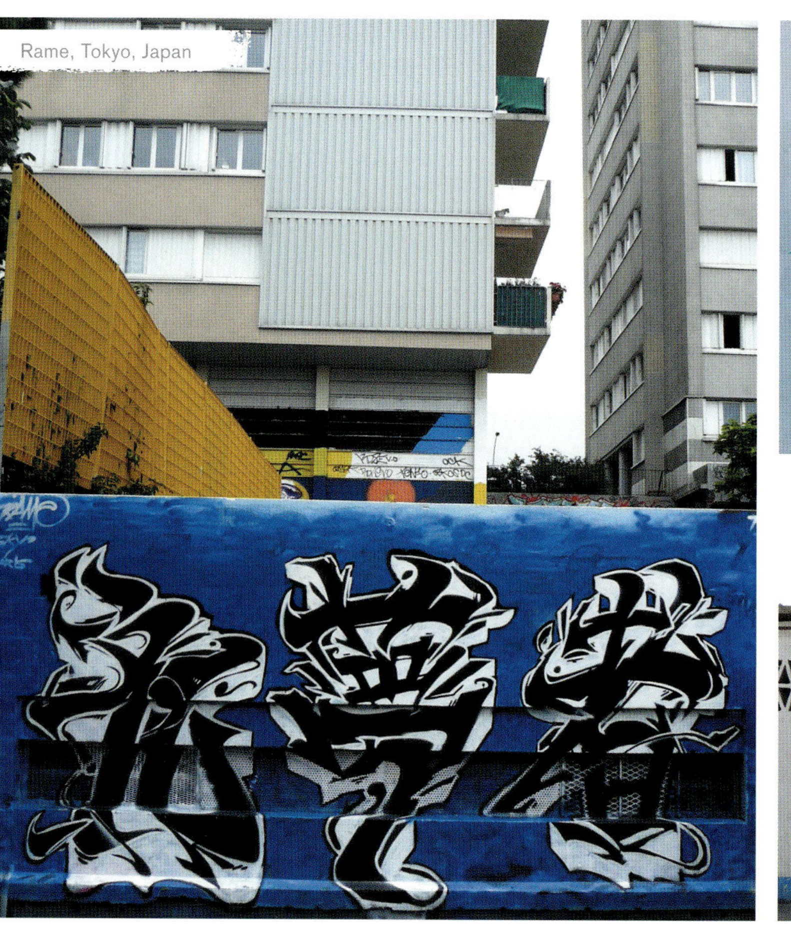

Rame, Tokyo, Japan

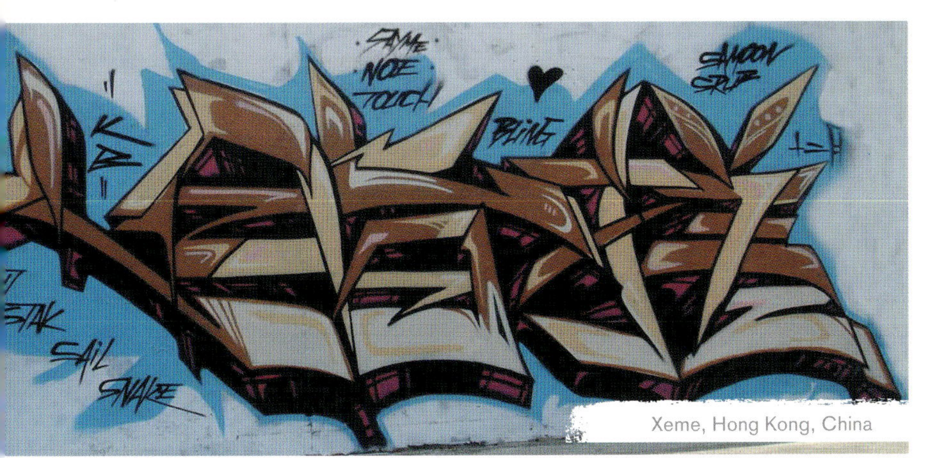

Xeme, Hong Kong, China

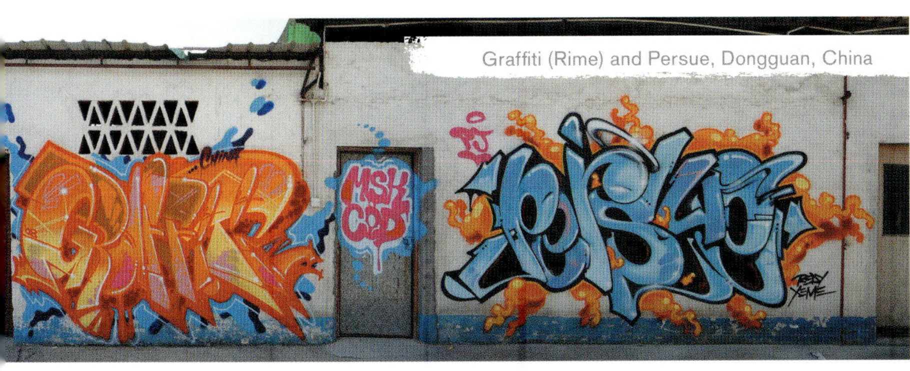

Graffiti (Rime) and Persue, Dongguan, China

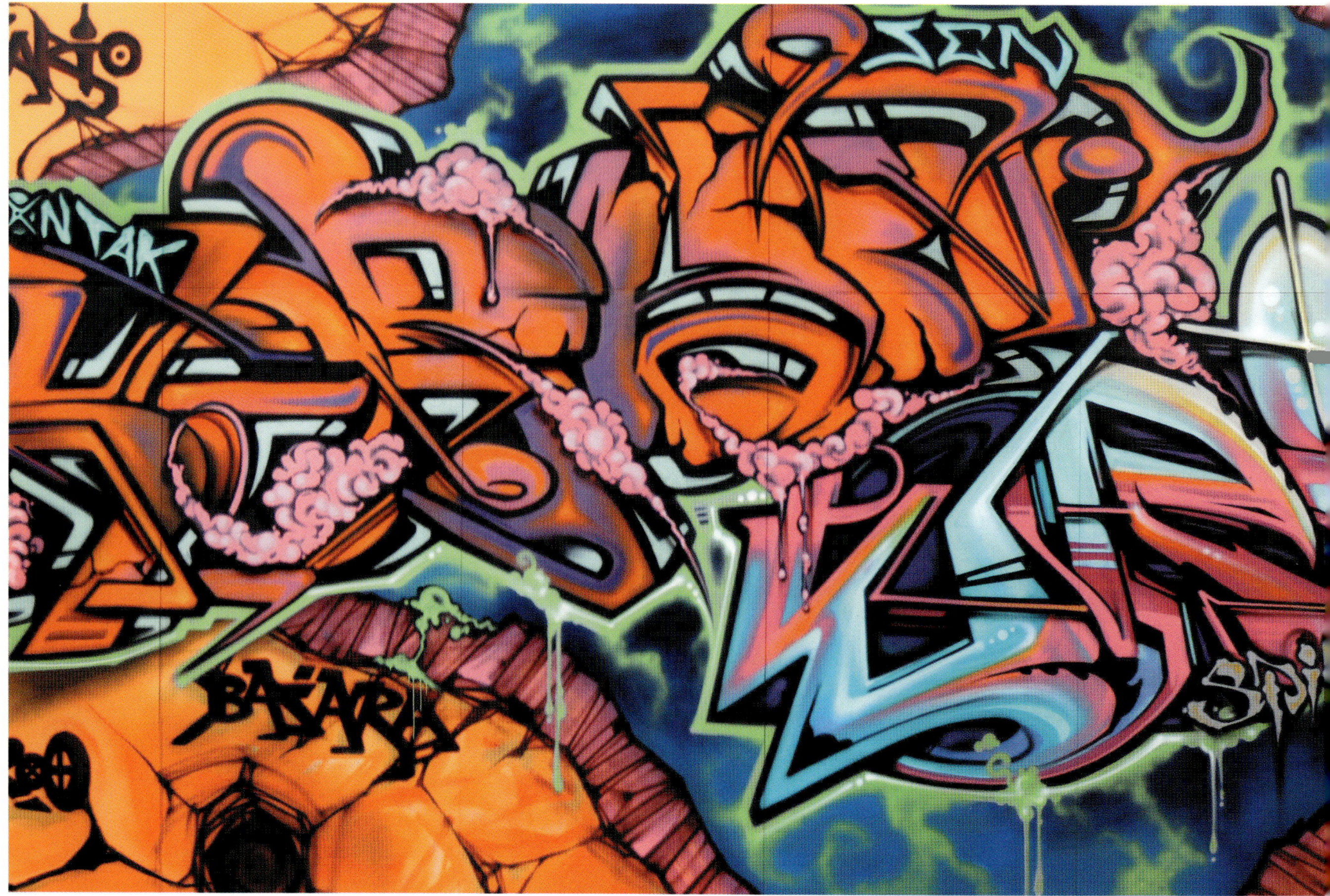
SEN
BASARA

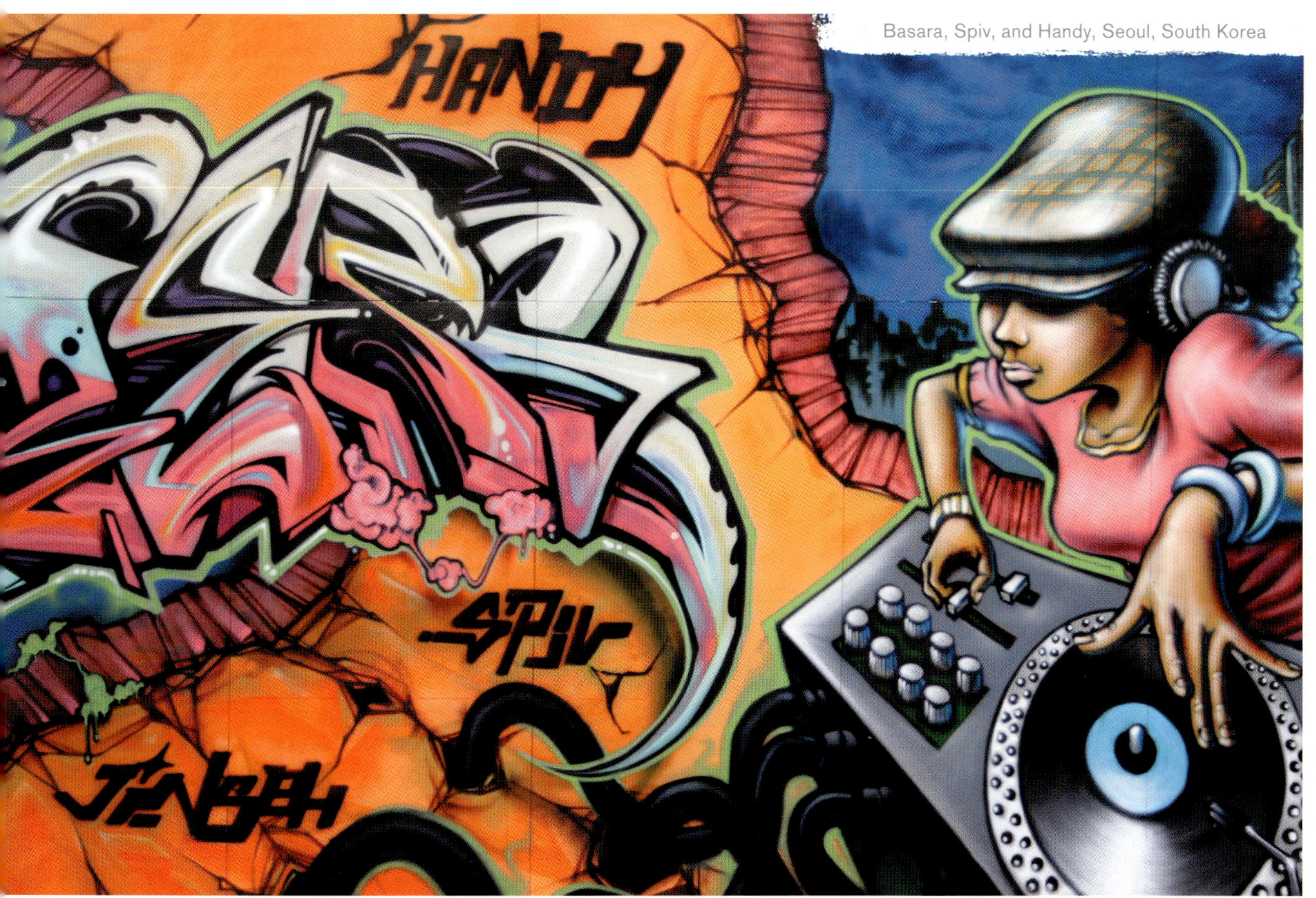

Basara, Spiv, and Handy, Seoul, South Korea

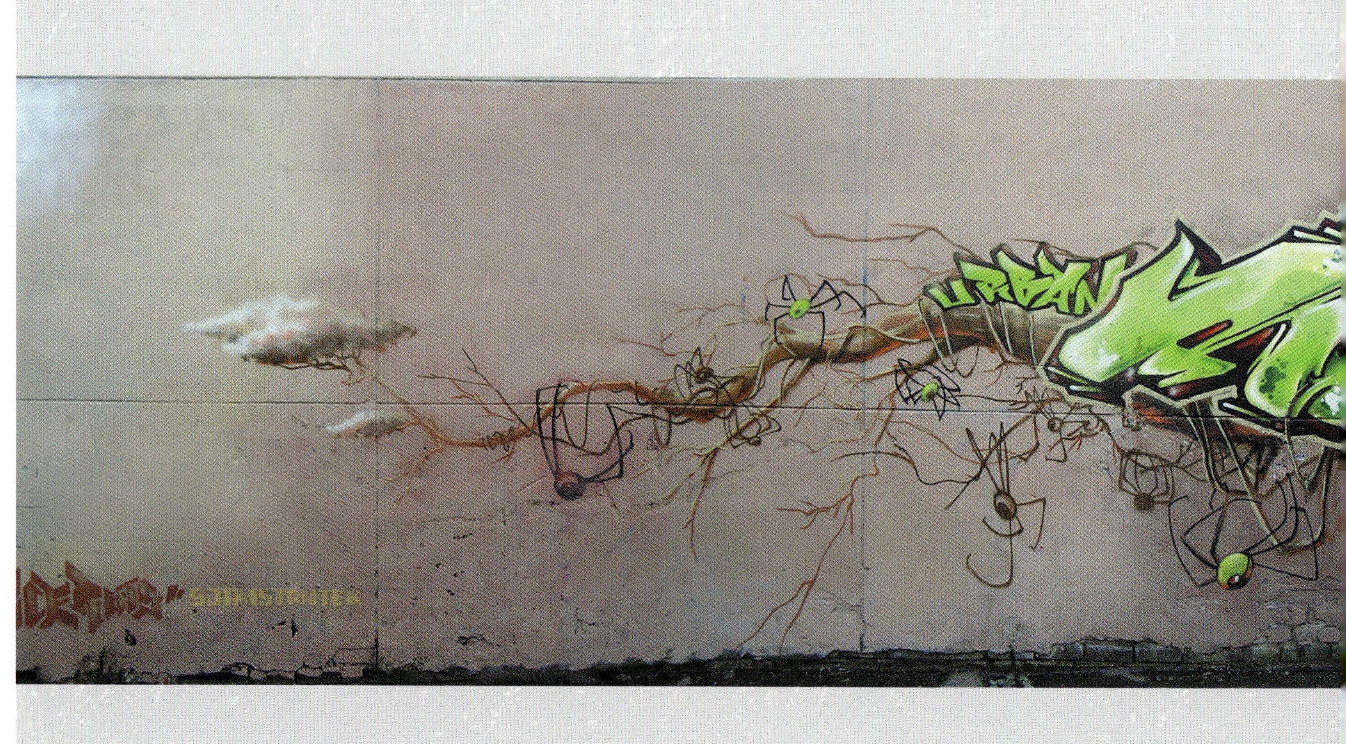
URBAN

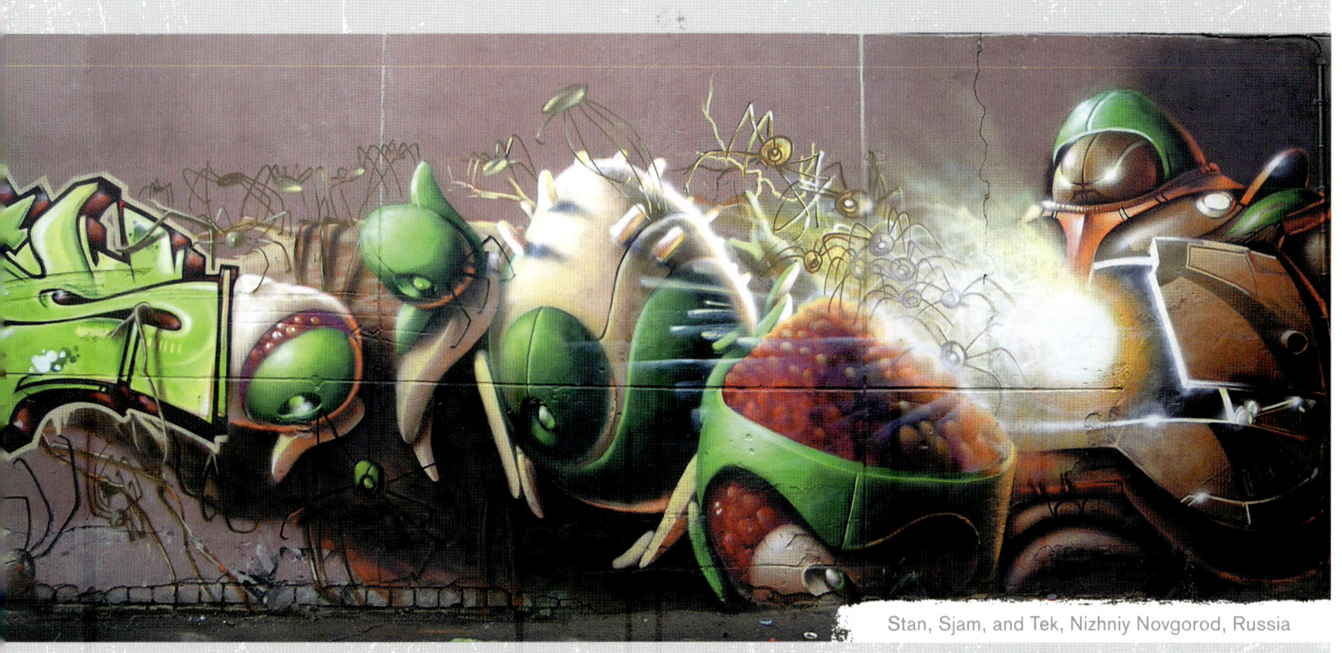

Stan, Sjam, and Tek, Nizhniy Novgorod, Russia

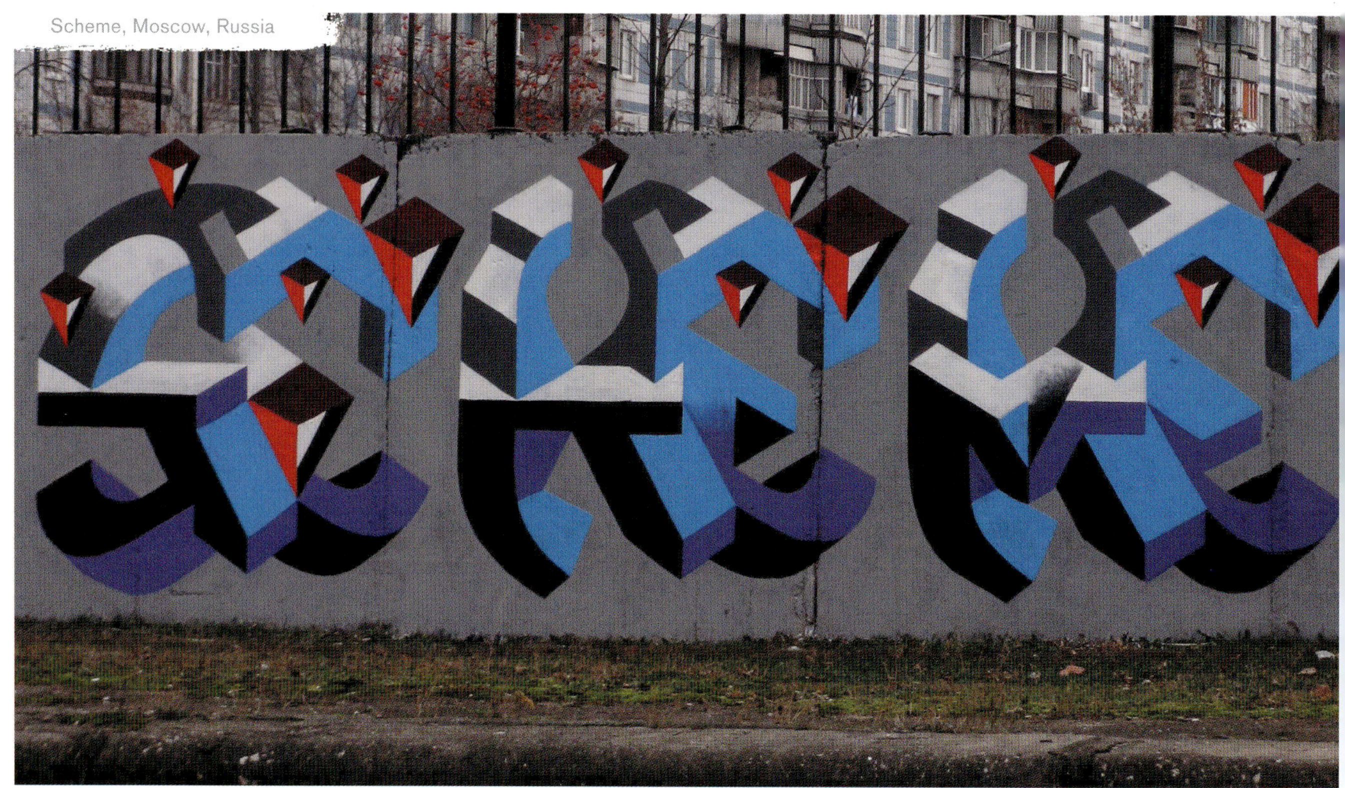

Scheme, Moscow, Russia

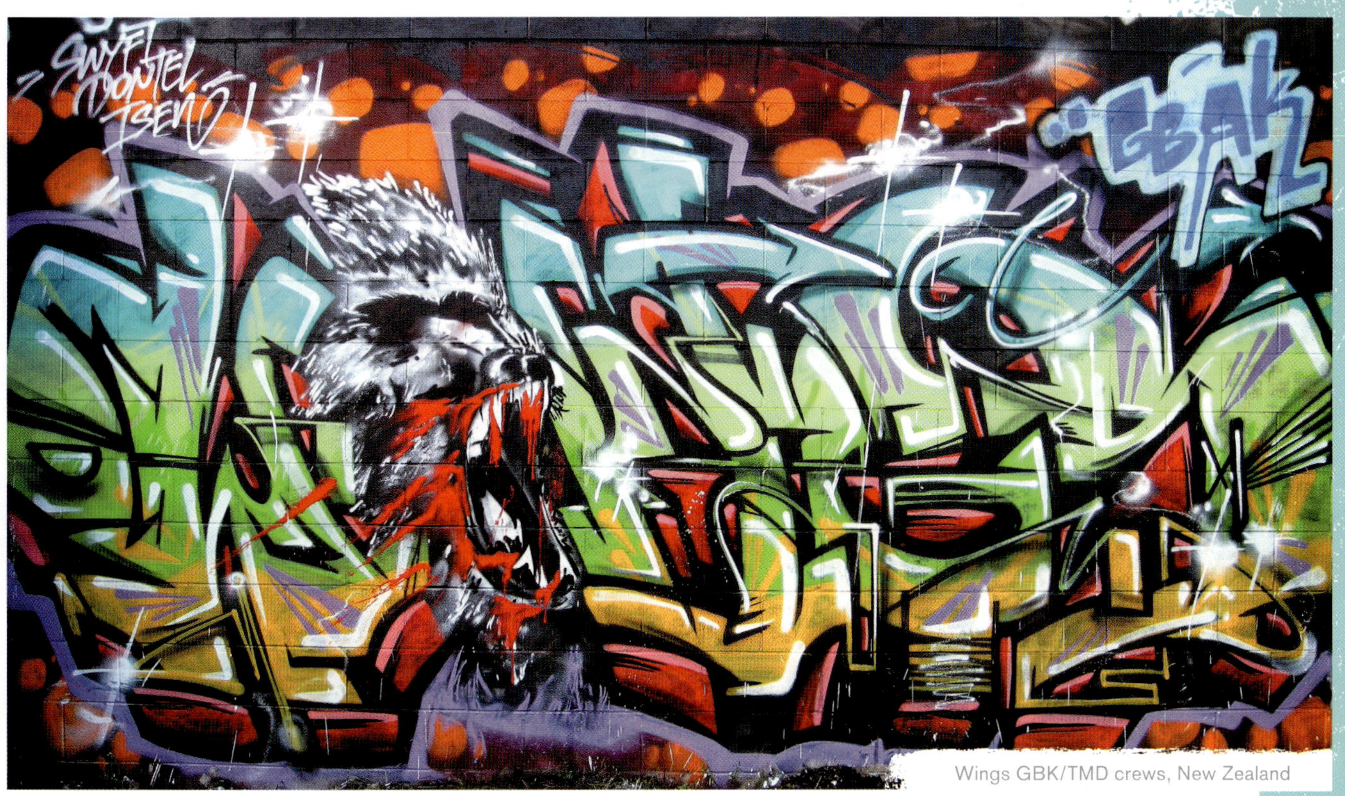

Wings GBK/TMD crews, New Zealand

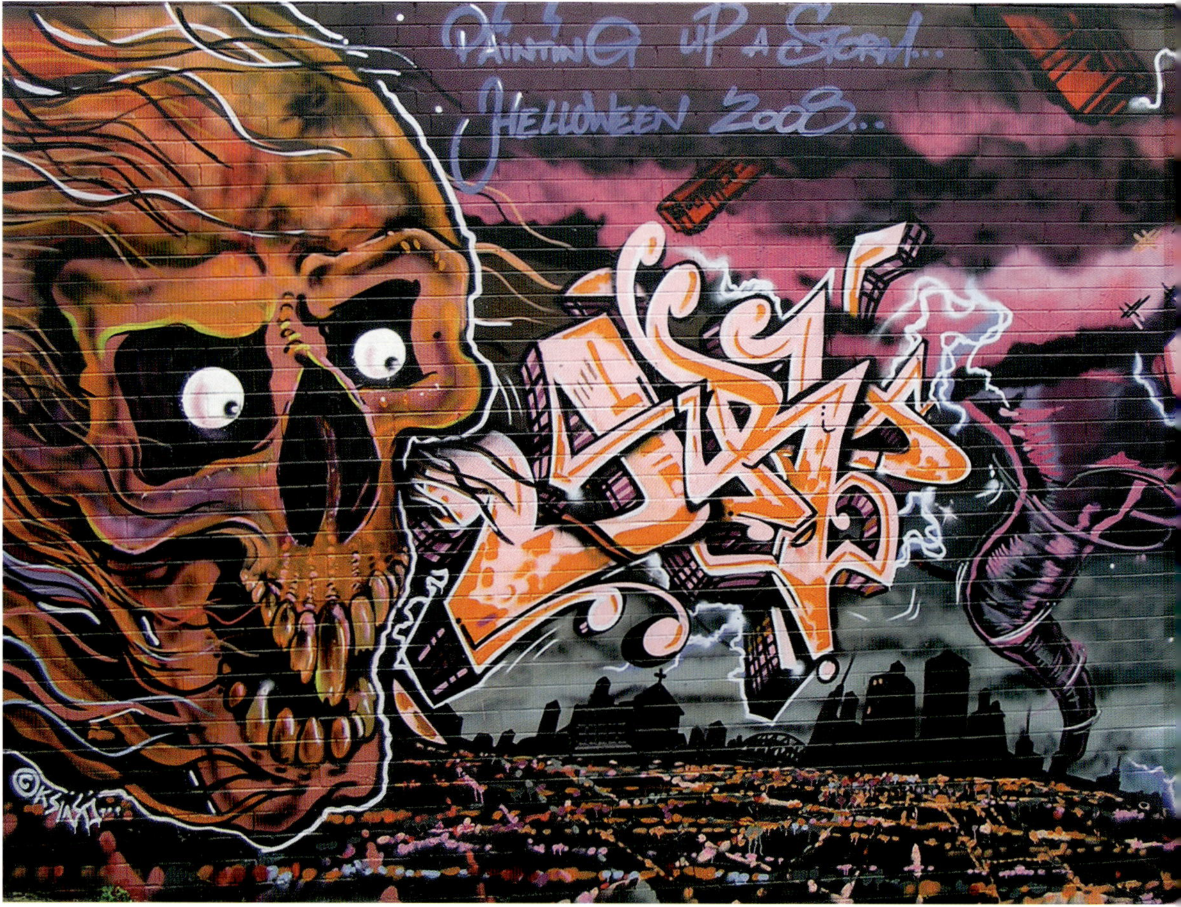
Painting up a Storm...
Helloween 2008...

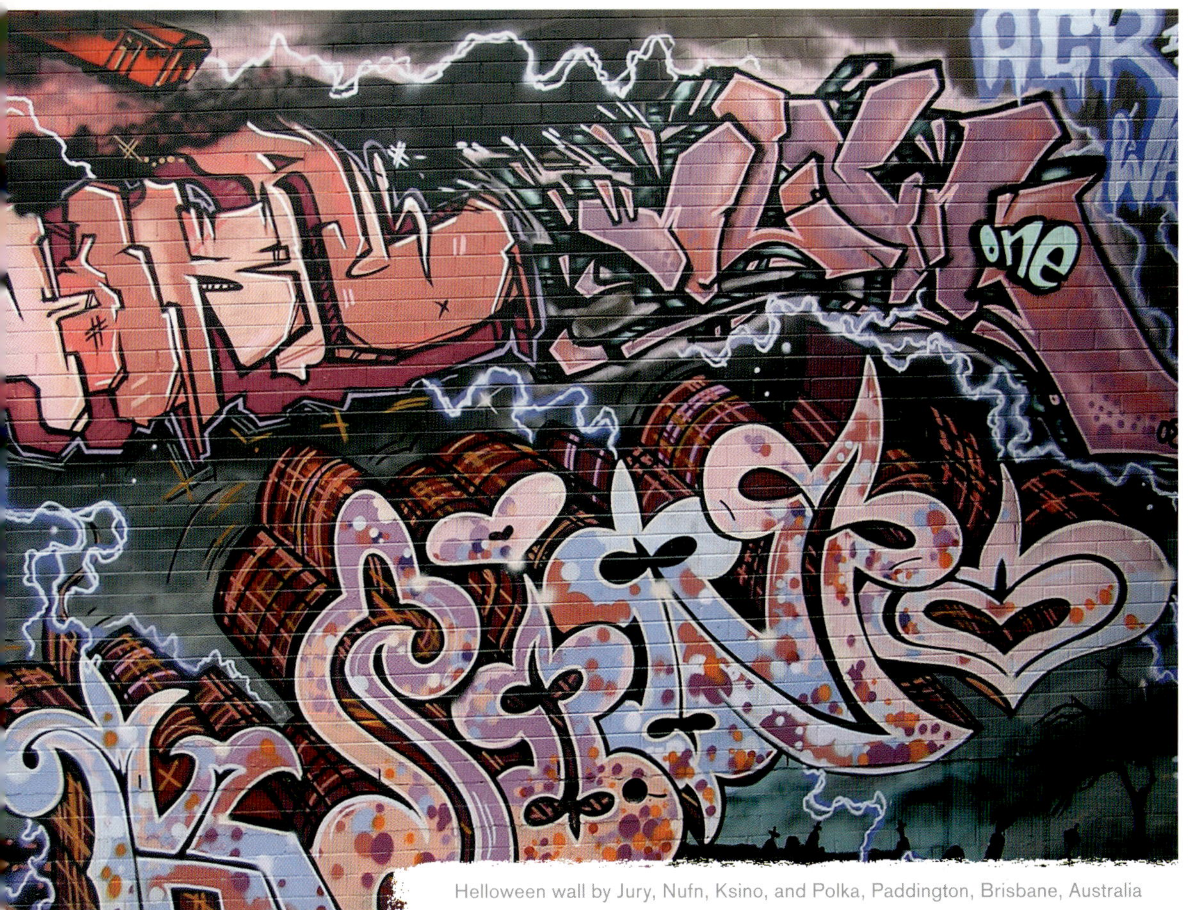

Helloween wall by Jury, Nufn, Ksino, and Polka, Paddington, Brisbane, Australia

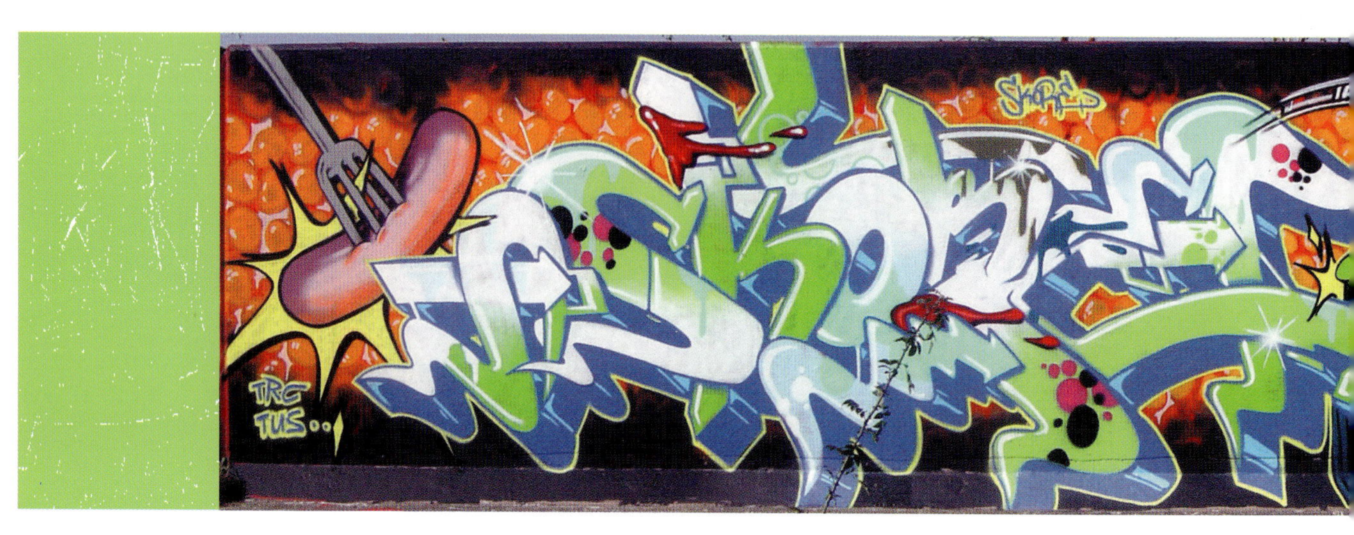
TRC
TUS

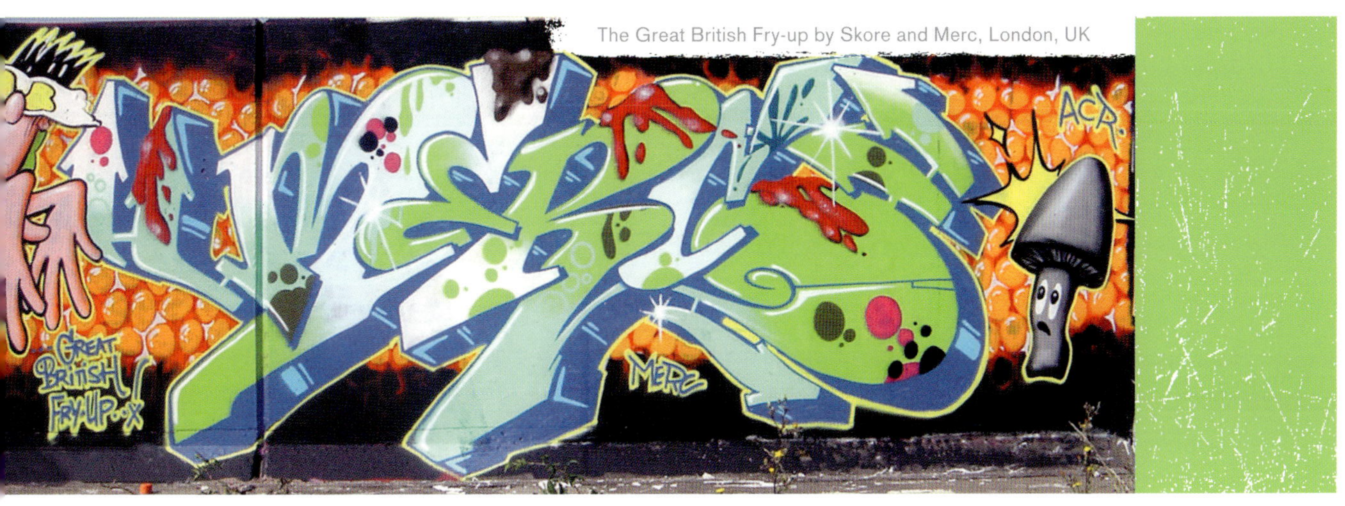

The Great British Fry-up by Skore and Merc, London, UK

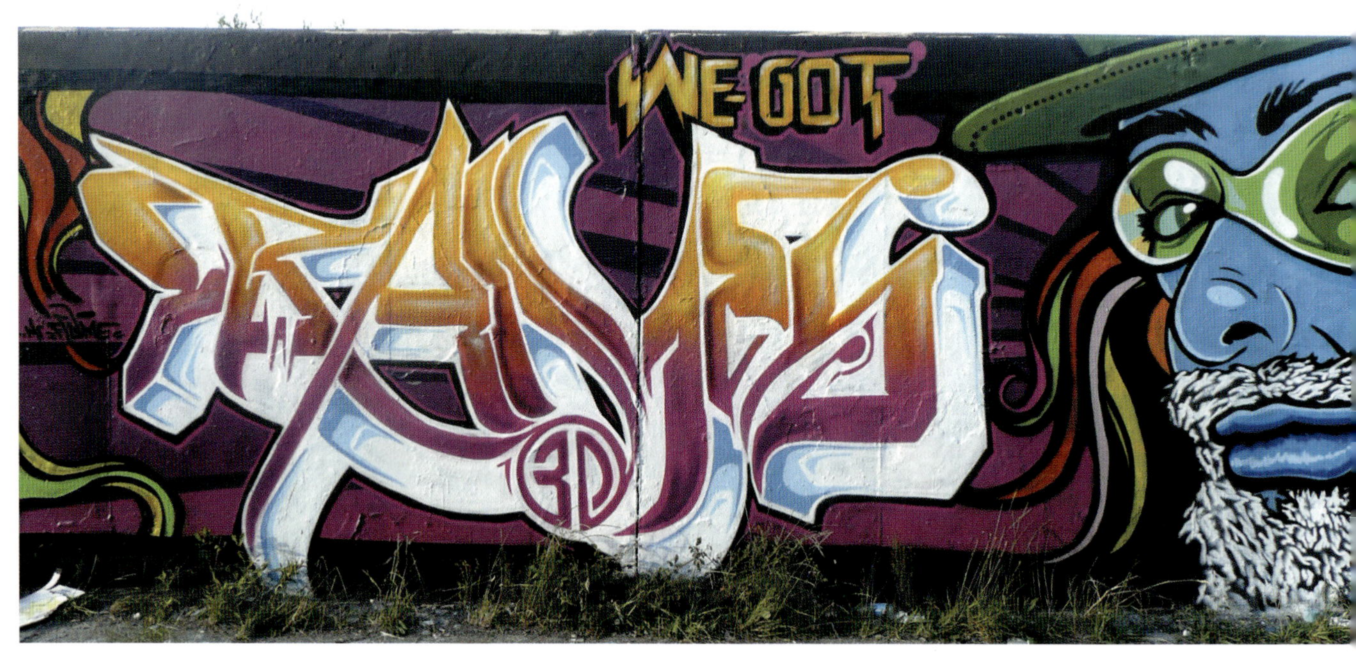
WE GOT

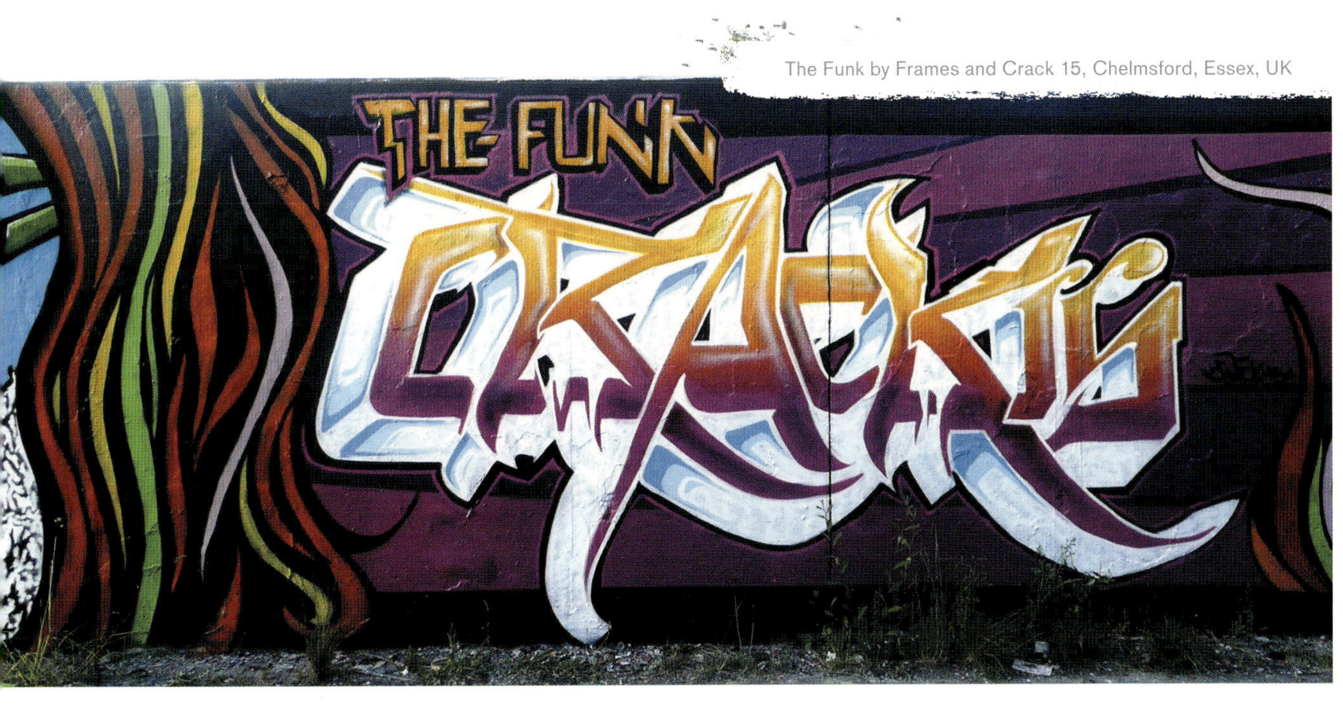

The Funk by Frames and Crack 15, Chelmsford, Essex, UK

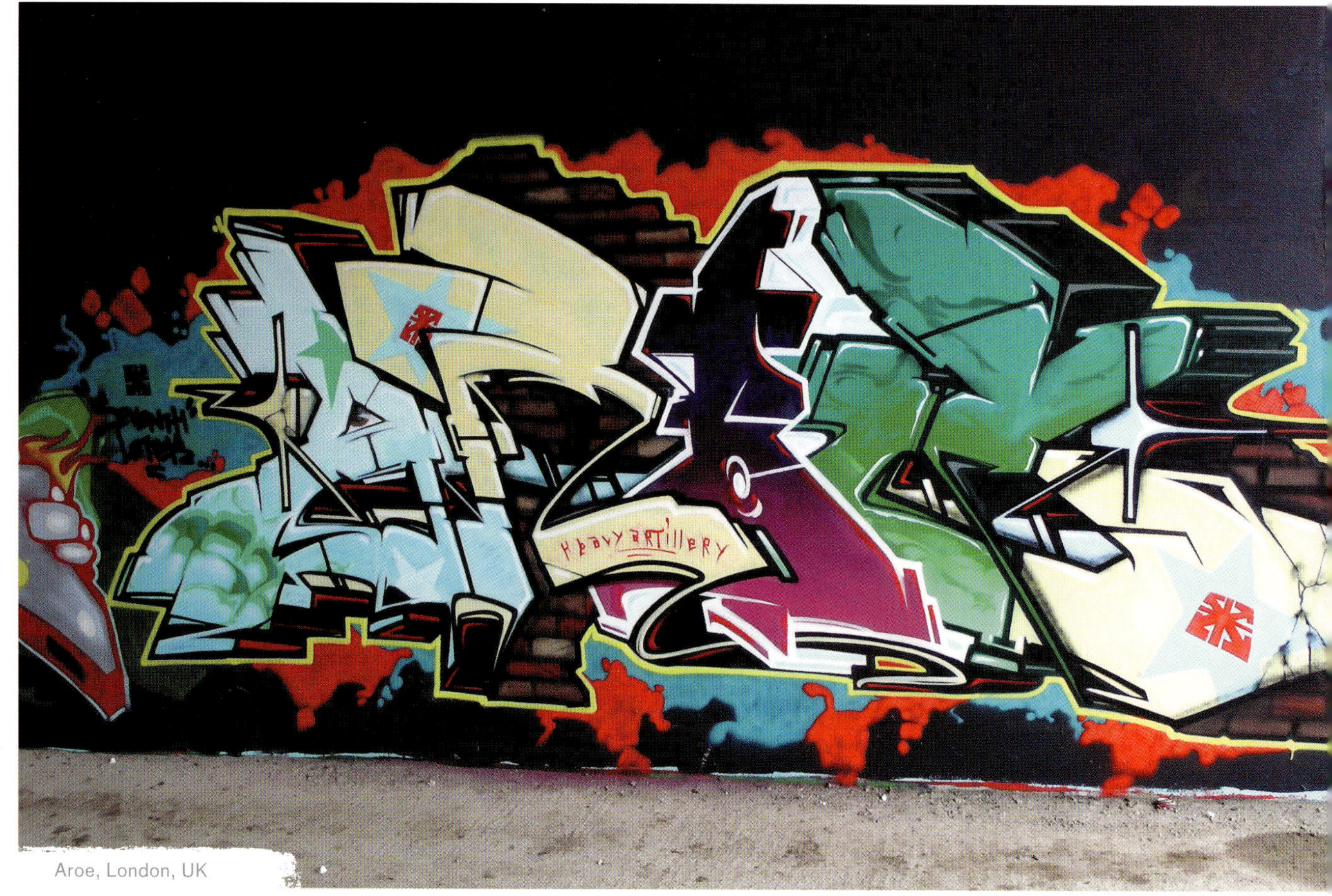

Aroe, London, UK

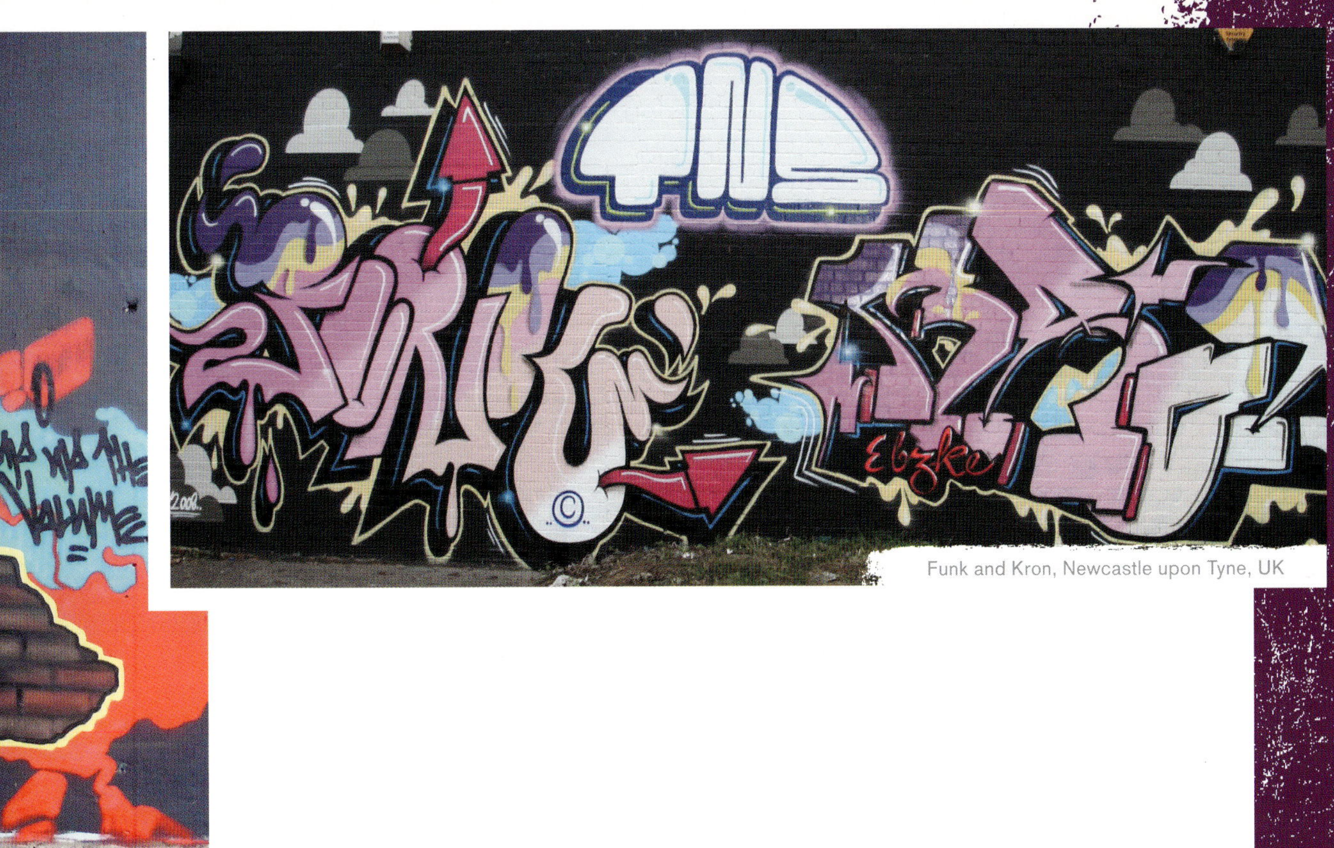

Funk and Kron, Newcastle upon Tyne, UK

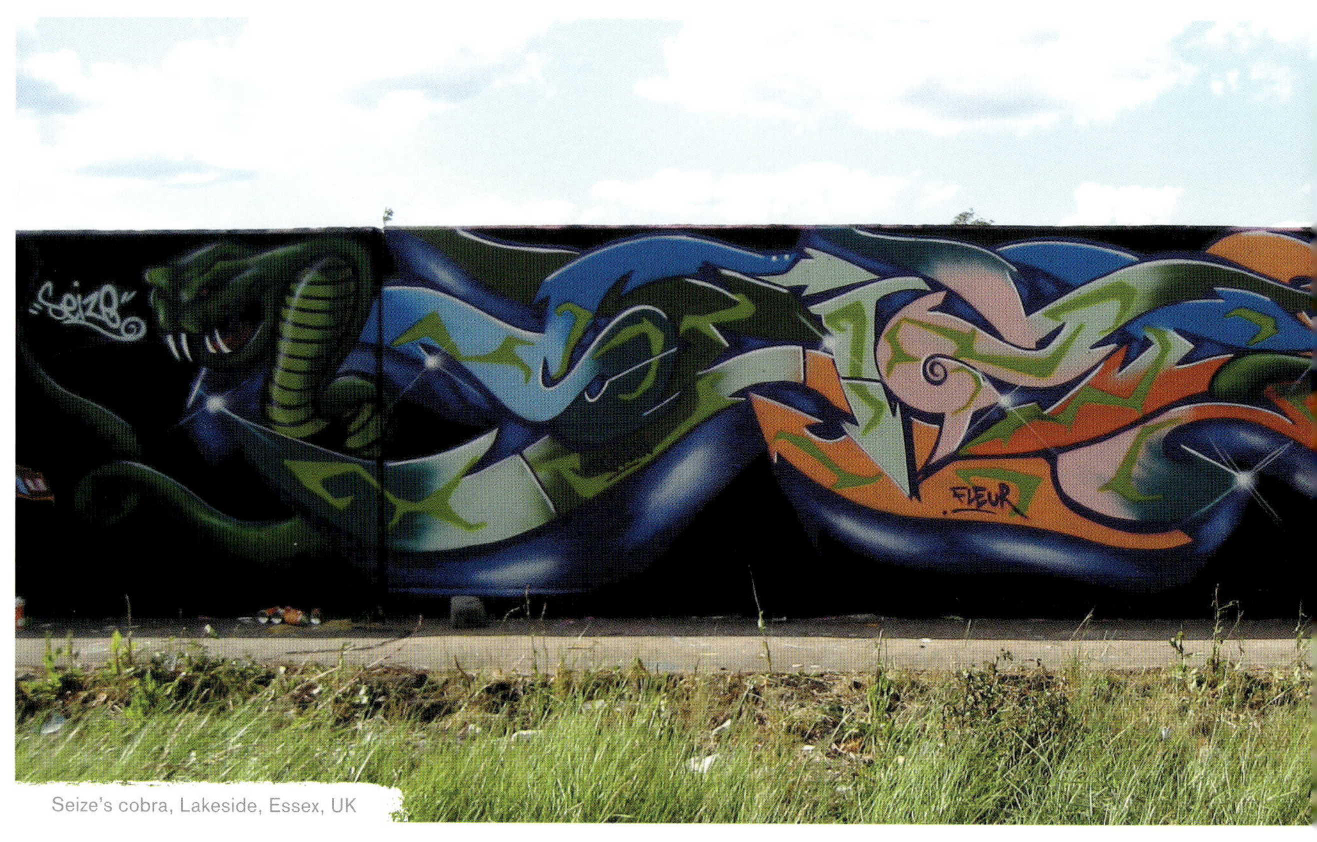

Seize's cobra, Lakeside, Essex, UK

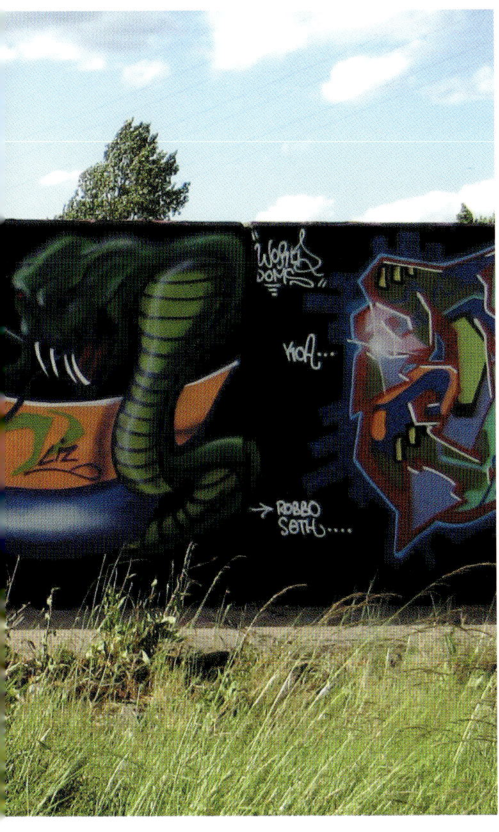

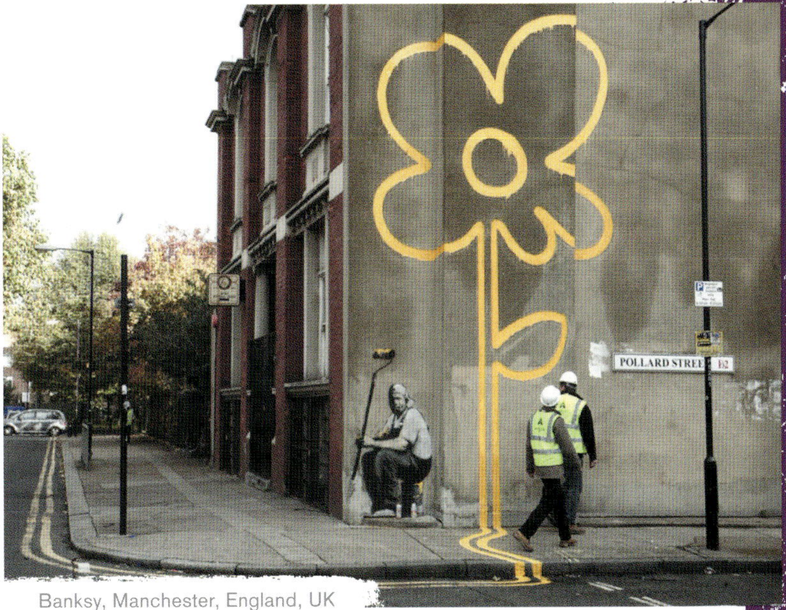

Banksy, Manchester, England, UK

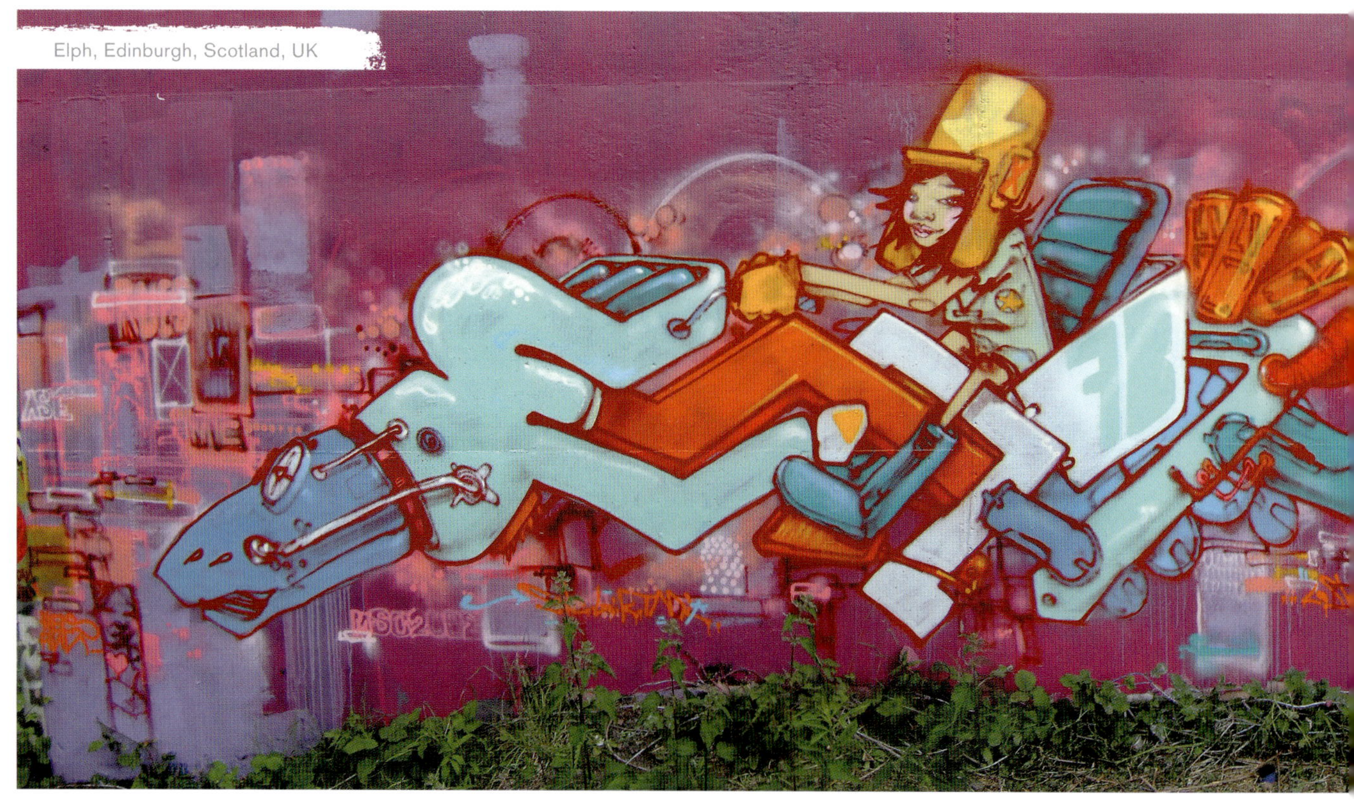

Elph, Edinburgh, Scotland, UK

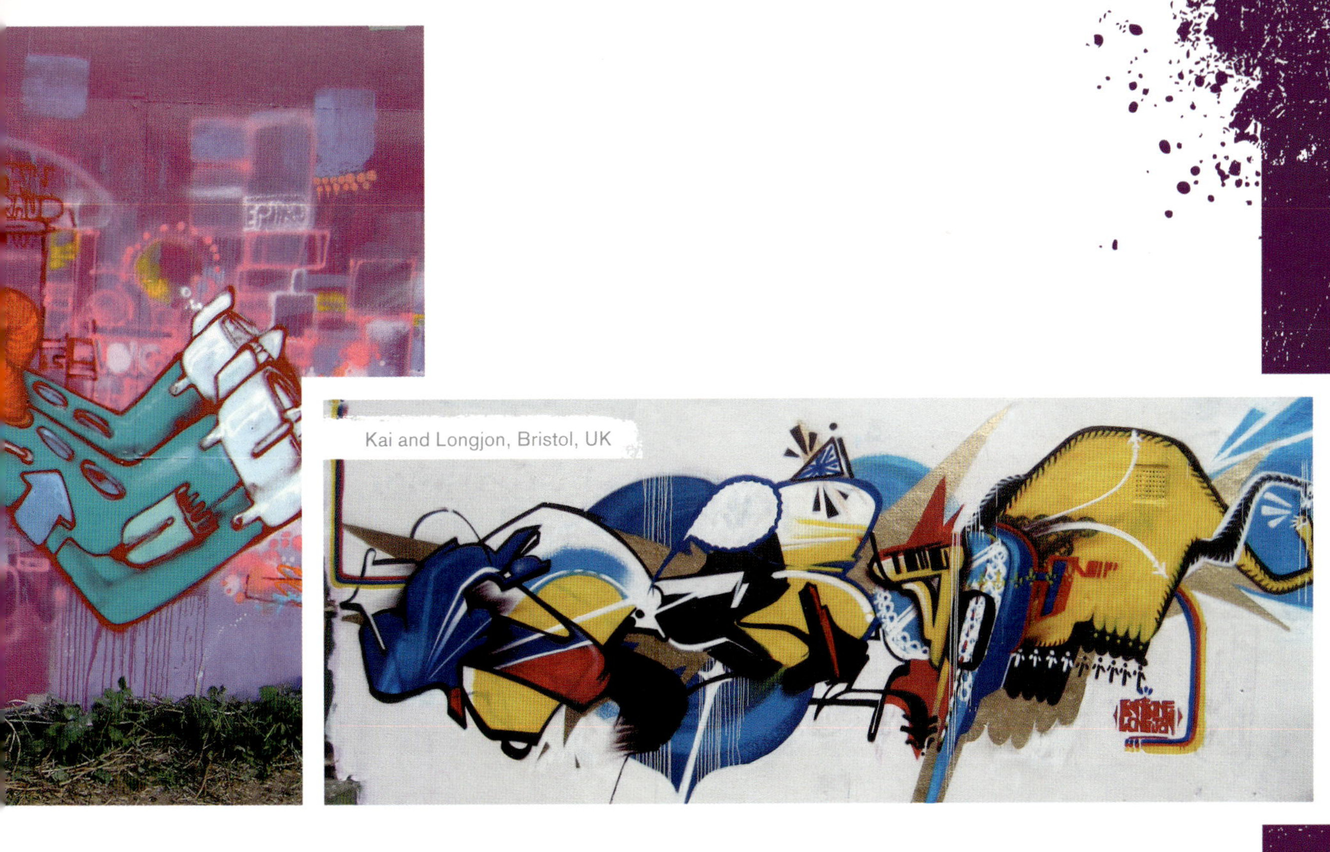

Kai and Longjon, Bristol, UK

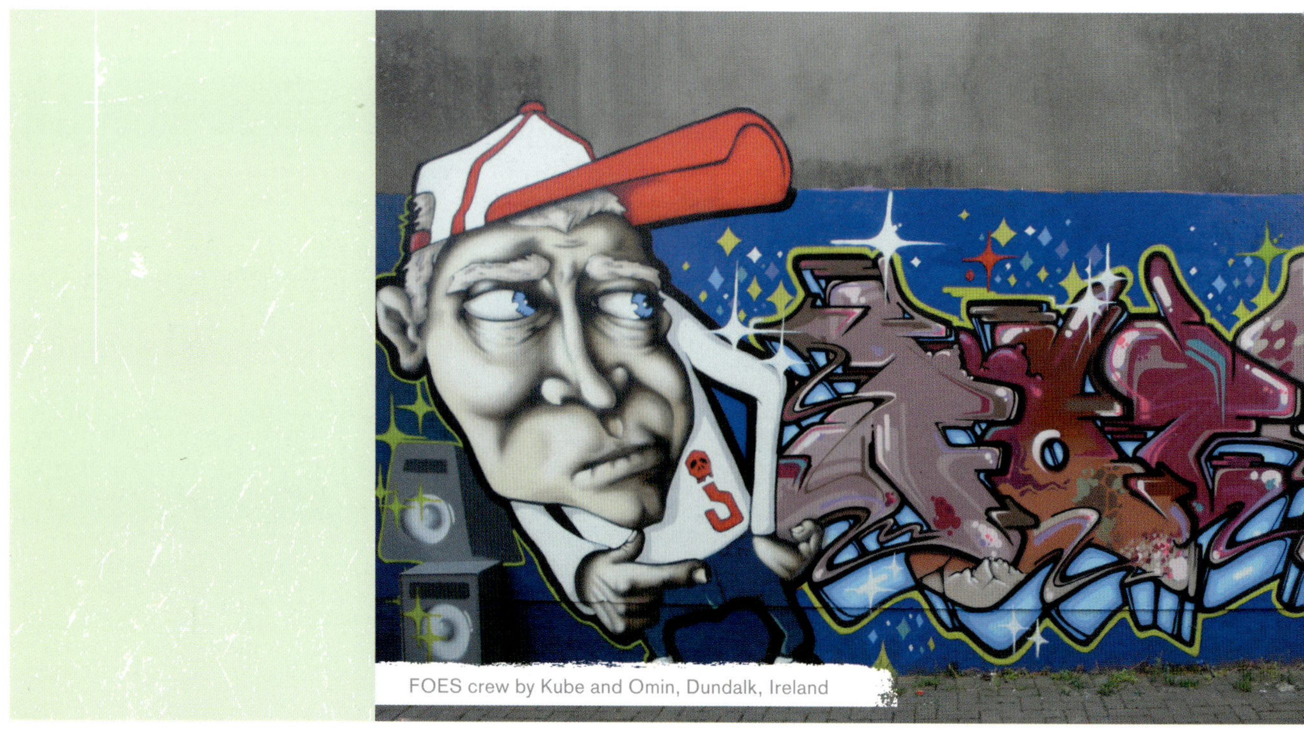

FOES crew by Kube and Omin, Dundalk, Ireland

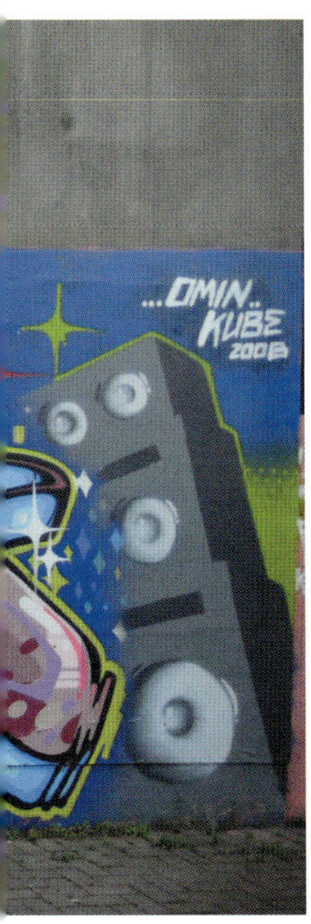

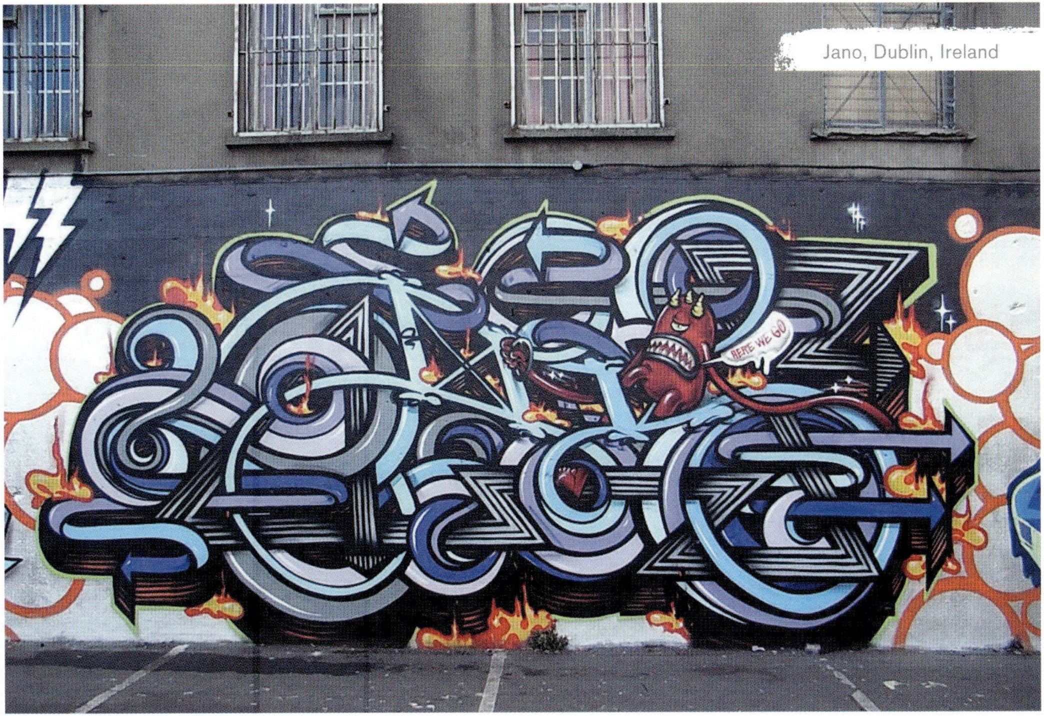

Jano, Dublin, Ireland

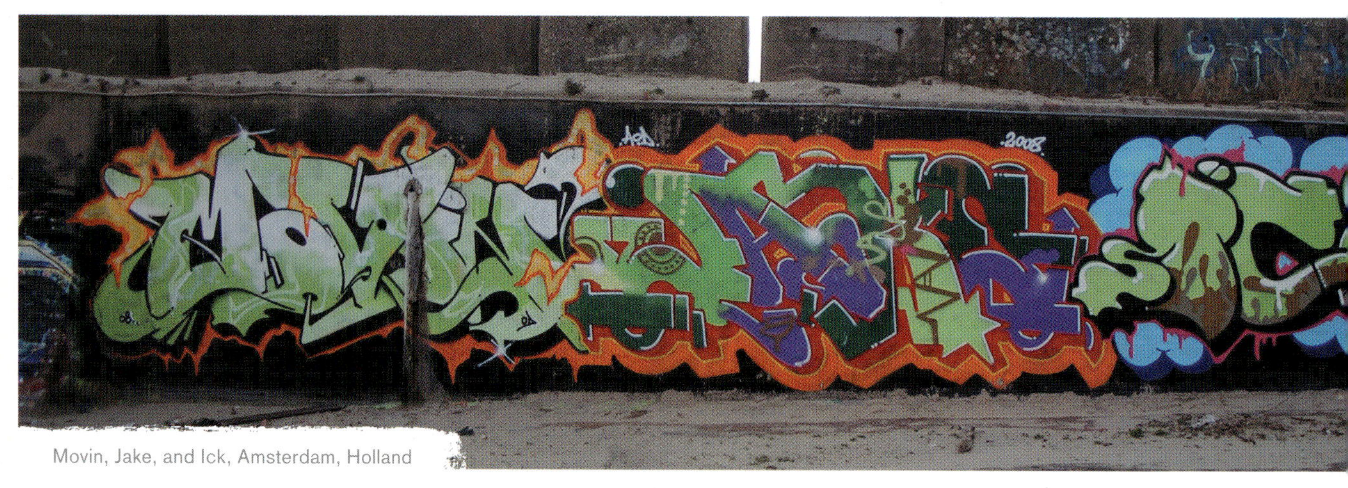

Movin, Jake, and Ick, Amsterdam, Holland

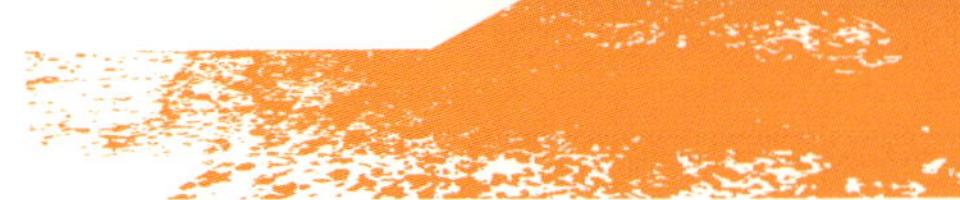

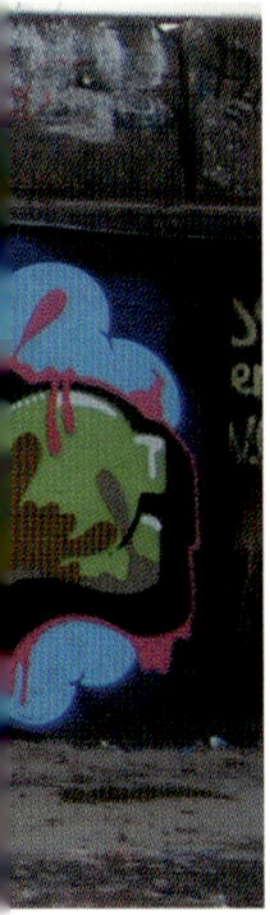

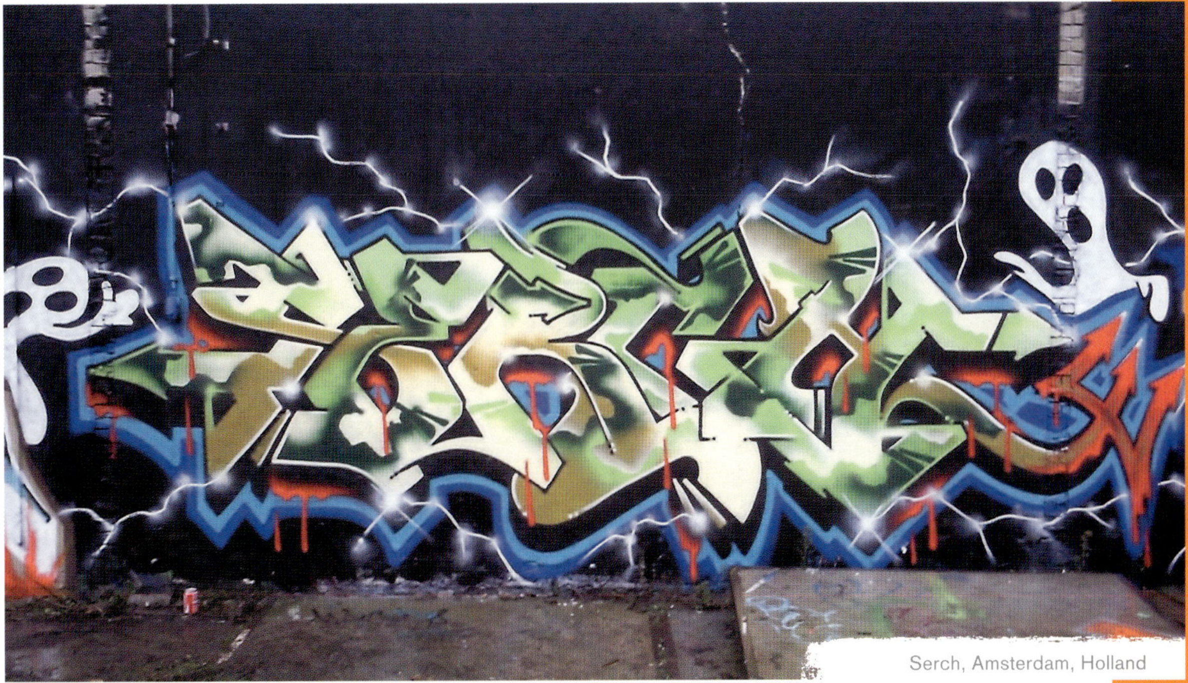

Serch, Amsterdam, Holland

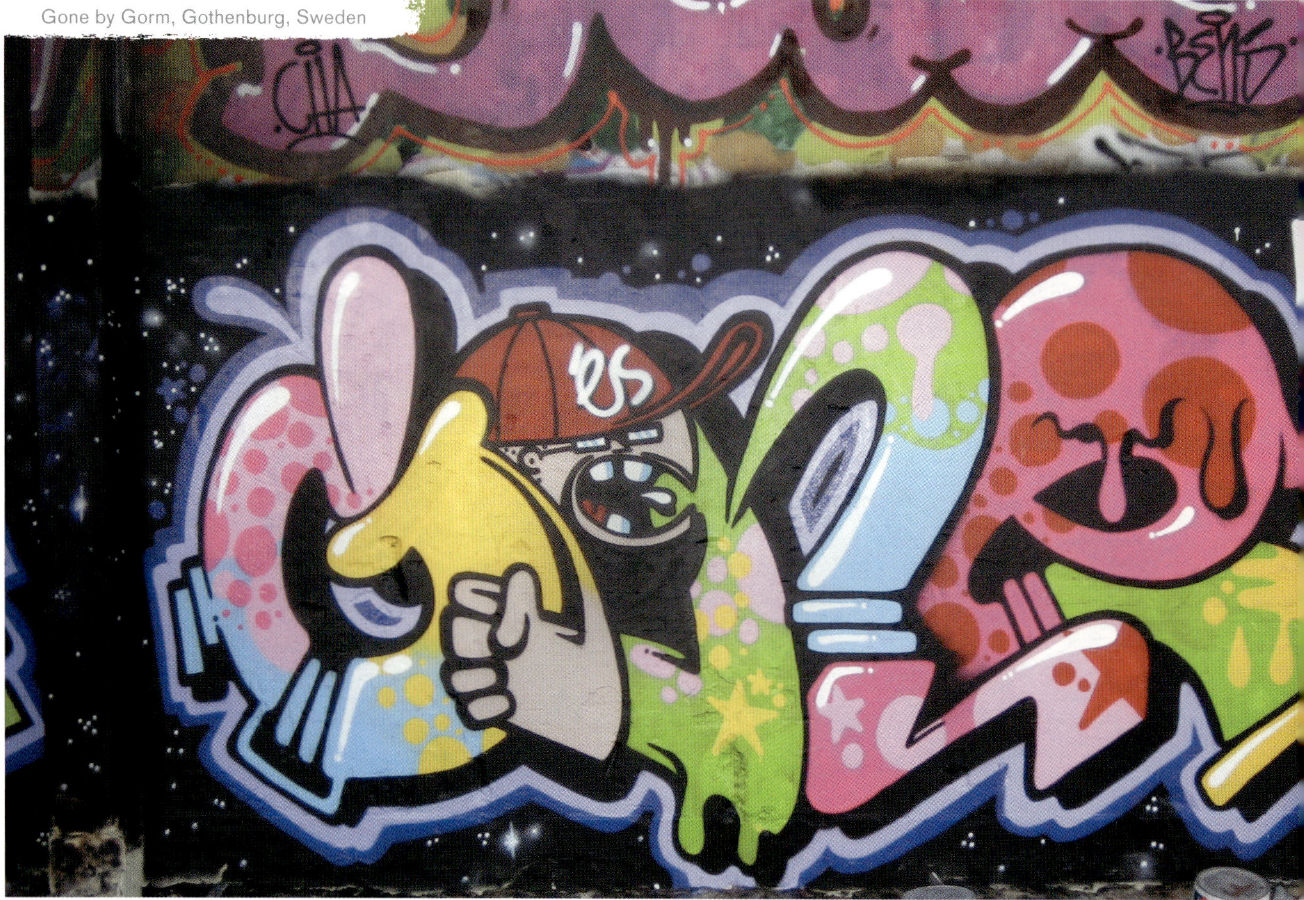

Gone by Gorm, Gothenburg, Sweden

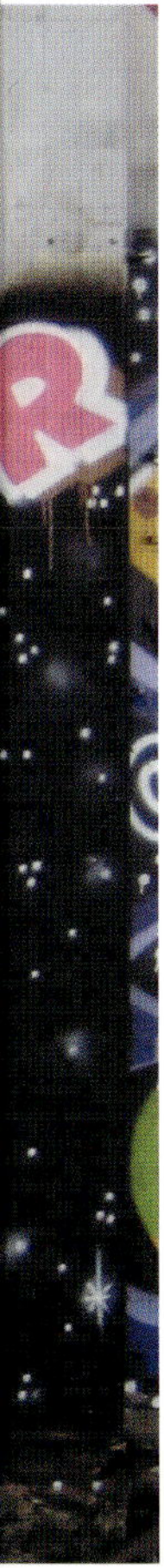

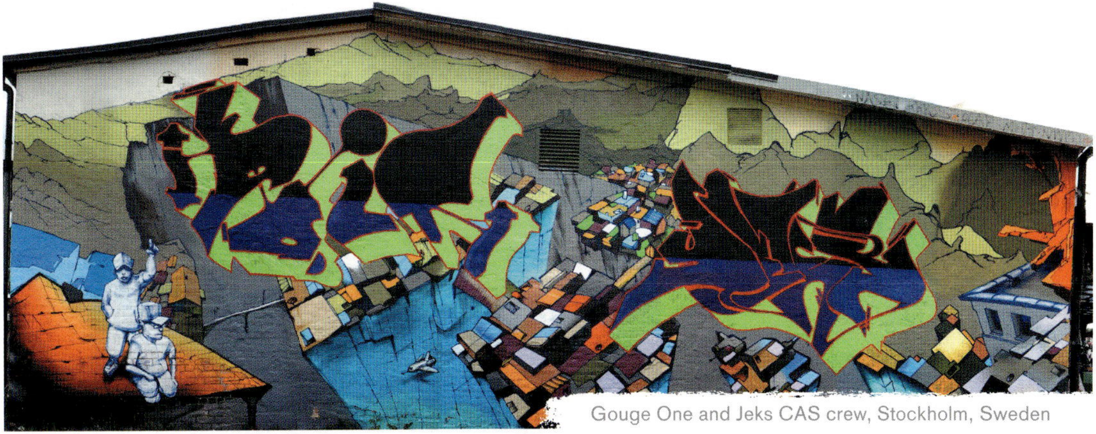

Gouge One and Jeks CAS crew, Stockholm, Sweden

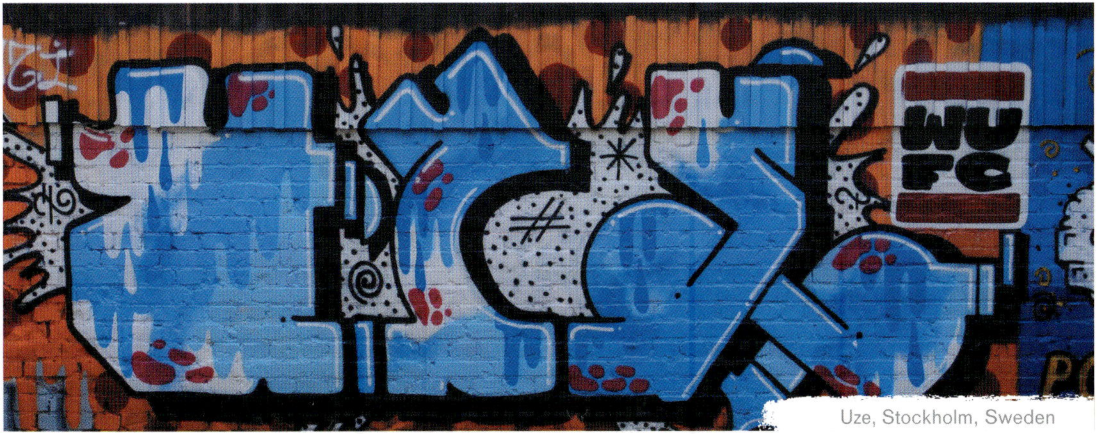

Uze, Stockholm, Sweden

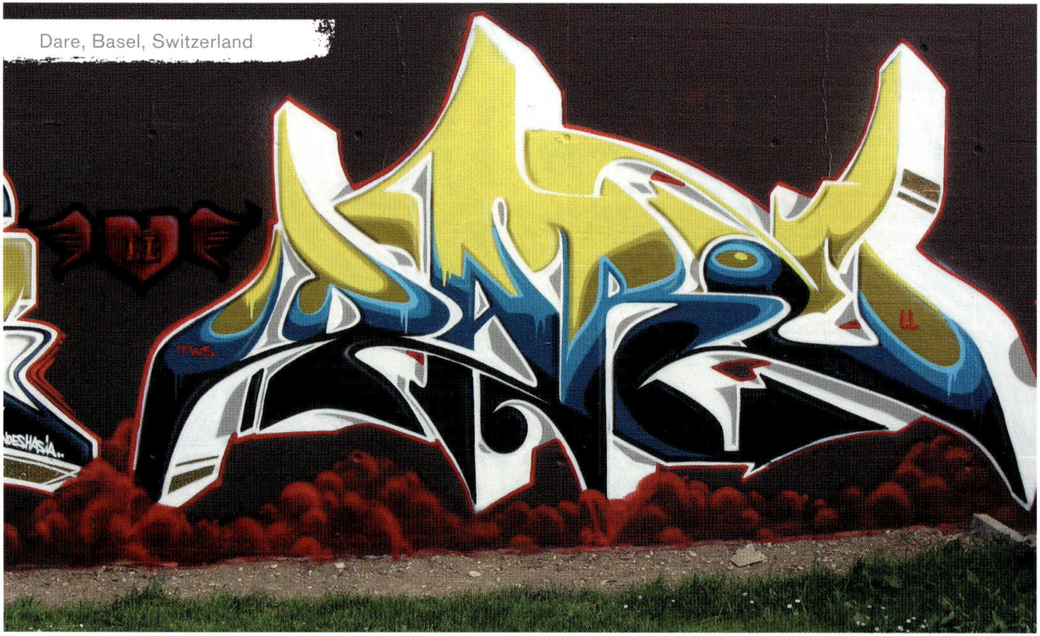

Dare, Basel, Switzerland

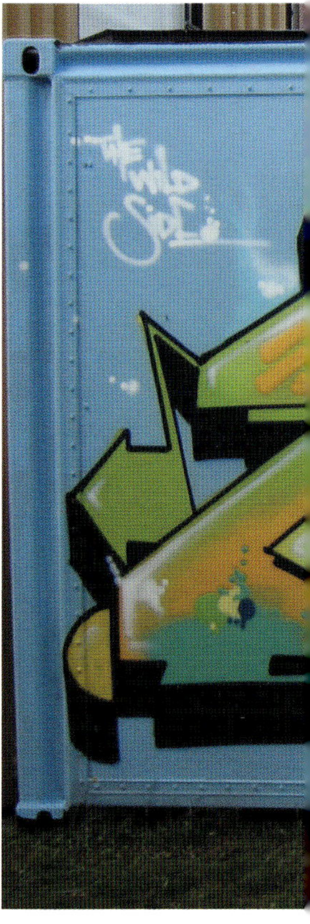

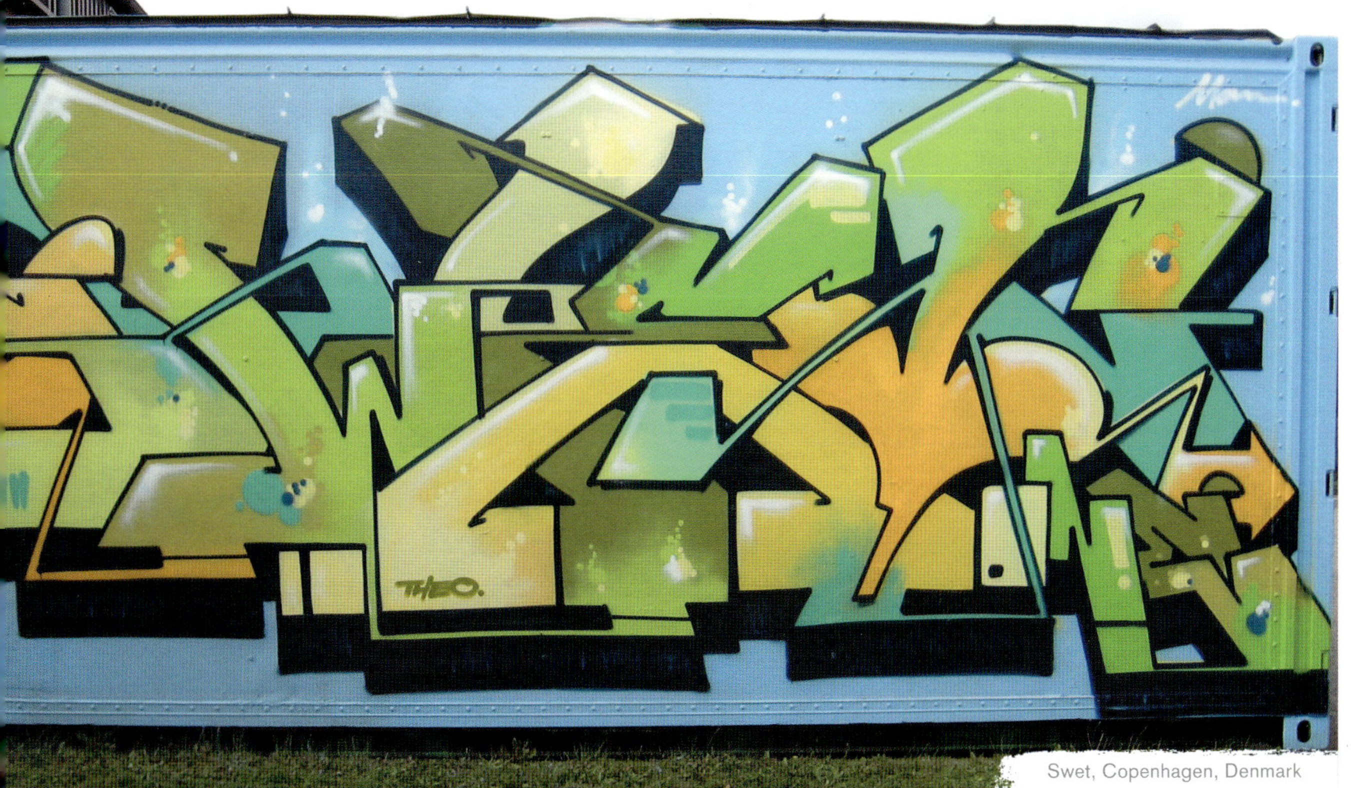

Swet, Copenhagen, Denmark

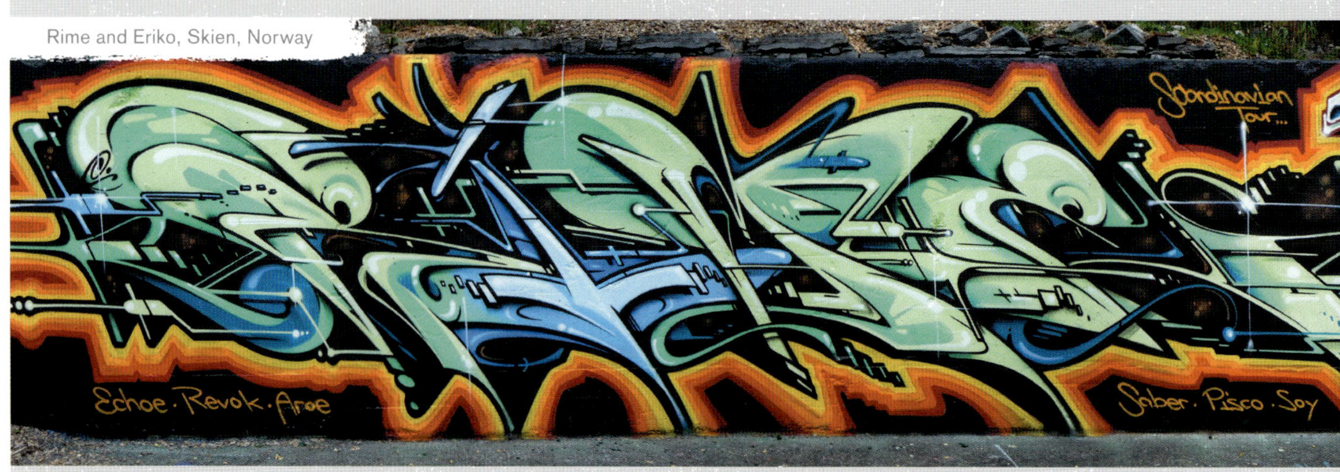

Rime and Eriko, Skien, Norway

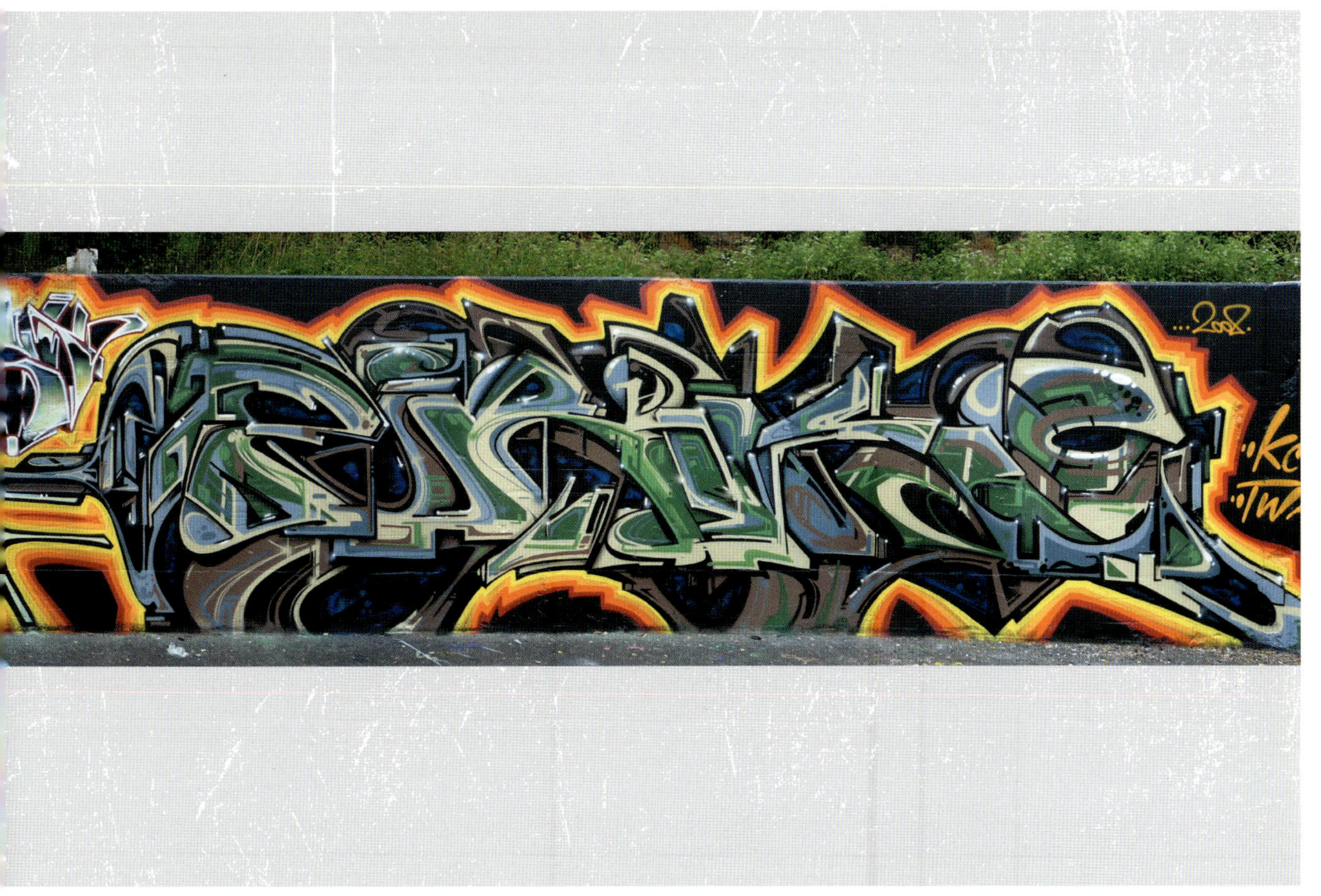
...2008.

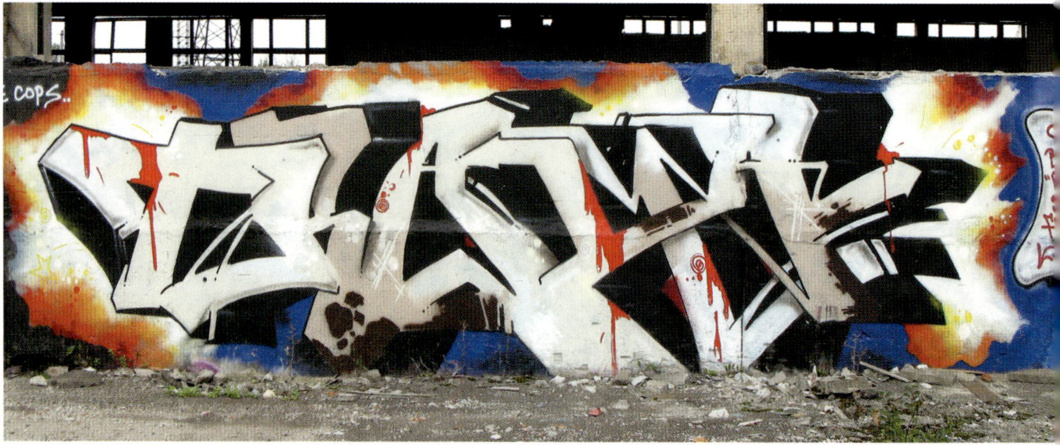

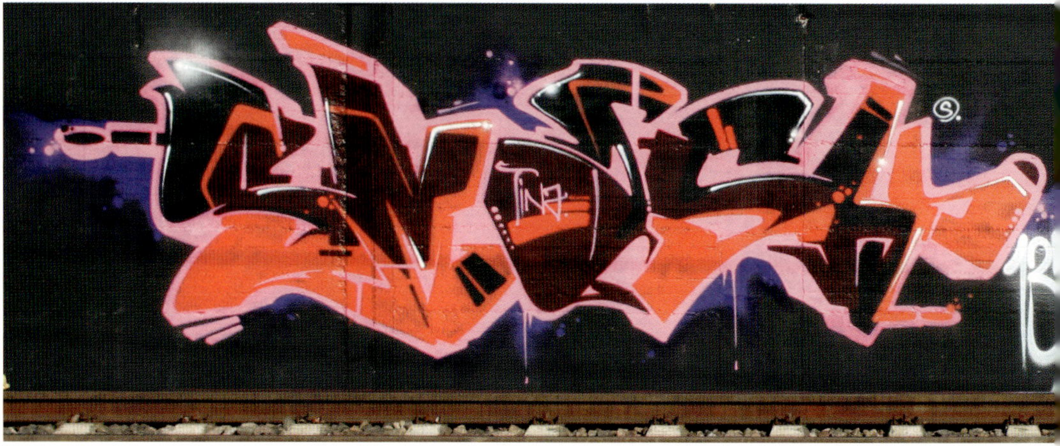

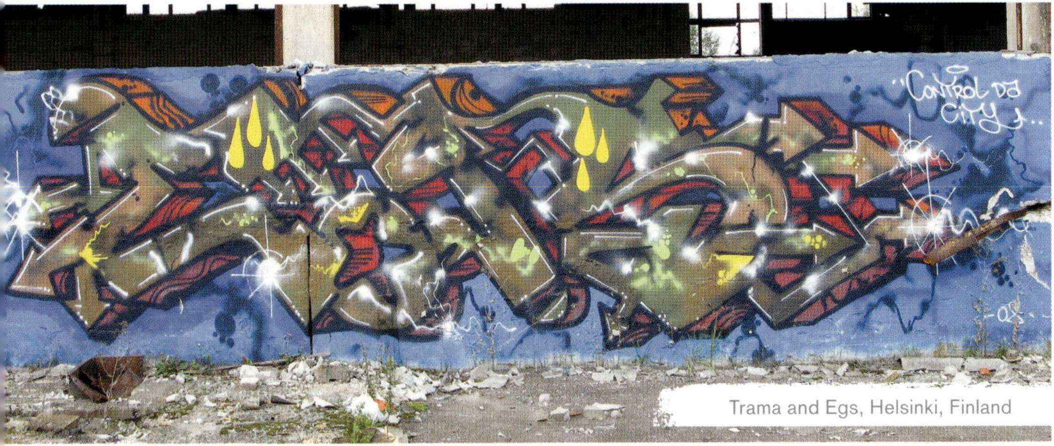

Trama and Egs, Helsinki, Finland

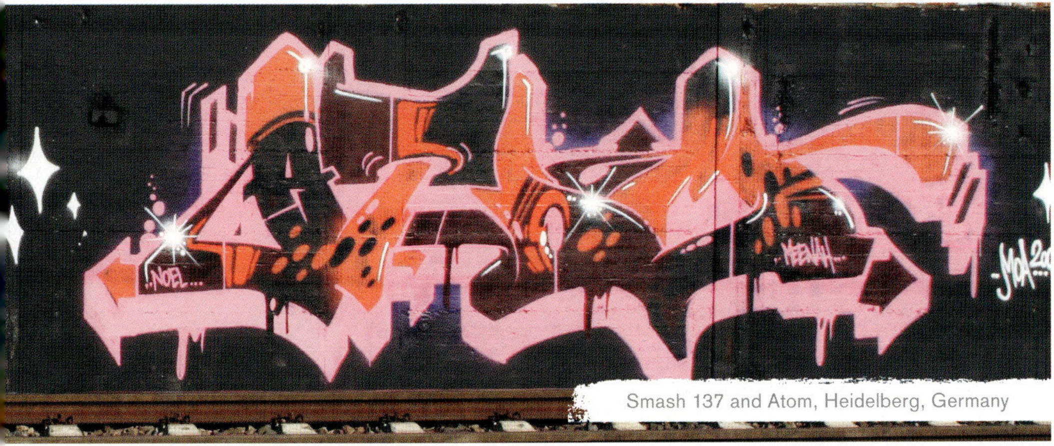

Smash 137 and Atom, Heidelberg, Germany

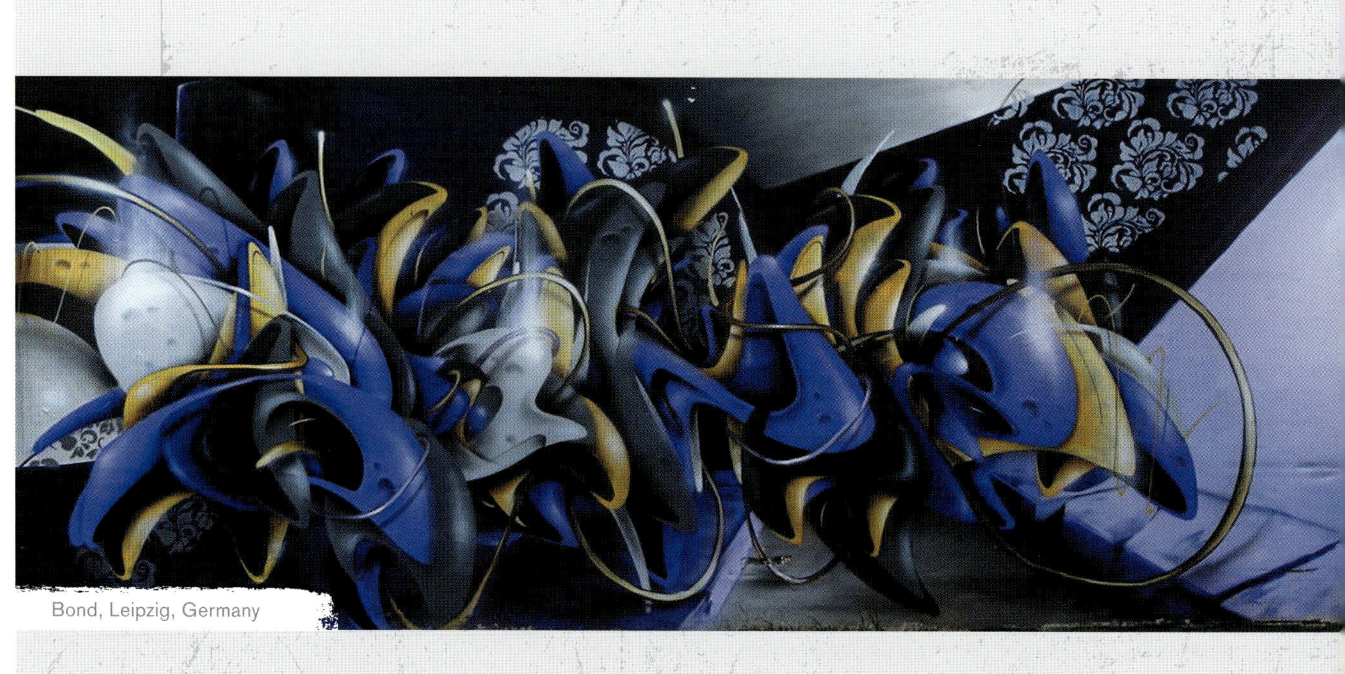

Bond, Leipzig, Germany

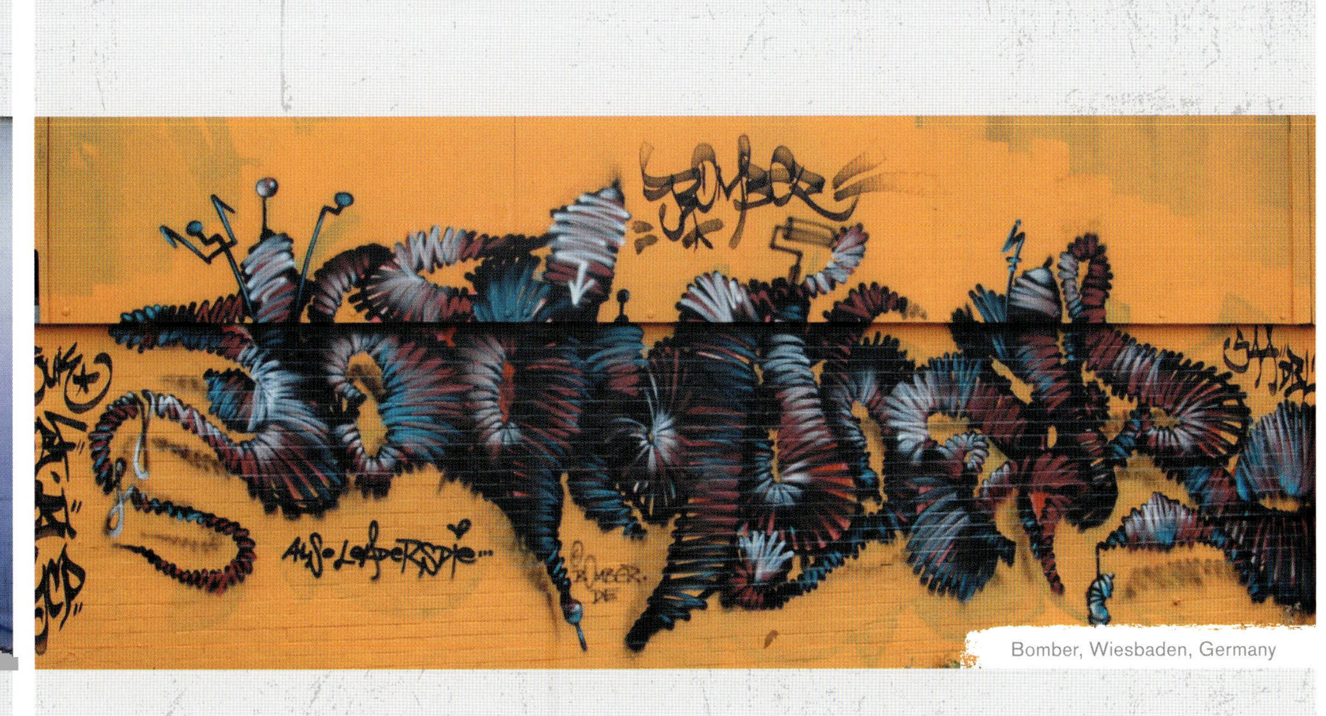

Bomber, Wiesbaden, Germany

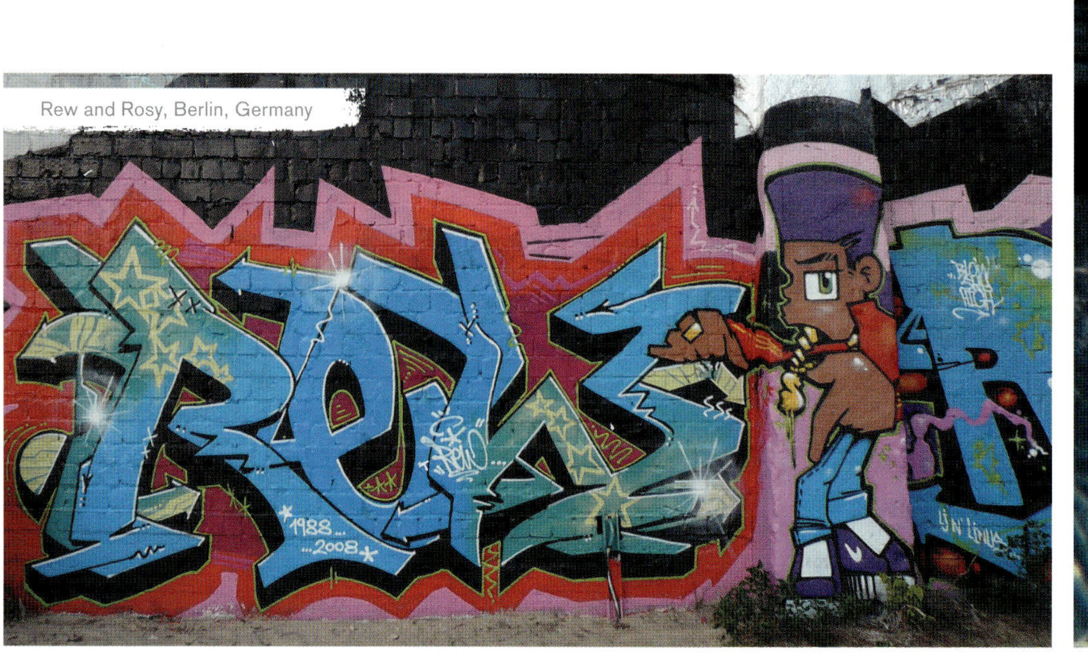

Rew and Rosy, Berlin, Germany

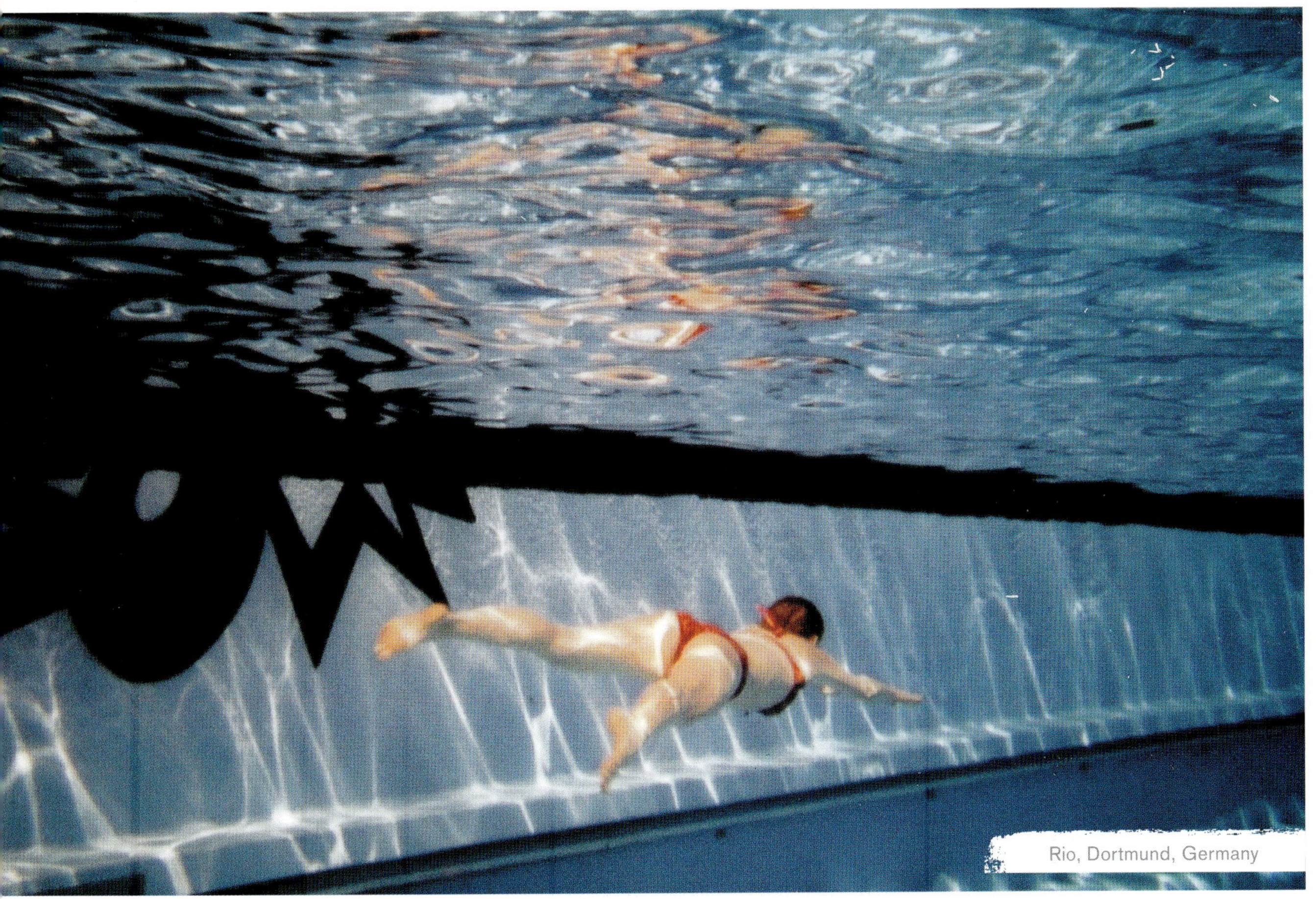

Rio, Dortmund, Germany

Kane, Phos, Fok, and Town, Berlin, Germany

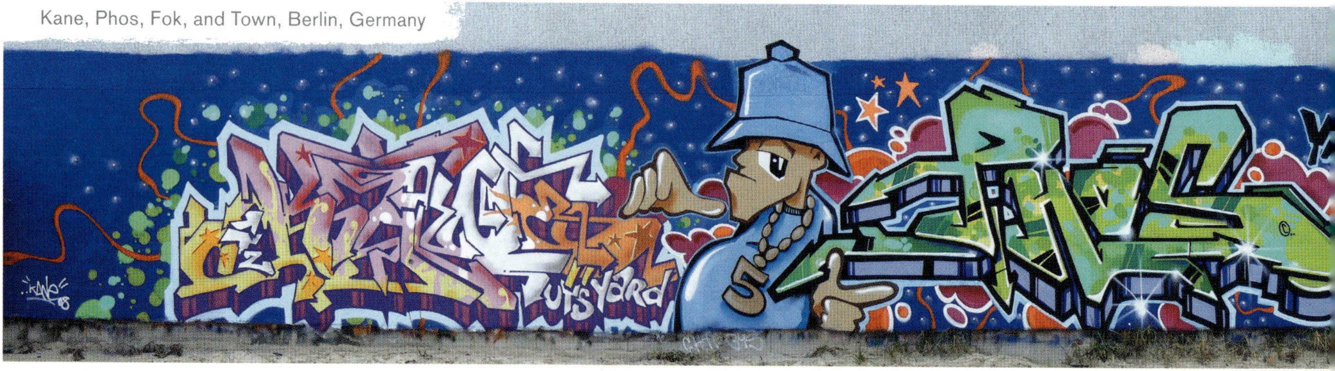

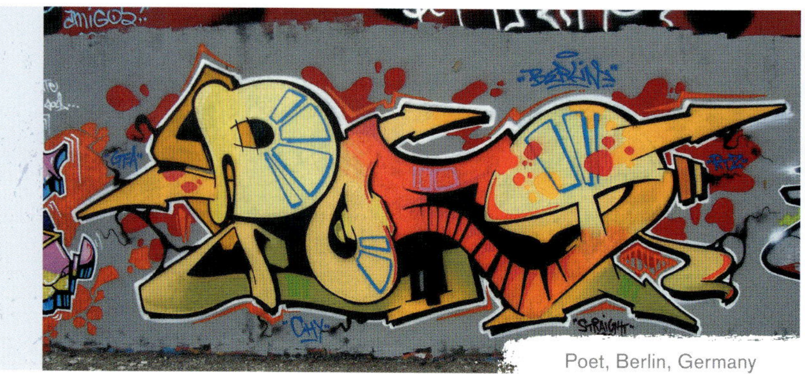

Poet, Berlin, Germany

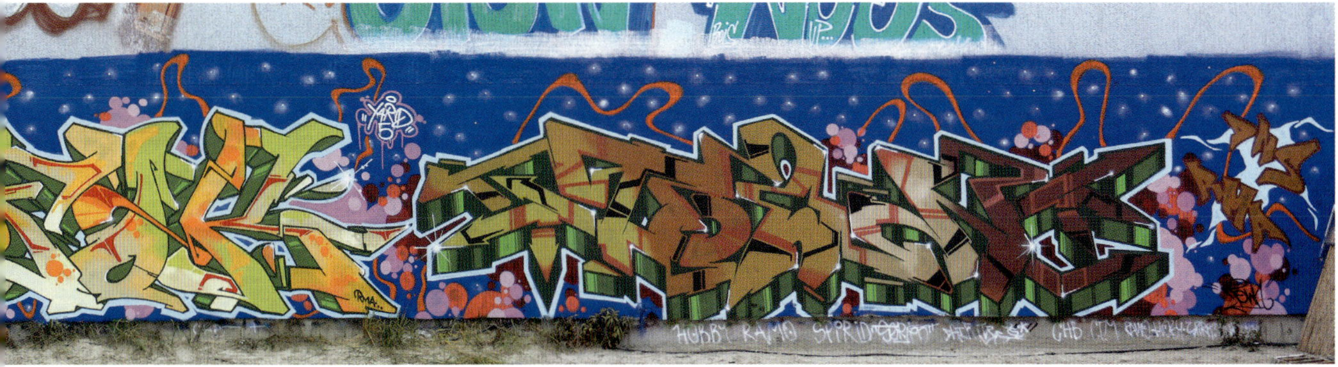

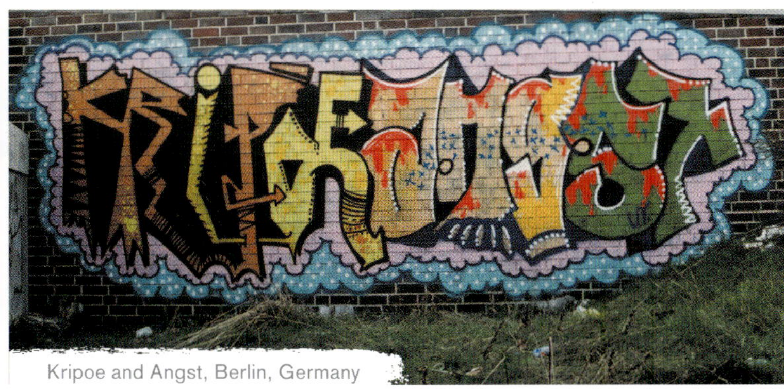

Kripoe and Angst, Berlin, Germany

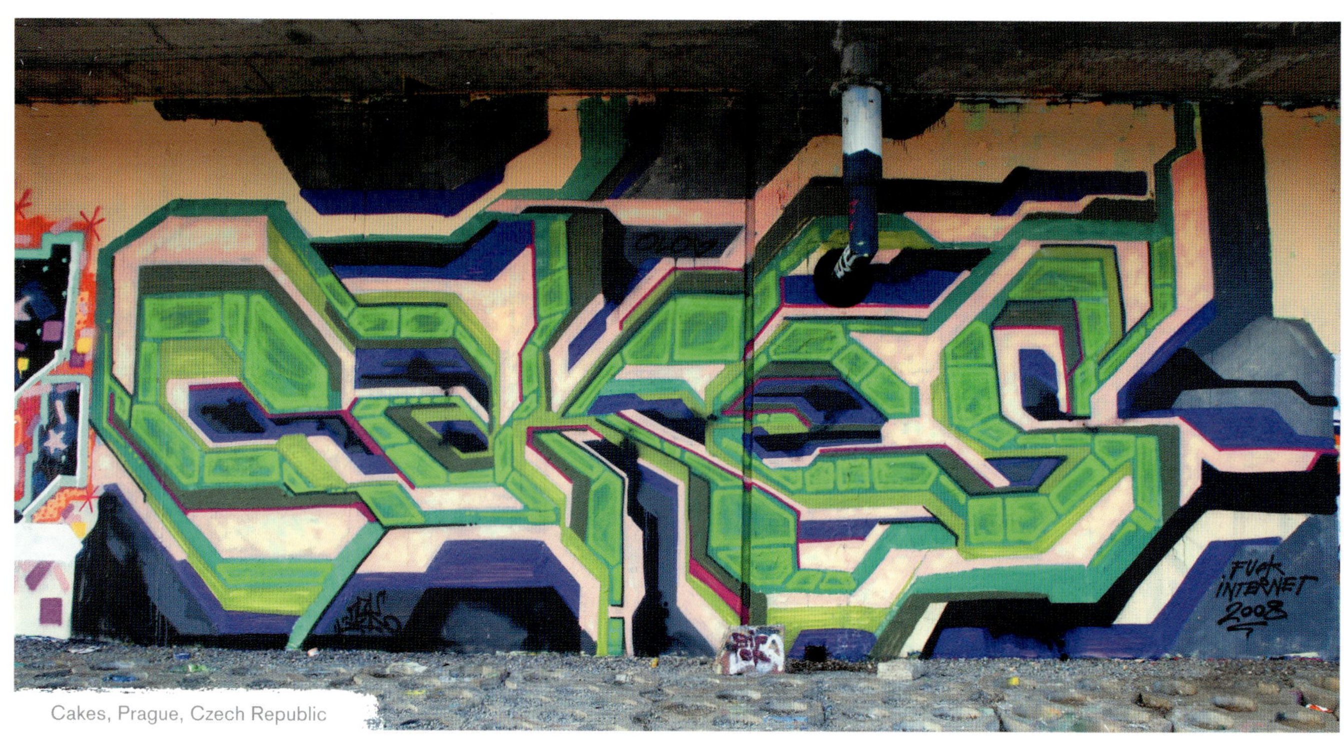

Cakes, Prague, Czech Republic

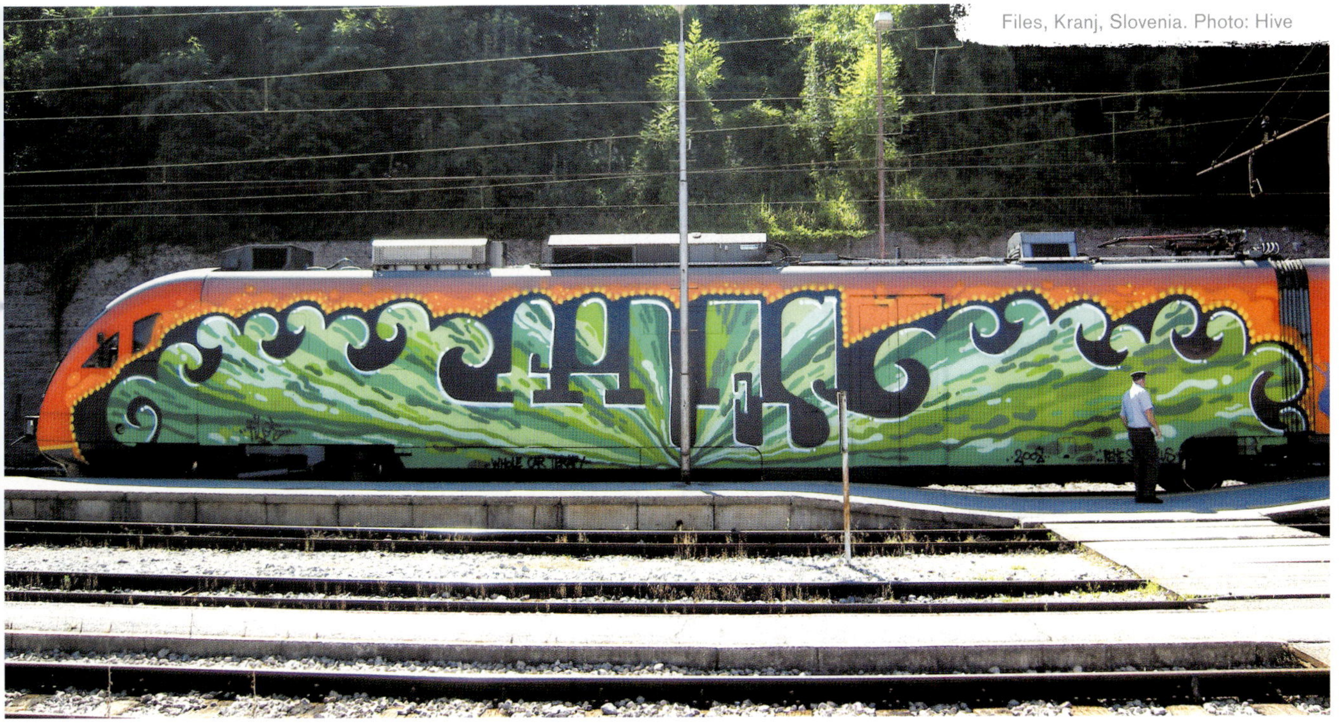

Files, Kranj, Slovenia. Photo: Hive

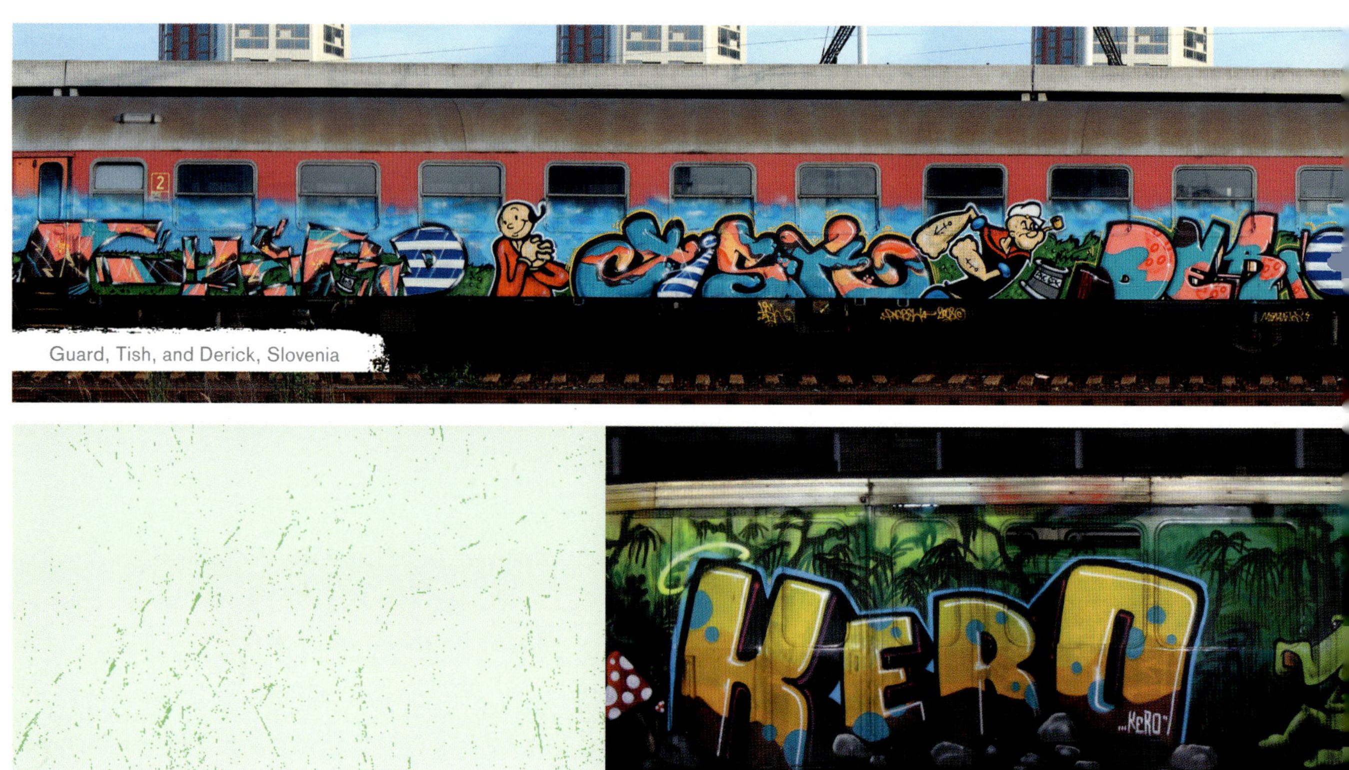

Guard, Tish, and Derick, Slovenia

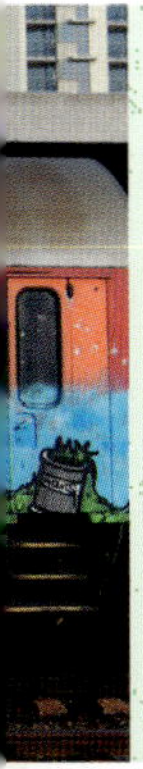

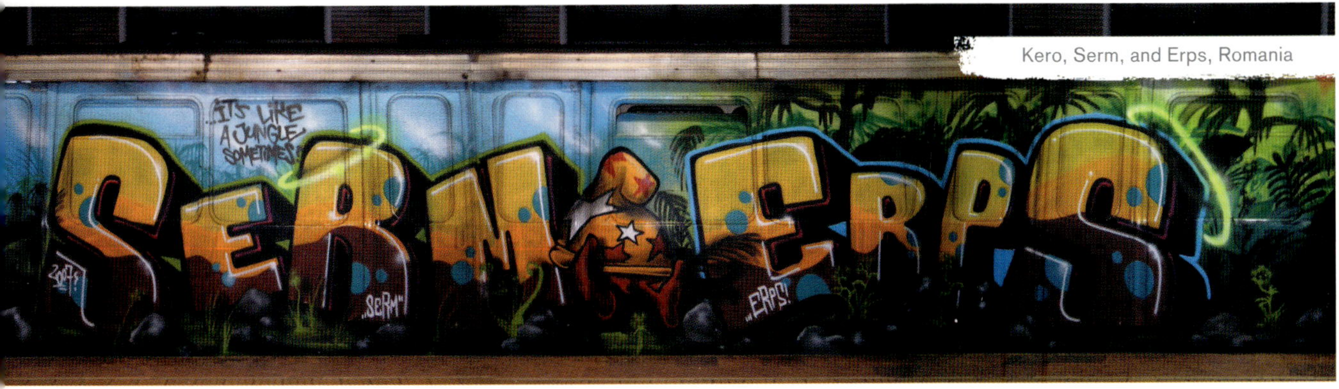

Kero, Serm, and Erps, Romania

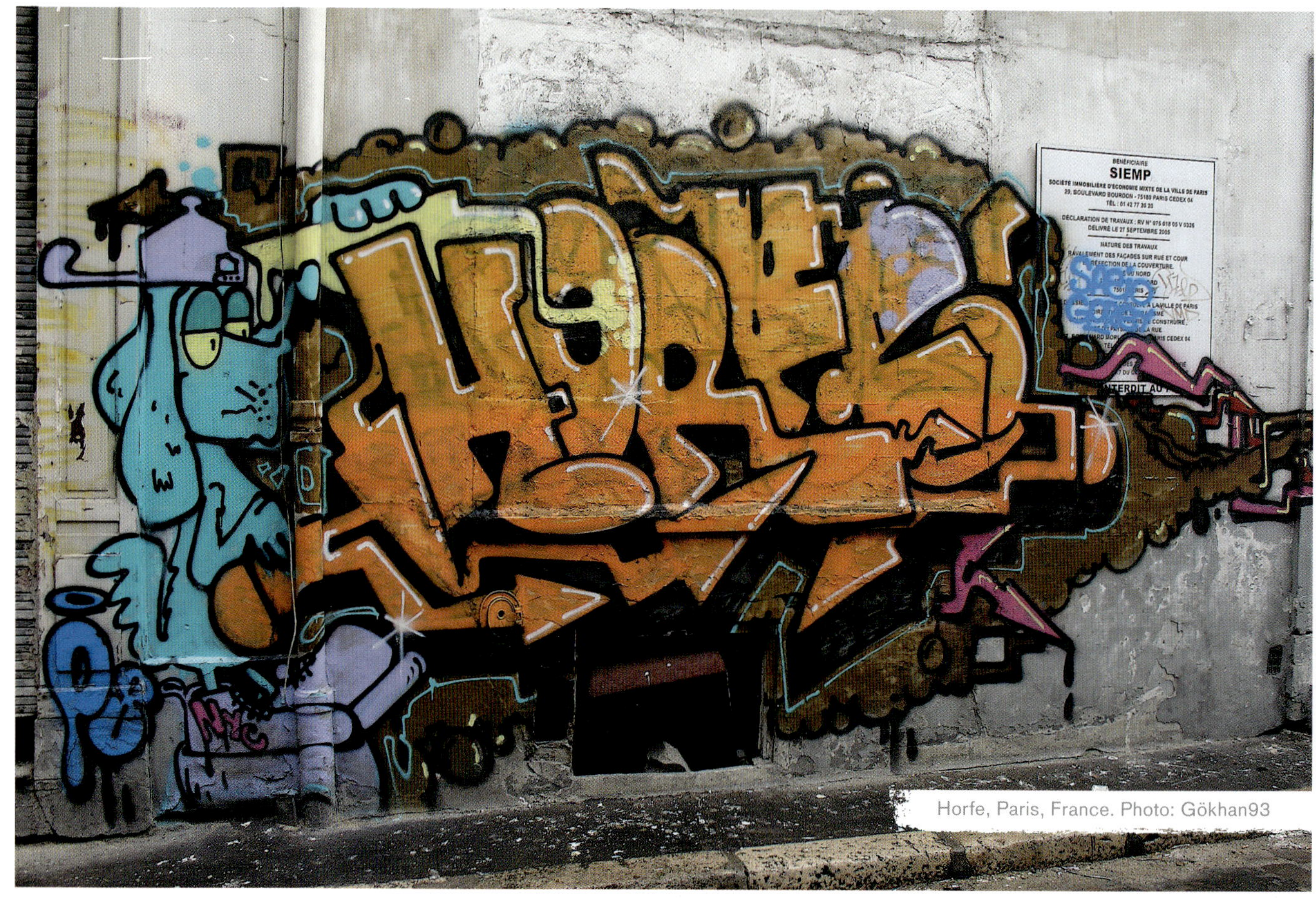

Horfe, Paris, France. Photo: Gökhan93

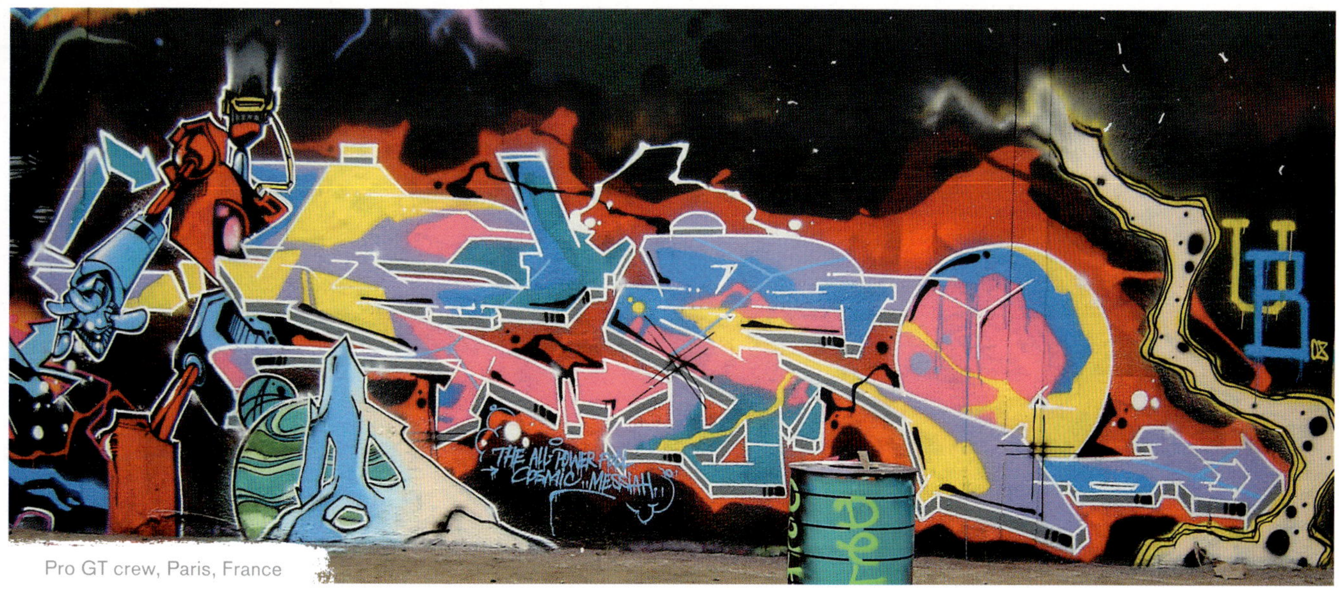

Pro GT crew, Paris, France

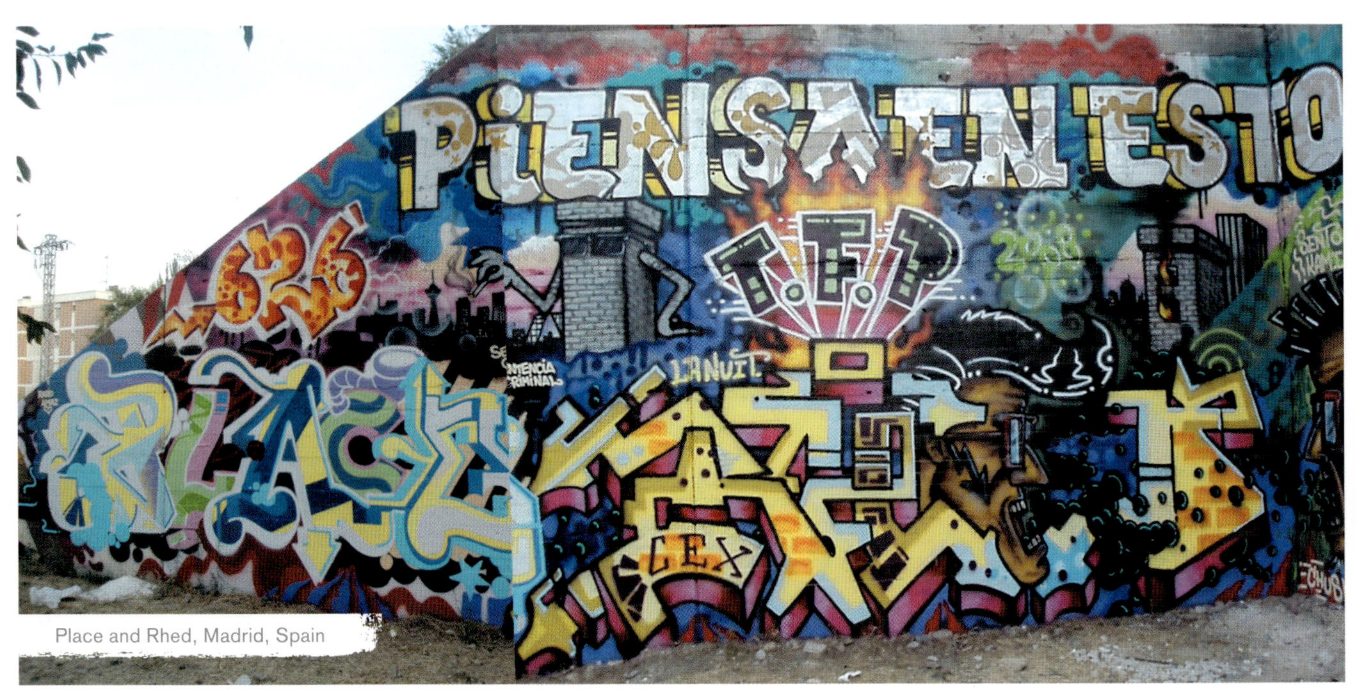

Place and Rhed, Madrid, Spain

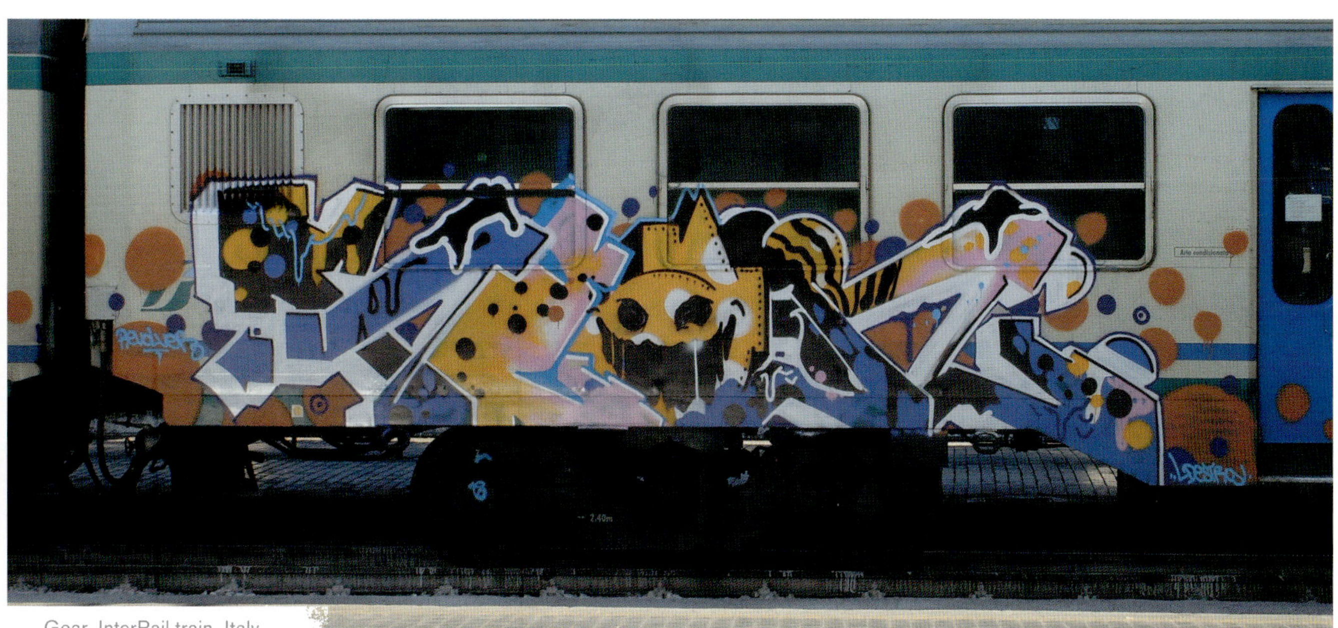

Gear, InterRail train, Italy

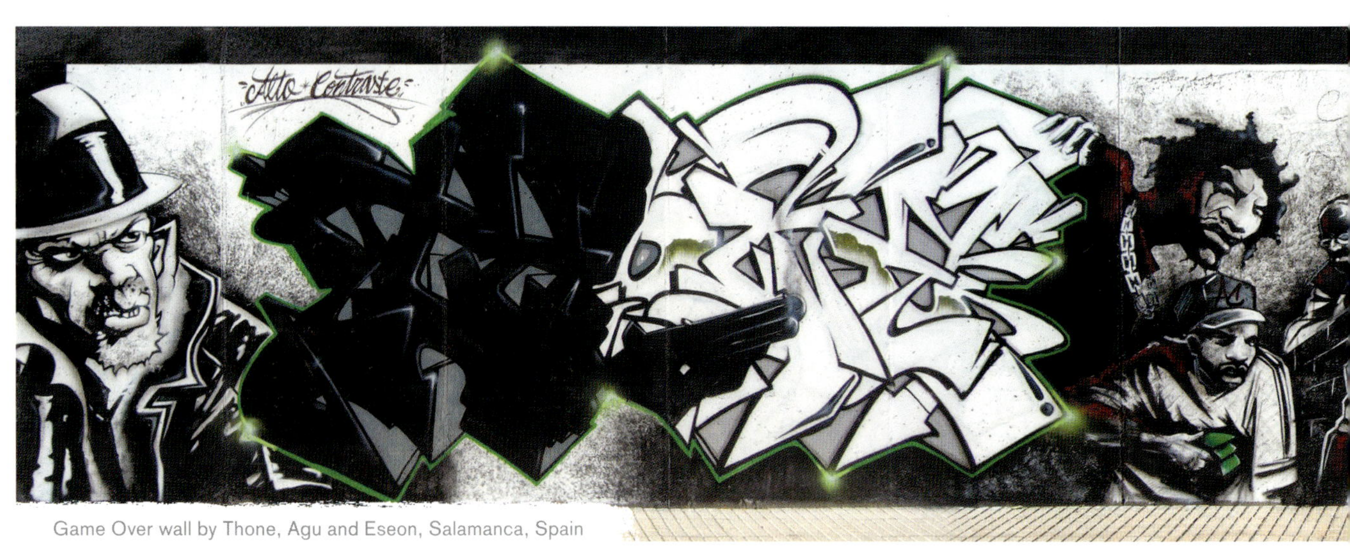

Game Over wall by Thone, Agu and Eseon, Salamanca, Spain

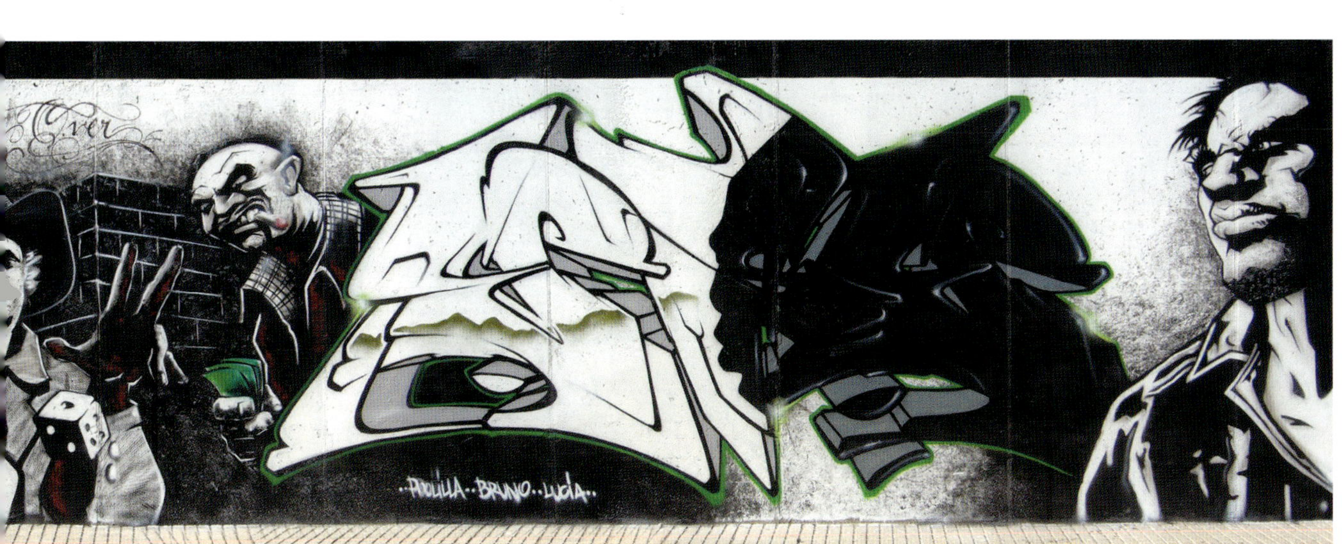
BRUNO
LUCIA

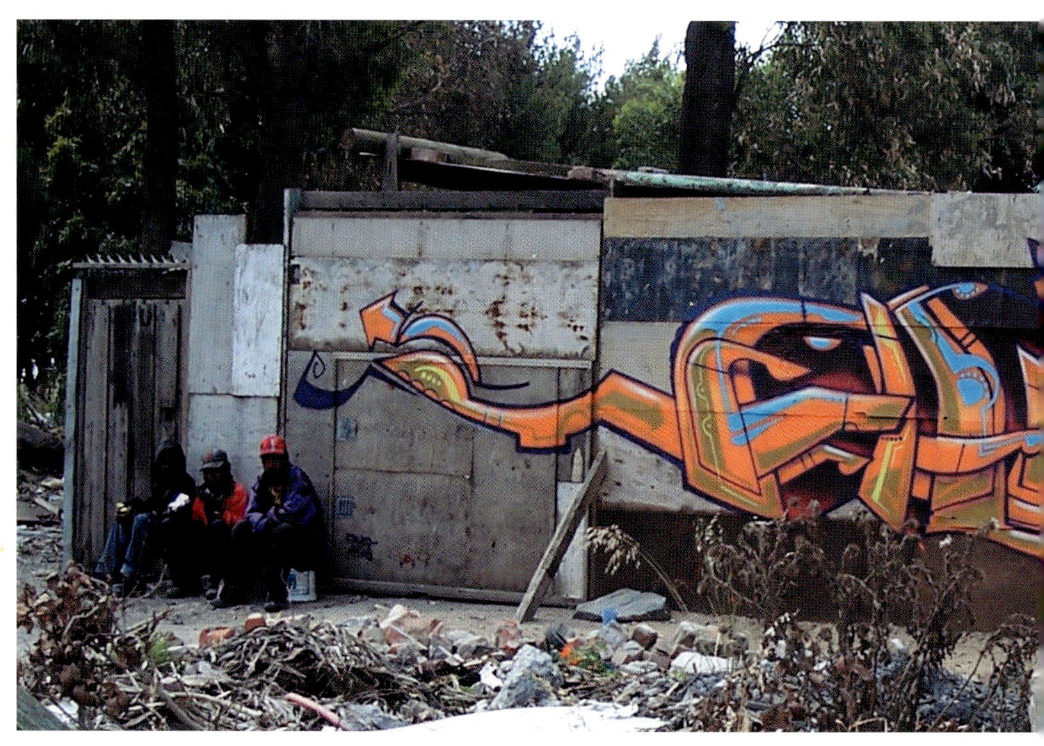

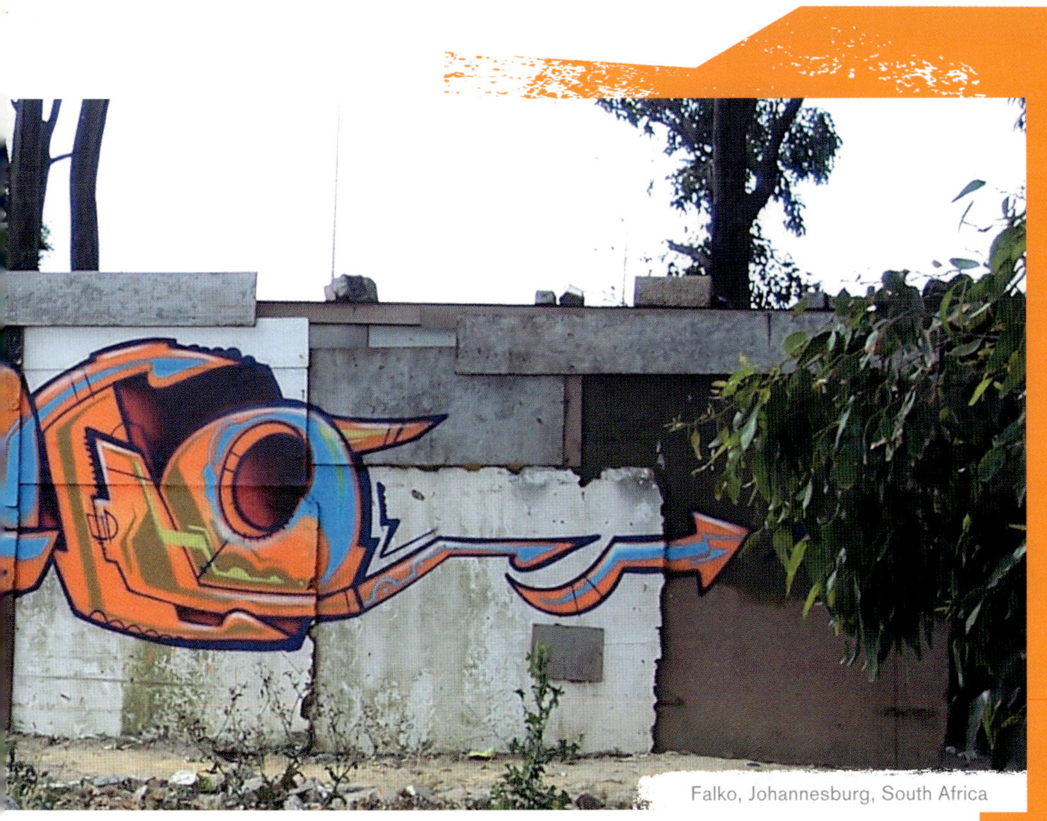

Falko, Johannesburg, South Africa

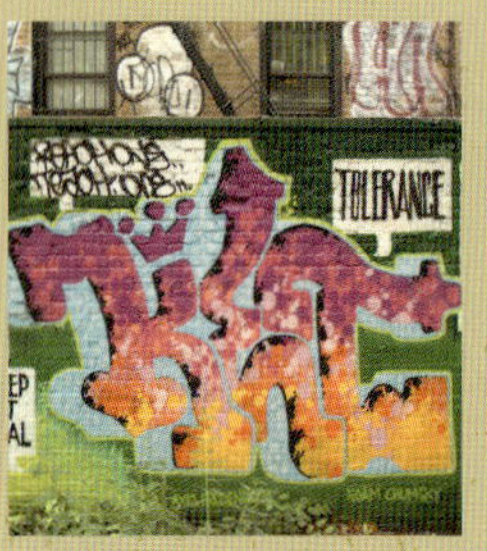

Ket started his art career at the age of fifteen, when he started taking photographs of the striking subway trains in Brooklyn. Since then, his pictures have graced the pages of many media outlets including *Rolling Stone, The New York Times Magazine, The Sunday Telegraph, The Source,* and *Stress.*

At seventeen, Ket was no longer content merely to document graffiti art; he wanted to create it as well. Once he perfected his tag, he quickly became a well-known graffiti writer both on the New York City subway lines and internationally. His painting has taken him around the world, where he has exhibited in major cities such as Munich, Berlin, and Copenhagen as well as documenting the graffiti movements there.

Today, he is active in his New York City community as a writer, graffiti historian, producer, photographer, painter and graffiti advocate. You can read his blog on www.12ozprophet.com and learn about his organization at www.thewallsbelongtous.com.

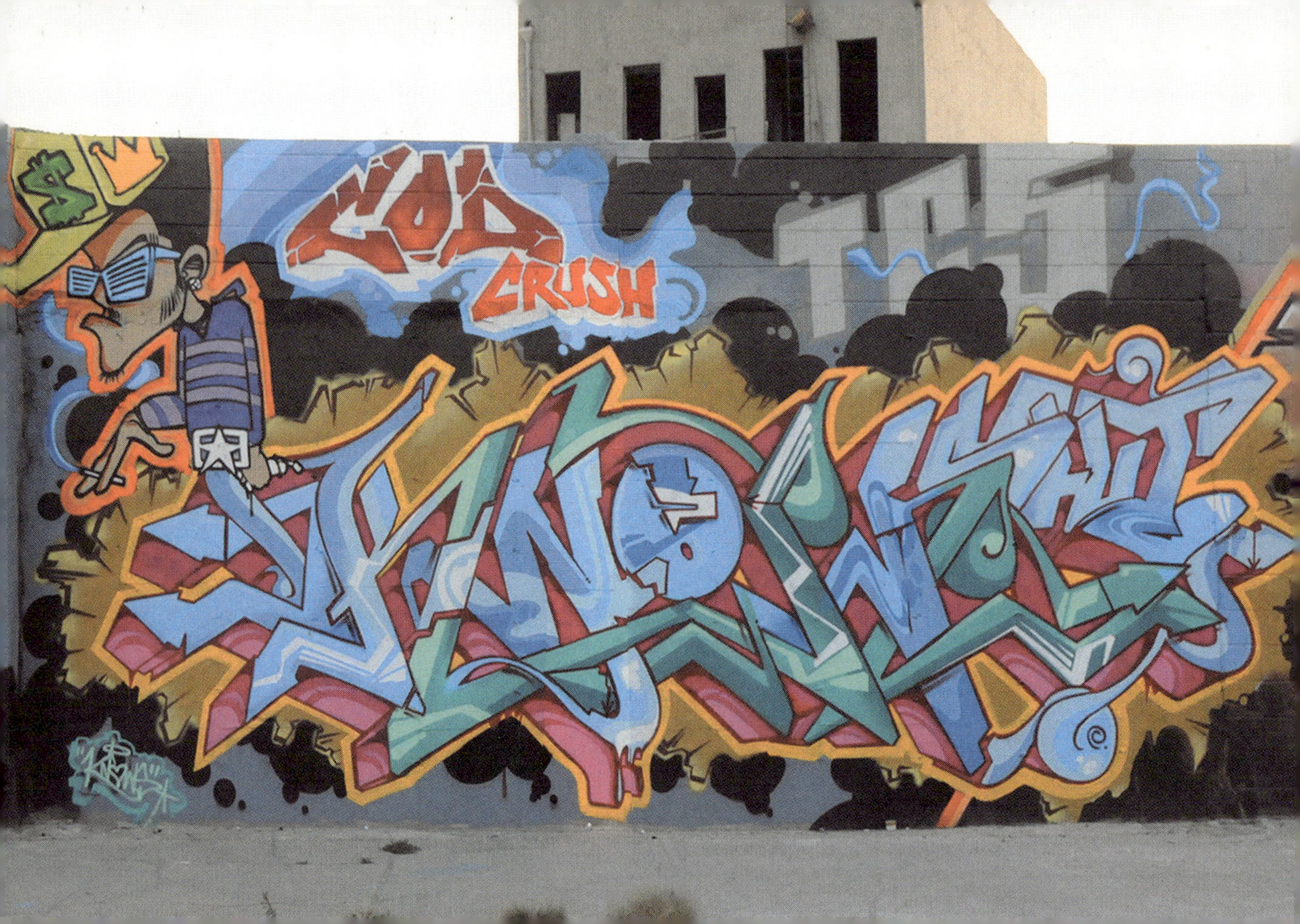
CRUSH